THEY CALL ME BABA BOOEY

Gary Dell'Abate

with Chad Millman

Spiegel & Grau
New York
2011

2011 Spiegel & Grau Trade Paperback Edition

Published in the United States by Spiegel & Grau, an imprint of The Random
House Publishing Group, a division of Random House, Inc., New York.

Spiegel & Grau and Design is a registered trademark of Random House, Inc.

Originally published in hardcover and in slightly different form in the United
States by Spiegel & Grau, an imprint of The Random House Publishing Group,
a division of Random House, Inc., in 2010.

Photograph credits can be found on page 303.

Library of Congress Cataloging-in-Publication Data

Dell'Abate, Gary.
They call me Baba Booey / Gary Dell'Abate with Chad Millman.
p. cm.
ISBN 978-0-8129-8189-6
eBook ISBN 978-0-679-60443-3
1. Dell'Abate, Gary. Radio producers and directors—United States—Biography.
I. Millman, Chad. II. Title.
PN1991.4.D46A3 2010
791.4402'33092—dc22 2010035302
[B]

Printed in the United States of America

www.spiegelandgrau.com

2 4 6 8 9 7 5 3 1

Book design by Christopher M. Zucker

To my beautiful wife, Mary:
I couldn't do it without you.
Thanks for your love and support.

To Jackson and Lucas:
You are not just my kids, you are my best friends.

To Mom and Dad:
I wouldn't be who I am without you.

God have mercy on the man who doubts what he's sure of.
—BRUCE SPRINGSTEEN, "BRILLIANT DISGUISE"

Contents

The Cure for What Ails Me

1997

"Why are you talking to me like this?"

Oh shit, I thought. I had just cracked open the back door of my house one afternoon in early March 1997 and heard my wife, Mary, asking that question. She sounded pissed and confused. She never sounded pissed and confused.

Mary is blond, kind, demure, and quiet. She is steady. I liked her when we first met because we didn't argue; we had conversations. I didn't do that with anyone else I knew. Ever. My entire life, from the time I was born to the first and only professional job I've ever had, producing *The Howard Stern Show*, has been built around chaos and confrontation. But Mary's world was full of happy, respectful people who treated her well. It had never occurred to her to ask, "Why are you talking to me like this?" because no one ever did. (I never asked because that's all *anyone* did.) Someone on the phone was yelling at her. And she was confused. Genuinely very confused, as if she didn't know the person on the other end of the line.

The truth was, she didn't, at least not really. But I did.

I knew who Mary was talking to the second I opened the door. It was my mom. My beautiful, warm, fierce, absolutely 100 percent certifiably crazy mom, Ellen.

You know that movie *Misery* with Kathy Bates, where she plays the nut job who kidnaps James Caan and breaks his ankles with a sledgehammer? There is a scene where it is raining and Kathy Bates's character looks uncommonly sad. "Sometimes when it rains I get really blue," she says. Well, *blue* was my mom's favorite word when I was growing up. Feeling blue. Having the blues. Bad weather, an argument with one of her six brothers and sisters, or a perceived slight from a neighbor could trigger it. When she felt fine she could gab all day long in a voice that sounded like Mary Tyler Moore with a Brooklyn accent. But if I asked her a question and her answers were short and curt or just a simple yes or no, that meant trouble. I knew a storm was brewing. It would lead to days and days of feeling blue, causing her to sleep in all morning because she had spent most of the night pacing. Or screaming. Or both.

She was clinically depressed, only no one knew to call it that at the time.

Early on, when Mary and I started dating and then got married, I did a good job of hiding my mom's instability. It wasn't too hard. She could be as tender as she was unhinged. When I was growing up she'd buy random gifts to keep around the house and pass out to my friends when the mood struck her. But those friends had also seen her end phone calls she didn't like by slamming the receiver down five or six times—*Bam! Bam! Bam! Bam! Bam!*—and then walk into her room, throw the door closed, and let out a holy, ear-piercing scream. They all understood how hot and cold she could run.

In high school my friend Frank said to me, "You know your mom's crazy, right?" I said, "Yeah." Then he said, "But she's your mom." He knew what the score was. My dad was an ice cream salesman, normal as can be. My mom was . . . not exactly normal. Frank and I laughed about it. I just shrugged my shoulders, as if I were raised in a '70s sitcom.

After Mary and I were married and then especially after we had our first son, Jackson, shielding her from my mom became pretty much impossible. Sometimes I would take the phone in my room and hide so Mary wouldn't hear me talking my mom down. It started to create a little trouble between us, in a way that wasn't at all like living in a sitcom.

And it came to a head that day in March, nearly five years after we were married. As Mom yelled at Mary for God knows what, I knew there was no more hiding it. That call was followed by one from my older brother Anthony, which ended in the two of us having a fight. And then came a call from my dad, which also ended in a fight. And finally there was one more call from my mom, which, yep, ended in a fight.

When the calls finally stopped, Mary looked at me and said, "Your head is so fucked up over your mom. You have to go see someone."

Mary was the one pushing me to see a shrink, and that really meant something to me. I don't think she has ever really believed in therapy, but I do. With a family like mine, I thought about therapy a lot, and it didn't frighten me at all. Everyone needs help at times. Howard and Robin talked about their own experiences in therapy plenty of times on the Stern show. Plus, I had lived in New York for a long time—almost everyone I knew was seeing a psychiatrist or went to a support group. My close friend Patty had always told me that seeing a shrink was a fantastic experience because you can get someone's complete attention for fifty minutes and they put your thoughts into perspective. I always liked the way she described it.

But Mary telling me to go get help was the push I needed. That's not to say it didn't freak me out—if my skeptical wife wants me to go, I must be really acting crazy.

First, I had to find someone. I had heard through the grapevine about Alan, a therapist that a good friend of mine and some people I knew in the music business had seen. The lead singer for a band I liked went to Alan, too. I felt like he was the shrink to the industry. That was cool. And when I called him to make the appointment he sounded like a regular guy, not someone playing Freud in the movies. I felt as though I could talk to him and he would be straight with me.

As soon as I made the appointment I thought to myself, *Now it's on, the adventure begins.* I was a little bit nervous. But mostly I had been so distraught I welcomed the change. I can only describe it as how I feel when I am sick and I make a doctor's appointment and I know that after I see the doctor I will feel better. I saw this as the antidote to what ailed me. If this went well I was going to be feeling better. I was excited.

Two weeks later, March 24, 1997, I had my first appointment.

That morning I was in my office at K-Rock at 5:35, as I am every morning. As the show's producer, I need to be in early and I need to know everything that happened in the world between when I went to bed and when I got to my desk. I checked emails and typed up a list of what was on the show that day. Howard showed up at 5:45, read the paper, and had some breakfast, then we chatted for about five minutes, a day like any other. I didn't mention that I was seeing a shrink that afternoon. Not a chance. I hadn't told my mother, my father, or my brother. I was not ready to share news like this on the show.

At 6:01 Howard went on the air. And at 6:05 he called me into the studio. "What are you doing to your hair?" he asked me. "It looks like you got caught in the rain."

"I put gel in my hair," I said.

Whenever you do something different, someone on the show will call you on it. The exhausting part is not knowing what "different" actually is. Do something radical and you know you will get killed. I once shaved my mustache and immediately everyone told me I looked terrible and that I should grow it back. I kind of expected that. But if I had any thought that putting gel in my hair that morning would warrant discussion on the air, I wouldn't have done it. In fact, I was wishing I hadn't.

"You put way too much gel in," Howard said.

"They put gel in my hair on the *Fox After Breakfast* show and I liked it, so I wanted to try it," I said.

We had done the Fox show to promote the movie *Private Parts,* which was based on Howard's book and had come out just two weeks earlier. It had debuted at No. 1. Being in the movie was a very happy thing for me. I went to the premiere with my parents, wife, brother, and sister-in-law. Mary and I walked the red carpet—heady stuff for a radio producer.

"It looks like it's lying on your wet hair," Howard said. "It makes your teeth look bigger."

"I think it looks okay," I said. "I'll go back to my regular hair tomorrow."

Then I left. And this is the flip side of working at the show. Was Howard just breaking my balls or was he doing me a favor? Was it good radio or was it the truth? Sometimes hurtful things were said and I'd talk to Howard during the break.

He'd say, "I was just doing a bit." I still wouldn't know if what was said on the air was the truth or if what was said on the break was a lie. It's a labyrinth.

But it's not why I needed to see a shrink.

My appointment was late in the day. I allowed plenty of time to get downtown. I knew that if you're late to see a psychologist the whole appointment becomes about why you're late. K-Rock was on the corner of Madison Avenue and Fifty-sixth Street and Alan's office was in Greenwich Village, near New York University. I gave myself ninety minutes to get there, because I wasn't sure if I'd find a parking spot. I was ready for the appointment and had been looking forward to it for two weeks. I was already convinced that peace of mind was just a handful of fifty-minute sessions away. But I'd be lying if I said my parking obsession wasn't just another part of the neurosis that was sending me to Alan.

I am always early. I don't like to be in a rush when going anywhere. I need to know where all the doors are, as they say, wherever I am. I like to scope out a scene. Surprises are not my thing. I grew up with lots of surprises, some of them nasty, every day. So the things I can control, I tend to try and control. I crave predictability. For instance, my drive to work is full of checkpoints that keep me comfortable. I pull out of my garage in Connecticut at 4:50 every morning. At 5 A.M., as I get on Interstate 95, I turn on 1010 WINS. If I hear the sports at 5:15 and I'm not on the Bruckner Expressway, I know I'm behind schedule. At 5:20 I turn on some music and no later than 5:30 I pull into the garage at the Sirius XM offices. I am at my desk by 5:35.

As I drove down Fifth Avenue to see Alan, I obsessed about the appointment. Who was this guy? What was he going to do? Was he going to ask me to lie on a couch with a piece of tissue under my head so I wouldn't get gel on the pillow? Would I click with him? What if I hated him? My friends who were in therapy told me I might have to see a few psychologists before I found one I clicked with. If that was true, then I'd have to talk to them again to find a new guy. Where was I going to park?

I pulled up to the address. I was glad it was a residential building instead of a crowded office tower. It was white and old and had a flight of marble steps leading up to a door with white pillars on either side. I drove around the block looking for a place to park and found a spot right away, which was a huge relief. Except then I had twenty minutes to kill. I sat in my car, listened to the radio, and thought about the appointment. I wondered who else might be in the waiting room. Would their something be more fucked up than my something?

When I finally entered the building, it was eerily quiet. There was no doorman, no one walking around. Just an elevator. When I got to the waiting room, there wasn't a receptionist, just some worn-looking furniture and framed posters of flowers on the walls. Across the room was a closed door, a mystery door leading to someplace else. I was alone, the only one with a fucked-up anything in the whole place.

And that's when I started wondering: *What the hell are we going to talk about?* I mean, I knew why I was there, but to get to that we were going to have to talk about a lot of other stuff.

Just then Alan walked through the mystery door into the waiting room. My first thought was, *Hey, it's Judd Hirsch as the shrink in* Ordinary People. He was in his mid-fifties, wore glasses and comfortable shoes, and had a thick New York accent. The guy just looked like New York to me. He reached out his hand. "Gary?"

I was the only one in the room, so I stood up.

"Nice to meet you," he said.

I followed him through the mystery door. We walked down a long, dark hallway with offices lining both sides. Each door had a sound machine in front of it running on static, so no one could hear what was happening on the other side. Alan's was the office at the end of the hall. My stomach buzzed with nerves, the good kind. I just couldn't help thinking that if the appointment went well, I was going to leave there feeling better.

"Right in here," he said, pointing to his office.

It was less luxurious than I expected, maybe even a little bit shabby. There was no oak library, no couch to lie down on, just a love seat, opposite a leather chair that Alan plopped himself into.

Then he leaned forward, rubbed his hands together like he was warming them up, and said, "So, why are we here?"

"Well," I answered. "Many people must sit on this love seat and tell you that their mother is crazy." I paused. "I have documentation."

He laughed and said, "*Okay.*"

For the next hour I told Alan my deepest, darkest secrets, things I had never shared during a life spent oversharing on the show. In fact no one—not Howard, Robin, Fred, none of the Stern regulars—truly knows how crazy my life was growing up.

Let me tell you, becoming Baba Booey wasn't easy.

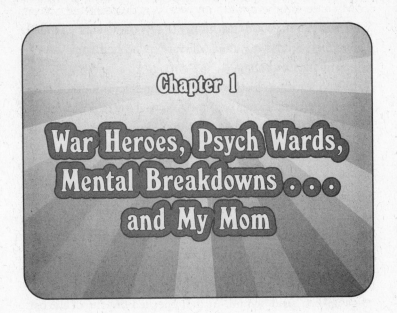

Chapter 1

War Heroes, Psych Wards, Mental Breakdowns . . . and My Mom

I STOOD ON THE AVOCADO GREEN CARPET of my living room in Uniondale, Long Island. My mom, Ellen, walked out of her bedroom, carrying an overnight bag she had just packed. Our house was a one-story ranch, and I watched her as she inched down the hall toward the living room.

She stopped just a few steps from me and bent down, practically kneeling on the carpet in her dress. She always cared about how she looked, no matter where she was going. "Come here," she told me. I was five years old and she wanted to tell me something face-to-face. I walked closer. She hugged me and said, "Mommy isn't feeling very well. I have to go away for a couple of days."

I knew she cried a lot. I knew she screamed a lot. And I knew people didn't do those things unless something was wrong. I thought she was physically sick and going to a hospital to get better.

My older brothers, Anthony, who was thirteen, and Steven, who was eleven, stood next to her. They knew what was really happening. So did my aunt Maryann, who had come over to watch us that afternoon.

When my mom let go of me she stood up, smoothed down her dress, picked up her bag, and followed my dad, Sal, out the front door. They were headed for the psych ward at Syosset Hospital.

My parents met in 1947 at Webster Hall, a dance place in Manhattan. He was twenty-two from Little Italy; she was twenty and from Bensonhurst, in Brooklyn. "He walked up to me and asked me to dance," my mom once told me. "I told him, 'I heard about all you fellas from Manhattan. You're all a bunch of gangsters.' And he said, 'Yeah, I checked my gun at the bar.' I thought, *how sarcastic.* That intrigued me.

"My friend Anne thought he was so cute—he reminded her of Humphrey Bogart. He had on a pin-striped suit and really did look like Bogart."

My mom was stylish, had a big smile, and loved mugging for a crowd or a camera. In every picture I have ever seen of her, from when she was young to today, she looks happy. There was never any sign in her eyes of the trouble behind them. On Saturdays when I was growing up, she'd spend three hours at the beauty parlor getting her hair colored and cut and then would sit with rollers in her hair under one of those huge dryers. She even had a cape and a hat that made her look just like Marlo Thomas in the opening credits for *That Girl.* She always liked to keep up appearances.

That was true when she was growing up in Bensonhurst, too. Her parents came to America from Sicily and Reggio Calabria when they were both kids. They met in Brooklyn and had seven children over fifteen years. The oldest one, Aunt

Josie, was nicknamed the General, because she did a lot of the child rearing. My grandmother worked as a seamstress and my grandfather was a construction worker (my aunts and uncles say he helped build the Empire State Building, but I think people say that about every construction worker from back then). My mom was the baby of the Cotroneo clan. The whole family lived together in a multifamily apartment building my grandfather owned.

But my mother didn't grow up rich. My mom likes to tell the story about how she wore nothing but hand-me-downs and had to put cardboard in her shoes because the soles had holes in them. She worked at Macy's while in high school and she'd bring her check home and hand it over to her mother, who cashed it and took all the money, except for a couple of bucks she kicked back to my mother.

None of the Cotroneos moved out of the building until long after they were married. Newlywed kids lived in one of the building's apartments until they could save enough money to buy a place of their own. Of course, most of them didn't move very far away. I had an uncle who moved to Los Angeles and an aunt who lived near us in Uniondale. Everyone else settled within a quarter mile of each other in Bensonhurst. Growing up we went to Brooklyn at least a couple of Sundays every month for huge Italian family dinners, the kind that began at three in the afternoon and started with three or four kinds of pasta piled with different meat sauces. That's when my aunt Angie, who probably never set foot outside Brooklyn, used to say to us, "Brooklyn is the best place in the world. I don't know why anyone would want to live anywhere else."

As close as they were, my mom's family loved arguing. It was like they couldn't stand to be too far away and then couldn't stand the sight of each other. Chaos reigned at those family meals. My father called them the Fighting Cotroneos.

His family was different. He grew up in a railroad flat in Lit-

tle Italy, on the corner of Mott and Hester. His family was qui-
eter and a little sadder. When my dad was small—"Too small
to remember all the details," he once told me—he had a one-
year-old brother who died from a throat infection. The funeral
was held in his parents' apartment.

My dad was always in great shape and kind of looked like a
low-level hood. There's a great picture of him and my mom
from their wedding in 1951. They both have ink black hair—
hers is down to her shoulders and his is slicked black. He's got
on a double-breasted black tuxedo with a white tie—he was a
dead ringer for Yankees shortstop Phil Rizzuto. They were
both rail thin, but my dad had butcher's hands. Thick and
strong.

He wasn't afraid of a fight, either. There was always tension
with the Chinese where he lived because Chinatown and Little Italy are basically right on top of each other. One night he
got into a fight with a kid from across Canal Street—which
separates the two neighborhoods—and beat the crap out of
him. A week later my dad saw the kid again, only this time he
was in the back of a police car, pointing at him. Two cops got
out, picked my dad up, and arrested him. He ended up spending the night at the Tombs, which is what they called the jail in
lower Manhattan. It deserved the nickname.

My dad was pretty smart. A junior high teacher recom-
mended him for Stuyvesant High School, one of New York
City's top public schools. "But I was always goofing around
with kids in my neighborhood, so I dropped out. Never graduated. You weren't supposed to know that," my dad once told me
when I interviewed him for a family history video.

He wasn't a thug—but he lived on the periphery of the mob
that ran Little Italy. And he liked to gamble. Even though he
grew up on the Lower East Side, my dad loved the Brooklyn
Dodgers. In 1951, when Bobby Thomson of the New York Giants hit a game-winning home run to beat the Dodgers for the

National League pennant, my dad lost a shitload of money. He was listening to the game on the roof of his building and was so upset he threw the radio over the edge.

Years later, I was signing autographs at an event and Giants hero Thomson was there, too, right next to me. I told him that story so he signed a picture for my father, which read, "To Sal, Sorry about the radio, Bobby Thomson."

My dad knew enough about gambling and the guys running the rackets in his neighborhood to know it wasn't the life for him. When World War II started he had just dropped out of high school so he decided to join the army. For more than a year he moved through the United States, training at Fort Dix in New Jersey, then in Illinois, and finally in Hawaii, "for jungle training," he said. When he finally shipped out to fight in the Pacific he thought he was headed for the Yap Islands, but the officers on the ship announced that plans had changed. They were headed for the Philippines.

My mother later told me that when the two of them went to see *Saving Private Ryan* it was harrowing; it put my dad right back in the war. He was seventeen when he landed in the Philippines. Unreal. When I was seventeen I was reading album liner notes trying to figure out who played horns on a Bob Seger record. My dad told me, "It was just like that movie. Guys were puking as they bounced around the waves. Then the front of the boat comes down and we run into the water and it's just every man for himself, guys were being killed right next to me on the beach."

He spent his war on the front lines as a medic, even though he hadn't even graduated from high school. It didn't matter. He wasn't doing battlefield surgery. His job was to patch someone together quick so they could stay alive long enough to get attention from the real doctors. Medics didn't have the option of ignoring it when one of their guys was screaming. No matter how bad the gunfire, they had to get low and go. And they were constantly under attack. "Banzai attacks," my father called them. They happened at night. "You don't hear them. It was hand-to-hand combat with bayonets. Every hill, every village was a battle."

There was one firefight he remembered that went on for two straight nights. They were under heavy attack, and my dad was in a foxhole when he heard someone yelling, "Medic! Medic!"

"We were dug in and the Japs were dug in and we were shooting at each other," he said. "Our men were hurt in the middle of no-man's-land and the officer called for me. I crawled out there, bandaged them up, gave them sulfur, and dragged one guy back at a time. I couldn't stand up because fire was coming constantly. It's all luck, who lives."

For that he earned a Bronze Star. Not that he wanted to discuss it. Ever. I remember when John Kerry was running for president my dad saw him on TV and said, "I don't like that guy." I asked him why and he said, "Because he's always talking about his medals." This was when the Republicans were claiming Kerry hadn't earned his Vietnam honors. I said, "Dad, he's being attacked. I thought if anyone would be on his side it would be you." But my dad said, "I don't care. You don't talk about it. Talking about it is wrong."

Later in the war, while in Okinawa, my father's unit was under fire and an artillery shell exploded above his head. A piece of shrapnel pierced his backpack and became embedded next to his lung. They shipped him out to a hospital, performed surgery, let him recover for a month, and then shipped him back to the front lines. "As they were giving us new weapons and clothes for a major offensive, we got word that Truman had dropped the bomb. The war was over. Two weeks later I came home."

I once asked my dad if he'd ever killed anyone and he ignored the question. But my older brother Anthony claims that, before my father died, he confessed to doing some bad things over there.

When he came home he hustled, delivering coffee around Manhattan, polishing costume jewelry, working as a proofreader for a publishing company. He was a young guy on the make. And my mom was a young woman with a little bit of sass. When I think of them courting each other I envision the movie *Goodfellas,* particularly the scenes in the nightclubs. My parents always used to talk about going to the Copa. I also hear my mom imitating her mother, who called my dad "the Mott Street gambler."

"When he would be coming over my mother didn't even say his name," my mom told me. "She just said, 'Is Mott Street coming over?'"

It wasn't that my grandma didn't like him. She was just wary of guys who dressed like gangsters, lived in the city, and courted her daughter. Still, that didn't stop my parents from getting married at a Coney Island Italian restaurant called Villa Joe's, in front of one hundred friends and family.

Naturally, after their weeklong honeymoon in Miami, they moved into an apartment in the Cotroneos' building in Bensonhurst. Their life together seemed like the beginning of their own American dream. "Back then," my father once told me, "your mom was normal."

The night after my mom went into the hospital, my dad and I took a ride to the Syosset psych ward. I was five, too young to visit her there, but my brothers weren't, and they had spent the afternoon with her. It was time for them to come home, and my dad thought the car ride would be a good opportunity to explain what was going on.

He never talked to me like I was a kid. I try to talk to my kids the same way—honestly. There were plenty of times when, after my mom experienced a screaming fit or broke down in tears, he told me I hadn't done anything wrong, that it wasn't my fault Mom was upset. And he made sure I understood it wasn't his fault, either.

Syosset Hospital was twenty-five minutes from our house. While driving, my dad said to me, "Your mom is sick. But not the regular kind of sick."

"What does that mean?" I asked.

"Her brain his sick," he answered. "And when she acts sad or angry it isn't her fault. She doesn't want to be like this." That sounded good to me. I knew enough to think that doctors made people better.

The hospital was a big, gray, stone building that was six stories high, tall for Long Island. We pulled into a circular driveway that was surrounded by flowers and then walked into the first-floor lobby, which was bustling with people. To a five-year-old, it was a fantastic place. The walls were painted a bright yellow; there was a gift shop and couches to play on and a vending machine in the corner. It wasn't a mental institution. It was exciting. And it was where my mother was, so it was where I wanted to be.

The door to the psych ward happened to be directly off the main lobby, and the entry was always protected by a security guard, who looked like he was defending Fort Knox. That's because it wasn't just a regular door, but something heavy that moved back and forth with wires and cables. You had to push a button that opened it. My father worked in the ice cream business—first as a deliveryman and then in sales—and I had been to his office in the Bronx. It had a blast freezer that was kept at 40 degrees below zero to store inventory. I loved that the door to my mom's room at the hospital looked just like the one at the ice cream factory. As I got older, I realized it also looked like the last line of defense in a cell block.

Since I couldn't go in to see my mom, I waited in the lobby with one of my brothers, while the other one was with her.

Then they'd switch, and the other one would keep an eye on me. This was our routine every other night for two weeks.

In the mornings a family friend from Brooklyn we called Jeanie Blah Blah made us breakfast and helped get us ready for school. We kids didn't know her real name. Everyone called her Jeanie Blah Blah behind her back because she never, ever shut up. She was like a utility aunt, an honorary Cotroneo who grew up near my mom and knew all the siblings. She wasn't married, smoked like a chimney, didn't work, didn't have children, and was always around. When someone needed some extra help with the kids, they called Jeanie Blah Blah. Once, she showed up at our door for a party and Steven yelled, "Jeanie Blah Blah is here." The adults practically died.

After school Jeanie gave us a snack and then for dinner my aunt Maryann, who was really my cousin but was closer in age to my mom than to us, either brought us food or had us over to her house since she lived nearby. Then, after dinner, we'd go back to the hospital.

In the car on the way there, we always sat in the same places: I was in the back behind Anthony, who sat where my mom would have been sitting in the front. And Steven sat behind my dad. We didn't talk on those trips. My mom was the chatterbox. I am a chatterbox. But my dad was always stoic. He even mowed the lawn in double-knit pants, collared shirts, and brown shoes. When my mom bought him sneakers he returned them and said, "These are for kids." Steven tended to keep to himself; he was the only person in my house who could find a way to disappear while he was standing right in front of you. And Anthony, at this point in his life, was full of rage and rebellion, a streak he was already prone to. I'm sure watching his mother deteriorate didn't help.

Instead of talking, we listened to the great AM pop station of the time, WABC. Music was something we all loved.

At the hospital, I would sit and wonder what was happening behind that ice cream freezer door. But as I waited with one of my brothers in the lobby, they never talked to me about it. They didn't talk to each other, either. While Steven and I shared a room at home, the age difference between us ensured that he and Anthony were much closer to each other than I was to them. Anthony tells me now the two of them never discussed what was happening, either, because they were too freaked out. They didn't want to go behind that door. But what were they going to do? It was our mom.

I saw her once. By accident. One of my brothers was coming out and the other was going in. I was sitting in the yellow lobby, bobbing up and down on my knees, peering over the back of the sofa, as I did whenever the cables started whirring and the door began sliding open. I was about to turn back around when, just then, I caught a glimpse of my mom.

She was shuffling to the front of the door, her black hair matted down in a way she would never let it be at home. There were paper slippers on her feet and a hospital gown hanging loosely from her shoulders to the floor. She tried to smile. She slowly lifted her arm to wave. Then one brother walked out, another walked in, and the doors whirred shut. And just like that, she disappeared.

Chapter 2

Blind Rages and Bedwetting

AFTER TWELVE YEARS IN BROOKLYN—only a couple of them spent at Hotel Cotroneo—my parents moved to Uniondale. For $21,500, they bought a 1,500-square-foot, three-bedroom, one-bath brick ranch with a basement. I was two years old when we moved in. My mom had a field of avocado green carpet installed over the wood floors. She covered the living room couches in sheets so no one messed them up. I think I saw the actual cushions of those couches five times in the twenty-three years I lived at home.

It was a tiny house. There was nowhere to hide. And the only constant was that my mom was completely inconsistent.

No one can pinpoint the day she started to change. No one in her family ever talked about her having a history of mental illness—despite all the intense arguing. Anthony says she was pretty with-it until he was about nine or ten. He says it was after I was born and when we moved to Long Island that she snapped.

Her stay in Syosset Hospital didn't change things. When she came home she was always sleepy and could barely get out of bed. The doctors had given her pills to take, but they didn't seem to be helping. I never felt angry with her. I never stopped believing my dad when he told me it wasn't her fault. It just seemed like the more that doctors tried to help her, the worse it got. I'd have grown up angry if she had been an alcoholic who never quit. But you can't tell someone to stop being crazy.

So we all learned to deal with it.

Some days I came home from school and before I could put my book bag down she had her coat on and was frantically looking for the car keys, practically buzzing around the house. Then she'd push me out the door, saying, "I've been waiting for you; we have to go, a lot of stuff to do." We'd drive to the Macy's in the Roosevelt Field mall or return a book to the library or drop something off at the Cancer Society, where she worked as a volunteer. Other days I'd walk in and she'd be at an ironing board in the kitchen, happily watching Mike Douglas on the Zenith she rolled in on the TV stand from the living room. Those were the good days, the enjoyable days.

Then there were the days when I'd get home and the house would be silent. By the time I was in school full-time, Anthony was in high school and Steven was in junior high. They had already been through my mom's up-and-down cycles and found ways to stay out of the house until dinner. I wasn't old enough yet. When I walked through the door it was just my mom and me. I knew the silence meant she was sleeping, or had spent most of the day sleeping and was resting. She'd slowly walk down the hall from her room to the living room, wearing her robe and looking tired. This is what happened when she was blue. She would tell me she was sick and tightly clutch her collar around her neck, complaining of a sore throat. Those days I had to play quietly by myself. I remember thinking to myself, *She is sick a lot.* Now I wonder if the physical symptoms were a part of her mental illness or the side effect of all the pills she was taking.

Somehow, though, she always pulled herself together for dinner. Our kitchen was tiny and decorated in avocado green to match the carpet. The avocado upholstery on our chairs matched the avocado fridge, which complemented the faux-oak table in the center of the room that seated six. I was always stuck at the end of the table right in front of the oven, and the door couldn't be opened if I was sitting at the table. When my mom had food to get out, I had to move.

Every night I and my brothers and my mom ate dinner together at six. I sat in front of the oven, Anthony sat next to my mom, and Steven sat by himself across from them. My dad sat at the opposite end from me. But he usually came home too late for dinner. We were not a family who ate out, except for the occasional Sunday trip to Borrelli's—the only place we deemed good enough to replace a proper Italian meal—or pizza at a place called Anthony's. But mostly, my mom cooked, and she was a great cook. Chicken cutlets. Broiled steak. She occasionally worked as a food demonstrator—meaning she was the lady in the mall with a microphone around her neck who made something in a wok and then handed out samples. I remember being in ninth grade when she did the wok demo. We ate Chinese three days a week. In tenth grade it was the pasta maker, which looked like a toaster with a hand crank.

Once we sat down, dinner lasted about five minutes and was almost always eaten in front of the Zenith. We watched the news, the Vietnam War unfolding on our screen as we shoveled food into our mouths.

It was actually television, more than food, that brought us together. None of us could believe it when *The Sound of Music*—Best Picture in 1965!—appeared on TV just a year later. We couldn't wait to watch it. It was an event! Saturday nights in our house were ruled by Carol Burnett and *All in the*

Family; Sundays belonged to Ed Sullivan. And then during commercials we talked about the musical acts, with my dad usually joking, "You call that music? That's not music!" Then he'd break into a Frank Sinatra song from the 1940s.

We all laughed, especially my mom.

When she was in a good mood and balanced, she was all love. She was very physical, and she would grab my friends and kiss them on the head and say, for no reason at all, "Oh your mother must be so proud." She'd be so warm, telling all the neighbors and my friends to come over, that her kitchen was never closed. The problem was, you never knew when that mood was going to change. She would spend three days being as warm and loving as anyone you'd ever seen. And then three days of being a normal mom. And then on the seventh day she'd wake up saying she was feeling blue.

Most people in their lives have "an incident" involving their parents, the moment when their mom or dad just loses it and rage trumps being rational. Well, we had "incidents."

Sometimes my mom would plop food down at dinner and then angrily bang some pots and pans while she washed them, before dropping them altogether in a loud clang. We never knew what had set her off. She'd walk into her room screaming and slam the door. You couldn't believe the words that came out of her mouth. Fuck, fuck, fuck, fuck. A sailor would have blushed. She'd come out, we'd think it was over, and then she would dial a number, usually one of her sisters, and fight with whoever could provoke her into a rage. Then she'd slam the phone down five or six times and go back into her room and scream some more. "These people think they live on an island," she liked to say. "Like you live all by yourself and can do whatever you want. They think they can pull one over on me, they think I don't know, they think I don't see. I see, I see what's going on."

The episodes didn't frighten me in a way that made me cower under the table or flinch if my mom came near me. I always loved her. But they affected me in other ways. How could they not? I had a bedwetting problem until I was in second grade. And I felt horrible about it. Not because my parents got angry with me or because my brothers made fun of me. Neither happened actually. I was too young for my brothers to think of me as a rival worthy of their torment. I just felt bad because I didn't know why it was happening. I was peeing in my sleep so often that my mom went to the drugstore and bought an expensive machine that connected to the bed. It had an alarm that went off whenever liquid hit the mattress. We never even connected it. That night my dad got home and said, "What good is that? If the alarm goes off when liquid hits the mattress, it's too late." My mom said she was going to return it and that's when Steven chimed in, pretending to be our mom calling the pharmacy. "Hi, this is Mrs. Dell'Abate, I'd like to return the piss machine."

One morning, showing a little frustration, my mom said to me, "You have to stop doing this." I said back, "I know. I want to." If I had known then what I know now, I would have said, "Stop screaming like a banshee and maybe I will stop peeing in my bed."

Mostly, when my mom lost it, Anthony, Steven, and I never said a word to one another. If she morphed at dinner, we just kept eating, giving one another looks. But we didn't want to talk because whoever spoke would draw attention to himself and become the target of her rant. Other than my mom yelling, no one said a word.

Blind rages like that only have to happen seven or eight times before you adapt and get used to it. Every explosion, we'd all just wonder how long the episode would last. Their length was never something you could gauge. My dad would get home, hear what was going on, and say, "Okay, this is what we get today."

From where I sat, it always seemed like my mom was the

one looking to pick a fight. One day she accused my father of cheating. I was at home when she called his office and started screaming at his assistant and the boss's assistant. When he got home he told her she couldn't call his office and yell like that. She screamed back, "I don't care!"

Mostly, though, when my father walked through the door and my mom started with him he'd say, "You know what? I am not going to fight with you tonight." Then he would sit in his chair and read the newspaper. She'd still try to pick a fight with him. Sometimes she would grab me and say we were leaving and moving back to Brooklyn. The first time this happened, it freaked me out. I remember crying. I wondered if I'd ever see my dad or brothers again. And where were we going to live when we got to Brooklyn? But I couldn't ask her any of these questions because she was ranting nonstop. Ranting and driving. We would be in the car on the Long Island Expressway. Then just as quickly as we had left the house, she'd get off the LIE, turn around, and take us home. We'd wake up the next morning and she'd act like everything was normal.

I learned to act like everything was normal, too. When I was a little older, my mom would scream and yell from the time I went to school in the morning until my dad got home at night. I would go to sleep and she'd still be screaming. She was manic. I wasn't sure if she ever slept. I'd curl up in the fetal position in my bed and scream into the pillow out of frustration. But then the next day, I had to get up. I had to forge ahead. What was I supposed to do? Wake up in the morning and fall apart? That was a survival skill. Maybe I thought if I got up and acted like it didn't happen—and she kept acting like nothing happened—then it wouldn't happen again. If everything was back to normal I preferred we go with that idea and hope it stayed that way.

Hope can be a powerful thing.

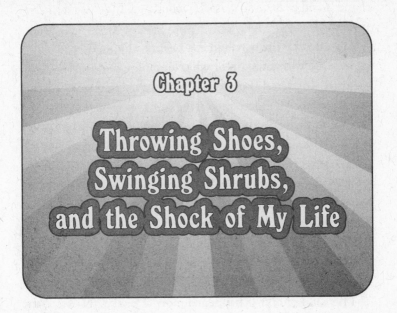

Chapter 3

Throwing Shoes, Swinging Shrubs, and the Shock of My Life

ONE COLD AND CLOUDY AFTERNOON in late fall, some time after my mom had been hospitalized, I came home from first grade and found her hurrying to get out of the house. Today was going to be that kind of a day, I thought. She put me in the car and drove me to a doctor's office. I had never been there before. I didn't know it was a psychiatrist.

She sat in the waiting room with me, sobbing hysterically, and when she was called in she just left me sitting there. She didn't think twice about that. But back then mothers smoked while they were pregnant and let kids ride without car seats. They didn't always think about their child's welfare. I waited, wondering if this doctor was going to make her feel better, but when she came out she was crying even harder. The doctor stood behind her. His name was Dr. Peck, and he looked like someone out of a textbook: heavyset with a tweed jacket, a Sigmund Freud beard, and glasses. I wondered, *Is this my mom feeling better?*

She cried all the way home, a twenty-minute drive. I didn't know what was going on or what kind of doctor she had been seeing. I wondered if they had hurt her or used scary instruments on her. At home the crying got even worse, and as she often did, she walked into her room and slammed the door. I heard her screaming, "Papa, I'm so sorry, I'm so sorry." But she didn't sound mad. She wasn't yelling at anyone. And this was strange to me. Normally when she acted like that she came back out screaming. But she wasn't mad, not at me or her sisters or my dad or anyone. I was confused, so I waited, until the light faded away and it turned dark. Then my brothers came home. And at 5:30 my mom came out and made us dinner. It was as if nothing had happened.

This kind of crying happened more after she got out of the hospital. This was also when she started to self-medicate. Her philosophy was, if the doctor told her one pill would make her feel less blue, then maybe she should take two.

She'd go to one doctor and get a prescription, then go to a different doctor and get a different prescription. Then she'd go to a third doctor for a third. She collected pills. Because she wouldn't level with any of the doctors, and because none of them knew about her other medications, it was impossible for them to diagnose her. That added to her downward spiral. When she moved out of the house years later, her medicine cabinet was full of pills. My brother Anthony, who packed her up, told me she had harder stuff in there than anything he'd ever found on the street when he was younger.

Because of what was happening at home, I was the kind of kid who wanted to evaporate in public. I never wanted any trouble, never wanted to draw attention to myself. I became very good at compensating so friends who came over couldn't tell what was happening with my mom. On the days she was feeling well, my friends and I hung out at the house. But if a buddy came over after school and it was one of her off days, I'd quickly say, "Hey, why don't we go to the park?"

But sometimes circumstances made that difficult.

My mother insisted on being the class mother for my field trips. This was incredibly anxiety-producing for me; she could have a meltdown at any moment. Plus, she was almost always late, which meant there was ample opportunity for a dramatic entrance. That alone would draw the kind of attention I wanted to avoid. The first few years I was in school, I had been safe. Then came my fourth-grade trip to the Empire State Building.

My class was leaving for the city on a bus a few hours after the schoolday had begun, which meant my mom would have to meet us at school. When it was time to leave, all the kids were sitting in their seats on the bus and our teacher stood in the front, checking his watch. There was no sign of my mother. My leg bounced up and down with nerves as we waited and waited and waited for my mom to show up. Finally the teacher said to me, "We're going to have to leave in two minutes."

Then my mom came screeching up in her car, threw it in park, jumped out, and ran onto the bus. She was panting as she said, "I'm so sorry, I'm so sorry I'm late." Already I was not invisible. I remember it being excruciatingly embarrassing. I didn't think it could get worse. Until we got to the top of the Empire State Building.

I was looking out over the city on the observation deck when I heard screaming. I turned around and saw my mom—with one high heel on and the other in her hand, gripping it as if it were a weapon—chasing some of my classmates. She was yelling at them to stop misbehaving and start listening. They were half laughing, half wondering why this woman, Gary's mom, was coming after them. At one point the heel on the shoe she was wearing broke and she started screaming at the kids for making her break her shoe. I wanted to go into a corner of the building and die. Or better yet throw myself off the observation deck. For the rest of that year kids asked me what was wrong with my mother. I was the kid in class with the crazy mom. My mom was oblivious to how that incident could scar a fourth grader for life. Instead, she'd bring it up and say, "Can you believe how badly those kids were behaving?"

But for the most part, no one outside of our house and immediate family knew the extent of what was happening with my mom. My dad didn't call the school when she was in the hospital to let my teacher know. And it's not like she walked around the neighborhood trading pills with other housewives or muttering to herself in her housecoat. Her manic incidents were isolated enough—once a week some months and none during others—that if you heard screaming from my house you'd just think someone was having an argument. Uniondale was blue-collar and Italian. Screaming was commonplace.

My mom's issues stemmed as much from her temper as they did from any mental instability. There was a line she crossed where one gave way to the other, like she couldn't find an off switch. One day we went to the A&S department store in Hempstead to buy me new school clothes. My mom tried to pay with a credit card that was in my father's name, but the saleslady wouldn't accept it. Naturally, my mom flew into a rage. She started throwing my clothes—which were sitting in a pile on the counter—at the lady. Those were followed by the black Chuck Taylor high-tops I had picked out. One of the Chucks hit the saleslady in the head while she was on the phone with security. That's when we sprinted out of the store to avoid getting arrested.

The temper problems meant that, even when my mom was in the right, she could occasionally wind up in the wrong. In our part of town she had a lot of friends, but she also had a lot of people she perceived to be enemies. That's how it was with her: Everything was black-and-white. You were her friend or you were her enemy.

Our next-door neighbors happened to be enemies. The houses on my street were practically on top of one another, separated by just a thin driveway. The older son next door was just a grade ahead of me and, for some reason, he had it in for me. He constantly beat the crap out of me. It became a regular topic of conversation in my house: What are we going to do about Gary getting beaten up? I was in third grade. Finally, one warm spring afternoon, my mom decided she was going to go next door and have a chat with the guy's mom. It was just like out of *The Brady Bunch*, when Peter was getting picked on and Mike and Carol went over to the bully's house expecting everyone to be reasonable. Except in my case they weren't.

With me on her heels, my mom walked over and knocked on our neighbor's door. I noticed a lot of kids playing ball in the street. I stopped by myself at the very edge of our property line, on the driveway, which meant I was still plenty close to listen to the conversation. I had never been in their house and was really anxious about being as close as I was.

Our neighbor opened her screen door but, instead of inviting my mom in, she stepped out onto the top step of the three-step stoop. My mom said, "I want your son to leave my son alone." So far so good, a perfectly reasonable request. Carol Brady would have been proud. Then our neighbor answered in a flip and casual tone: "Maybe your son can defend himself."

Uh-oh.

I can't remember who dropped the first F-bomb, but in a matter of seconds they were flying. The neighbor was yelling, "Fuck you!" My mom yelled it back. And then . . . my mom pushed her. My first thought was, *Let's get out of here now, Mom. This isn't working. We should walk away right now!* I knew that my mom would get herself worked up and it would be impossible to stop this thing from escalating. There would be no turning back.

Our neighbor couldn't believe she had been pushed. She stood there, her mouth open, like she was watching a scary movie. Only she was in it. Now people were starting to gather around. The kids who had been playing ball on the street dropped their bats and stared. Then my mom took it to another level. There were shrubs and a flower bed just to the side of our neighbors' stoop, underneath a big bay window. As the woman stood there, my mom reached down and pulled up some shrubs. She must have caught a glimpse of the roots, because she decided that they might make a good weapon. Then she started bashing our neighbor with the shrubs. Dirt was flying everywhere. By now the neighborhood parents were in the street watching, too. They were fascinated, amazed, horrified, and stunned. I was petrified and embarrassed. *This is not what we came here to do,* I thought. My mom had started out in the right, and now she was beating our neighbor with her shrubbery.

Someone must have called the cops, because the next thing we knew, a squad car pulled up with the lights flashing. *Really? The cops?* Now I was freaking out. My dad wasn't home. My brothers weren't home. I figured the cops were going to haul her off. I didn't cry—I wasn't a yeller; that would just draw more attention to me—I was just kind of frozen, waiting to see where it all went. My stomach ached.

One of the cops put my mom in the back of the cruiser. The other one had a talk with our neighbor. After several minutes the two cops got together and conferred. Then they released my mom. What were they going to do? Arrest two housewives?

As we walked into the house, my mom didn't say a word. It was almost dinner, so she went into the kitchen and started to cook. She was moving on. But it wasn't that easy for me. The next morning at school a bunch of kids came up to me and said, "I heard about what your mom did. She's crazy."

They weren't cruel. I wasn't teased about it or ignored on the playground. And weirdly I wasn't *that* embarrassed. It ran so much deeper than that. I just wished someone could fix things. I wondered: *How do we get it to stop now and forever? Can't someone do something?*

When I was older, around eight or nine, my mom went back into the hospital. This time her stay was shorter—I don't even remember visiting her—and Anthony was old enough that he was put in charge of me and my brother until my dad got home from work. But when she got home, the pattern was similar to the first time she went away: She was lethargic. She slept a lot. She self-medicated. She still had mood swings, fits of anger, and moments when she couldn't stop crying.

Nothing the doctors tried seemed to work. And I know now they tried everything.

I was in ninth grade when I began to understand what my mom went through, what those visits to the hospital were all about. The movie *One Flew Over the Cuckoo's Nest* had just been released and my aunts and uncles were talking about it. They wondered how realistic the electroshock therapy scenes were, and then I heard one of them say, "I wonder if that's what it was like for Ellen."

What the fuck! Electroshock therapy! On my mom! Twice! I went to see the movie right after that conversation. In one scene, hospital workers grab Jack Nicholson and strap him down to a gurney with giant leather belts. They rub Vaseline on the side of his head and attach what look like a pair of headphones to his temples. When they flip the switch, he buckles and gyrates. I realized he would have flown across the room if he hadn't been strapped in. My mom was half his size. If this grown man was shaking and convulsing, what must this have done to my mother's body? Holy shit. I was seriously scared for my mother. I wasn't surprised the treatment didn't help her; I wondered if it made things worse. At this point Anthony and Steven were long gone from the house. They didn't talk about my mom's treatment when they were around and, even if they knew what was happening, there was no way they would discuss it with me. So I just tried to process everything as well as I could. It didn't make me any less frustrated when she was struggling, but it did make me more sympathetic. Years later, when I saw *Changeling* with Angelina Jolie, I cried. The ECT scene in this movie was even more graphic. The orderlies took their time buckling her in. And the fact that the character was a woman—and a mother—going through it made it harder for me. If *Cuckoo's Nest* was a discovery, *Changeling* was reality.

I guess I buried those memories for a long time—it all feels like it happened a hundred years ago—and I hadn't really shared them with anyone, other than my shrink, as an adult. But one day at work early in 2010, I was hanging with Jason Kaplan and Jon Hein in an area we call the bullpen, which is just rows of cubicles. We were talking about our mothers and I said to Jason, "You can't believe the shit that I went through."

Jason said, "Yeah, I've heard you and Howard talk about it on the air. What is it about your mom that was so crazy?"

In a flip way, I told him the story about visiting my mom in the hospital the very first time—as if to say, look at what I went through and I am fine. Suddenly I got choked up and abruptly ended the story. I was embarrassed. I thought, *Maybe I'm actually not fine about it.*

Or maybe it's just that I still can't believe what my mom went through.

Chapter 4

My Hippie Brother, My Gay Brother, and Me

MOST MORNINGS WHEN I WAS A KID, I'd wake up, roll out of bed, walk into the kitchen, and find my mom sitting at our faux-oak table. She'd be smoking a cigarette, drinking some coffee, and watching the news on TV. Then she'd fix me breakfast. Cheerios and milk, my favorite. As long as I had that, I was happy. But by the time I was in fourth grade, my mother slept in more and more. By the time I was in junior high, she didn't bother getting up at all. Part of it was the depression and part of it was that I was the third child and she decided I could take care of myself in the mornings. She'd make me my lunch the night before and leave it in the fridge. I never even thought it was strange until one morning, before school, a friend stopped by to walk with me. I was rummaging through the refrigerator looking for cream cheese and he said, "Where's your mom?"

"Sleeping," I said.

Then he asked, more curious than accusatory, "Why isn't she making breakfast for you?"

"I don't know." I shrugged. "She sleeps in."

In my house, mornings were the quietest times of the day. Everyone, it seemed, found a reason to get out of there as quickly as possible. My dad was off to sell ice cream before sunrise. And my brothers, well, when we were all living under the same roof, I can't remember many times we had breakfast together. They always left early and came home late, just before dinner. "It was traumatic living in a house like that," Anthony said.

I couldn't blame either of them for wanting to escape the chaos. Especially Anthony. Steven was a bit of a golden child, very smart and very quiet. But Anthony was trouble. For a long time—before and after my mom went into the hospital—she accused him of making her sick, yelling, "It's your fault I am crazy, you're making me crazy because you are so out of control!" She wasn't wrong: Anthony kind of *was* out of control. In eighth grade he stayed out all night without calling home. When he was thirteen he used to hang with a buddy whose older brother was in a motorcycle gang called the Pagans. Anthony and his pal went to the gang's parties and acted as mascots/waiters, bringing everyone beers until the sun came up. They thought they were the coolest kids in the world.

When he was sixteen Anthony asked my parents if he could go to Woodstock. All his buddies were going. Naturally my parents said no. That day they left him to babysit me—Steven was old enough to be out doing his own thing during the summer—so there was no way Anthony could sneak out. At least that's what they thought. It was early in the morning and, while he watched the Woodstock coverage on TV, Anthony got so riled up he said, "I'm going. Gary, go pack your bag." I was eight years old. So I wrapped a bunch of toys in a rag and tied it around a stick, like a hobo. Anthony helped me. We walked out of the house and headed to Uniondale Park, where Anthony and his friends hung out a lot. The place was nothing special—some baseball fields, some tennis courts, and a lot of benches for the teenagers in town to sit at and figure out how to get into trouble.

I couldn't believe it. I was going on an adventure with my older brother to this far-off land called Woodstock. It sounded interesting and fun and grown-up. And since Anthony was in charge and said we could go, I figured everything we were doing was allowed.

At the park Anthony saw some friends. A bunch of them were talking about heading up to the concert. Another group was already on their way. Now Anthony was really pissed. I could hear him going, "Harrumph." He looked at me, said, "Let's go," and dragged me and my hobo sack through the park. At the opposite end of the park, beyond some trees bordering a grassy field, was the road that led to the Southern State Parkway. We were going to stick out our thumbs and hitchhike to Woodstock. Seemed like a good plan to me.

We stood on the side of the road for five minutes. Who knows what people thought when they drove by. A sixteen-year-old kid with hair that hung down to his shoulders and an eight-year-old boy holding a stick and handkerchief filled with toys. No one stopped to pick us up or ask us if we needed help. Eventually I heard my brother start harrumphing again. They were audible groans. "Fuck it," he said. "I can't do this." He started to turn around and then stopped. This time he said, "Fuck this, I have to go to Woodstock." Then he stopped again. Finally he mumbled, "I can't do this. Dad will kill me."

He grabbed me by the arm, walked us back through the trees, and led us to the bench where his buddies had been sitting. We stayed there the rest of the day.

I totally looked up to Anthony. He was older; he hung out with kids who smoked and looked cool. And when my mom made Anthony take me with him to Uniondale Park, which was often, none of them cared. I wasn't a pain in the ass. They found me interesting, someone they could teach. One night Anthony had a party in our backyard—which was only slightly bigger than a pitcher's mound. His buddies who were in a band provided the music. My parents mostly stayed inside but I had been excited about the party all day. So I wandered out and saw two of my brother's friends sitting in a back corner, with their backs to the house. I walked over and asked, "What are you guys doing?"

They were smoking cigarettes and, without saying a word, one of them handed me his and said, "Here, try it." I was eight or nine years old and I idolized these guys. I took a puff and practically hacked up a lung. But I was so excited to be doing what the big kids did, I ran into the house and told my mom, "Guess what? Guess what? I just tried a cigarette."

That was the end of the party. My dad sent everyone home and my mom sent me to my room, where I cried and kept asking, "What did I do wrong?"

Other than my mom, Anthony was at the center of most of the drama in my house. He was a teenager struggling with a lot of heavy personal shit in the late 1960s, an era that happened to be tailor-made for kids looking to rebel. Uniondale was just like any other town in America that was divided by the Vietnam War. There was a deli owned by a veteran with a sign in it that read, "America, love it or leave it." Meanwhile, the teenagers were walking around with long hair and flashing peace signs. Anthony had a pair of purple bell-bottoms and a matching purple shirt that he loved to wear. Whenever he did, Steven called him "Antoinette."

Anthony saw himself as a revolutionary, but he wasn't quite old enough to spend his life traveling around the country protesting. Instead he went into the city and hung out at the offices of the Youth International Party, where he met radicals like Abbie Hoffman and Jerry Rubin. He picked up literature on how to organize rallies and stage sit-ins at his school. At one of them he led a group of two hundred students who refused to move from the lobby. The teachers didn't call the cops—they called the parents. When my mom came down and heard Anthony had been the ringleader her mouth curled up and she said, "I knew it." Then she dragged her oldest son out of the lobby by his very long hair. "It was a scene, all the way around," Anthony said.

The war was a big deal in our house. Every night we watched footage on the news during dinner. It also pitted Anthony directly against my war hero dad.

My father was always so calm and stable, a straight line through a storm. The only time he seemed to lose his cool was when he and Anthony fought about Vietnam. Even though I had no idea what the war was about, I couldn't believe how passionately the two argued. Their relationship was so black-and-white. My brother was a lefty like Meathead from *All in the Family*—as liberal as liberal can be. My father was no Archie Bunker, but he was a conservative, decorated World War II veteran. He really did believe that the president of the United States knew what was best for us. He was actually crushed by Watergate because he just didn't think the men who ran the country were capable of doing anything wrong.

Anthony's rebellions seemed like a slap in the face, not just to my father, but to all the men he fought with. By the time Anthony was a senior in high school he and my dad were fighting constantly. It came to a head the Easter Sunday before he graduated. I remember it so clearly because, as usual, the blowup came at the worst possible moment—for me.

My favorite TV program as a kid was *Wonderama*, a legendary show that aired on Sunday mornings for twenty years. It was hosted by Bob McAllister and for more than three hours it featured kids participating in games in the studio, along with cartoons and *Three Stooges* segments. The show was filmed in New York and it was my dream to be in the studio audience, but the waiting list for tickets was three years long. One day, miraculously, we were able to get tickets through a family friend. Even better, the show taped on Tuesdays so I would have to miss school.

Leading up to the big day I practiced the *Wonderama* theme song day and night. I thought about what it was going to be like to see Bob McAllister in person. I wondered if I would get to play my favorite game on the show, Snake-in-a-Can. I was ten years old; this was the biggest thing that had ever happened to me.

My mom, my friend Gary Bennett, and I left for the city early in the morning. As we waited on line to get in, Bob McAllister walked right by us and waved. A bona fide celeb! When we finally got inside I was amazed at how small the studio was, but when we all sang the theme song I couldn't believe my ears and eyes. The singing was actually piped in over the loudspeakers and Bob was lip-synching!

Watching from home I always thought the stage must be huge because each segment appeared to be filmed in different parts of the studio. I was wrong about that, too. There was only one stage. It took ten hours to shoot a three-hour show because they had to strike each set before putting up another one. We spent most of our time in the audience waiting.

But I did get picked to be in a game. Since it was the Easter show there was a bit where they had piles of chocolate Easter eggs with all kinds of toppings, from hot sauce to whipped cream, set up on tables. My job was to walk around the audience, take orders, and then bring everyone their eggs. I wore an apron, but it was easy. Everyone got his or her eggs, and I got to be on TV. When I was done they gave me a Spirograph, which was even better.

. My mom made the show, too. In one segment kids made

Easter bonnets out of paper hats and she was chosen as a model along with a handful of other moms. The hats were so gaudy and looked exactly like something someone would wear at a baby shower: full of ribbons and piled high with glued-together scraps of paper from a crafts table. Even though my mom was one of a half-dozen women on the stage, she posed like she was a star, camping it up with the great big smile I saw in every picture she took. It was fun to see her so happy. They shot so many close-ups of her she was actually recognized by a hot dog vendor in the city after the show aired.

By the time we left the studio it was eight o'clock at night and I had a goodie bag filled with a bagel, Hostess cupcakes, a T-shirt, and my beloved Spirograph. It was the greatest day of my life. I couldn't wait to see the show.

The show aired on Sunday. This was before VCRs and DVRs, so the only way to see it—the only way to find out if I had made it on TV—was by watching it when it aired.

But it wasn't meant to be.

Minutes before the show I turned on our big RCA in the living room. That's when my dad and Anthony chose to get into a crazy, knock-down, drag-out argument about Anthony joining the army after he graduated. My dad was demanding it; Anthony was defiant. I turned the volume up but they only yelled louder. I moved closer, my nose inches from the screen, and I still couldn't hear. Soon my mom was crying and wailing, too.

"Well, if you don't like it here then you can move out!" my dad yelled.

"Fuck you, maybe I will, because you can't talk to me like that!" Anthony screamed.

Oh no he didn't! My mom dropped F-bombs all the time, but no one in my house ever said the word back to my parents. Even for someone as used to cursing as I was—I heard it so often, to me it sounded like white noise—this was impossible

to ignore. The greatness of watching myself on TV and the entire *Wonderama* experience would have to wait.

Anthony moving out? The idea seemed impossible. He
hadn't graduated from high school. He didn't have a job.
Where was he going to go? But none of these minor inconve-
niences stopped him. After that last exchange, my father was so
stunned he didn't have time to react. Anthony stomped into his
room, grabbed his sleeping bag, threw some clothes out of his
window onto the front lawn, and left. He was gone. It was devastating on two levels: I didn't get to see myself on TV, and I
didn't know if I'd ever see my brother again.

I never did get to watch the show. Years later, while shooting
Private Parts, I met an extra who was friends with Bob McAllister's daughter, who kept a tape of every show. Of course, she
never labeled them. Four different times Bob McAllister's
daughter looked through her stack of tapes but she couldn't
find my episode. I did, however, get a chance to speak with
McAllister. In 1994, four years before he died, he called in to
the Stern show to say he thought it was okay for the government to control what kids could listen to. Howard hung up on
him.

For weeks after Anthony left, I had no idea where he was
living. No one in my house spoke to me about it. I don't even
know if my parents knew where he was. Then one day at school
a kid who always used to shake me down, Alan Franklin,
stopped me in the hallway. He lived in the slums in Uniondale.
"Hey," he said, "your brother is living next door to me. Gimme
a quarter."

Soon after that my brother came by the house to see me. He
still wanted nothing to do with my parents, but I was just his
little brother, I didn't do anything wrong. One day he picked
me up and brought me to his new place, right next to Alan's.
There were twelve white guys who looked like hippies in the
middle of this run-down, black neighborhood. Everyone in the

living room was wearing a dashiki and smoking something. One of them had a water bed and I remember thinking, *This isn't a house where a mother lives.* Which is exactly why my brother moved in.

Eventually he tried to make peace with my parents. A week before he graduated he went to see them. Everyone apologized. He wanted them in the crowd when he received his diploma. But as he walked across the stage that night, he couldn't resist making a personal statement against authority. When the principal offered him a handshake, my brother blew past him. I didn't even notice it, but my parents did. Anthony was going out with friends after the ceremony and when my parents and I got into our car I could tell everyone was mad—the silence was thick with tension—so I asked what was going on. My mom said to me, "Did you see that Anthony wouldn't shake his principal's hand?" They were mortified.

It was a couple of months before they all spoke to one another again.

For all of Anthony's outward rebellion, Steven was the one my mom worried about most. "It's the quiet ones you've got to look out for," she used to say.

Everyone always said that Anthony and I were my mother's kids, while Steven was my father's. He was thinner than we were and, although he had dark hair, he had fairer skin. He was also so much more chill. The arguing we did in the house wasn't his scene at all. But he had a wicked sense of humor that tickled my mom and helped him get away with stuff. One year he got her a T-shirt that read, NOT A WELL WOMAN. If Anthony or I had given her that shirt she would have blown her top. But because Steven did it, she thought it was hysterical.

Until Anthony moved out, Steven and I shared a room. We had our *Brady Bunch* moments, like when we'd split the room in half with tape. Only he'd always get the side with the door and I'd have to give him a special pass if I wanted to get out and use the bathroom.

Anthony's drama was out in the open and in your face, but Steven's was bubbling inside. He didn't have screaming matches with my parents. He studied hard, made the honor roll, and was a member of the National Honor Society. He had orange crates full of records—there were hundreds in there—and he'd listen to them for hours by himself on the record player in our living room.

One day, seemingly out of nowhere, he proved my mom's intuition right. When he was a junior in high school he came home and announced that he had gotten a girl pregnant. This almost killed my folks. Their firstborn was a hippie who moved out of the house at seventeen. And now their second born knocked up a girl. To this day I can't say for certain what happened after that announcement. I'm pretty sure the girl must have had an abortion. Every family has secrets, and in mine they were always kept from me because I was the youngest. But there is no way my family could keep quiet if there were a grandchild out there in the world who had been put up for adoption.

One night in Steven's senior year he snuck out of the house and went into the city with his friends. He never came home. When my parents woke up the next morning and he wasn't there they called the police. They were frantic, pacing the rug, praying Steven would walk through the door.

When the cop arrived he didn't seem too concerned. This was Long Island—teenagers blew off curfew for a night in the city every weekend. But he still opened his pad and took notes on what Steven was wearing, what his frame of mind was, and the last time my parents saw him. Then, as the cop started to tell them that he'd probably show up any minute, Steven walked right through the door. He was wearing the clothes he had on the day before and looked like he hadn't slept.

My mom ran to him, hugged him, and then shouted, "Where the hell have you been?"

Steven was vague. "I don't know," he said. "Some Colombian's house."

"I can't believe you were at Columbia House!" my mom screamed.

"No, Mom," Steven said, faking exasperation. "Columbia House is a record club. I stayed at a Colombian's house."

We didn't know it at the time, but there was a reason he was being deliberately vague about where he had been. Steven was gay.

Who knows? Maybe that's why he was always so quiet and a little more aloof than the rest of us. Maybe that's why he liked to disappear while the rest of us swirled in the tornado. We all centered our lives around managing my mom and learned how to do that in a way that allowed us to function normally. Steven was not only learning to cope with her breakdowns, he was also trying to figure out who he was—and not in the way that most teenagers discover themselves, like Anthony's rebellion.

Being gay wasn't a phase Steven could grow out of or a lifestyle choice he could reject. It was as much a part of him as the heart in his chest. And at that time, as a senior in high school, I don't think he had come to grips with it yet himself. How could he? He wasn't that far removed from getting a girl pregnant. And it was the 1970s; people weren't out and comfortable the way they are today.

While he was living at home, Steven didn't tell us anything. After he graduated from high school he moved out of the house—no drama, no fight, he just walked across the stage, shook the principal's hand, and moved into Manhattan. I'd visit him at his apartment about once a month. He was driving a cab then and, one afternoon, while I was waiting for him to come home after his shift, I decided to snoop around his place. I get antsy just sitting. I like to stand up and walk around and go places. As I rifled through some stuff in the bathroom I noticed a bunch of gay men's magazines in the cabinet. I was shocked, and a little scared. I worried that at that moment someone was going to come walking through the door. I quickly shoved them back in the cabinet and walked out of the bathroom. At the time, it never occurred to me they were Steven's. I assumed they belonged to his roommate.

For a long time, the only person who knew the truth in my family was Anthony. Steven had told Anthony he was gay when he moved into the city after high school. For years, Anthony kept pushing him to share the news with the rest of us, but that wasn't Steven's style. I'm sure he was afraid of how my parents would react. He also hated the idea of making a scene. He'd been watching drama unfold his entire life and had worked hard to sidestep it. It just wasn't his way.

But when I was a freshman in college, Steven decided it was time to tell us—or maybe he just got tired of Anthony pestering him. He called Anthony and said, "Okay, I'm ready for them to know." Then he said, "You tell them." So Anthony did.

Anthony was convinced my mom would lose it and my dad would sit at the kitchen table and stoically accept it. But it was the other way around. In that moment, my dad seemed stunned and in a state of disbelief, while my mom was totally accepting. I'm not surprised. As long as my mom could focus her worry, she was strong. It's when things were good and she looked at her own life that she started to lose it.

A couple of nights later I went to Anthony's place on Long Island and he told me, too. He was as blunt as Steven was reluctant. As I sat down in his living room he blurted out, "You know Steven's gay, right?" I just said, as casually as I could, "Oh yeah, of course, I know." But I had no idea. I was blindsided. I remember leaving Anthony's and walking to my car feeling numb. It was just so shocking. It didn't help that Anthony had said it so matter-of-factly. For a day or two I desperately wanted to call Steven and tell him that I knew and that I loved him and that no matter what, he was my brother. But he would have hated that. I would have been doing it for me, not for him.

I realized that he tried to come out to me once, in his own way, a few months earlier. He'd invited me to a Sylvester concert at the Felt Forum, the arena attached to Madison Square Garden. Sylvester had a couple of big disco hits, like "Disco Heat" and "You Make Me Feel (Mighty Real)."

When we arrived I didn't pay much attention to the crowd. Then Sylvester made his entrance, like a black Liberace. He was super gay. He wore a full-length mink coat, was accompanied by a twenty-five-piece orchestra, and opened with an orchestral version of "Disco Heat." Suddenly, I was surrounded by the Gay Pride Parade. Everyone started jumping up and down, blowing police whistles. I thought I must be the only straight guy in the room besides my brother.

The truth was, as much as I loved Steven and accepted that he was gay, I wasn't entirely comfortable with homosexuality. This was 1980; none of us had heard of AIDS yet. No one in our lives was gay. Gay people lived . . . somewhere else. So the idea that my own brother was gay was something I struggled with at first. I couldn't call my friends and discuss Steven's situation with them. They're good guys, but we were a bunch of Italian guys from Long Island. We called each other fags as an insult. I didn't see the upside of telling them. After a while, though, I started to feel like the closeted gay guy in the locker room who joins in the jokes because he doesn't want anyone to know his secret.

My mom, as strong as she was the day Anthony told her, had

a hard time with it, too. I remember sitting at the kitchen table with her one night shortly after finding out and she asked me, "Do you know about Steven?" I nodded and she just started crying. Then she said, "What did I do wrong? What did I do wrong?" I told her she didn't *do* anything. She raised three boys; two were straight, and one was not. She hadn't done anything different with Steven than she had with me and Anthony. "How could it be your fault?" I asked her. She seemed comforted by that.

Steven and I never did have a conversation about it. The fact that he was gay always went unspoken. Instead he'd just talk about his life in ways that let me know he wasn't trying to hide anything anymore.

While I was in college and still living at home Steven usually came back to Long Island once a month or so to visit. He'd arrive on a Sunday morning with his friend Howard. They never stayed overnight, probably to avoid having to answer questions about sleeping arrangements. We all assumed Howard was his boyfriend, but Steven never made a declaration and we never asked. Looking back, it seems crazy. My mom had no problem hiding in Anthony's closet to catch him smoking dope, but she couldn't bring herself to ask my brother if he had a boyfriend.

Howard was ten years older than Steven and looked exactly like the Marlboro Man, with a chiseled, weathered face. My family loved when he came over, especially my mom. He was such a good cook she even let him help her in the kitchen. I know this is going to make me sound like a dick, but the two of them were the ungayest gay guys I had ever seen. There was nothing flamboyant about either one of them. When Howard and my brother stopped seeing each other a couple of years later and my brother brought someone else home, the dynamic was the same: Anyone who came into the house with him was loved and accepted; nothing about it was ever awkward.

What I enjoyed most about Steven's visits was watching him play with Anthony's son. I always remember thinking to myself, *This is going to be awesome when I get older, have kids, and move to the suburbs. Steven is going to be that fantastic, magical uncle who comes to visit every weekend.*

I thought we had time for all that.

Chapter 5

Casey Kasem, Countdowns, and Columbia House

MUSIC WAS INCREDIBLY IMPORTANT in my family. It was always blaring in the house, even at the most insane moments. Often it seemed like the only thing that actually put us all on the same page.

We had one record player and it was housed in a cabinet that was as big as a piece of furniture, like something you'd keep in the kitchen to store all your really good china. It was waist high, had four sliding doors, was stained a light brown, and nearly covered an entire wall of the living room. It would have fit perfectly on the set of *Mad Men*. At opposite ends of the piece were the speakers, also built into the cabinet. These were killer speakers; you could see them vibrate if you turned the music up too loud. The receiver and the tuner sat in the middle compartment on a shelf. Below them was the turntable. You could pile a stack of records at the top of the spindle and, as the one on the bottom finished playing, another would drop down.

If the bottom stack became too big, the music sounded like it was being played at half speed. A few years ago I saw the same system in an antiques store. The owners called it an "art deco" piece and were selling it for seven thousand dollars.

My parents and my brothers each had their own pile of albums. My dad was a sucker for the Columbia House record deals and he'd send away for opera and big-band stuff. He loved Tommy Dorsey and Harry James, and would try to teach me the differences between musicians. My mom played Ella Fitzgerald, Frank Sinatra, and Billie Holiday, her favorite. Everything she sang brought me down. Years later I learned that Billie Holiday suffered from depression, too.

Anthony was on the edge of what was radical. I remember he came home with the Frank Zappa record *Freak Out!*, which had some psychedelic images of Zappa surrounded by other washed-out-looking musicians. To me it looked scary and dangerous. When my dad listened to it he went into his "What the hell is this?" routine. He'd say that about anyone whose voice wasn't smooth as glass. The first time he heard Bruce Springsteen he said to me, "This guy can't sing." And he's right. Springsteen is a stylist; my dad was used to crooners.

When I was in grammar school, I started to track the Top 40 as intensely as I did Mets box scores. In fact, the Mets might have been the only thing that mattered to me as much as music. They had won the World Series in 1969 when I was eight years old, the exact moment my fandom was cemented. The players on that team—Bud Harrelson, Tom Seaver, Tommie Agee—were my idols. But the difference between music and baseball was that I only cared about the Mets, not any other major-league team, and my opinions were limited to being mad when they lost and happy when they won. I did not think about how Ed Kranepool could raise his batting average. But with music I cared about everything. Knowing all about it made me a part of the conversation in my house whenever my family watched Ed Sullivan or took a ride in the car or teased Anthony about his Frank Zappa obsession.

When I was around ten years old I had a paper route delivering the local Long Island *Newsday*. I had sixty houses on my route and I couldn't carry all the newspapers on my bike, so I "borrowed" a grocery cart from the local supermarket and stored it in my backyard. A lot of the other paperboys got rides when it rained, but I was out of luck. My dad was always gone before I was up and my mom . . . well, you know.

Anyway, the Sunday *Newsday* came in two sections. One I had to pick up on Saturday and the other was dropped off at my house before dawn on Sundays. It was my job, in the early morning hours, to put the two sections together before I delivered them. But first I had to check out the Billboard Top 20, which was printed in the Sunday entertainment section. I'd sit on the living room floor surrounded by stacks of newspapers and spend five or ten minutes studying the chart. There weren't a lot of changes from week to week, but it felt like following a horse race to me. The chart always listed the songs with their current rank and the previous week's ranking. I liked to see which songs were dropping and which ones were climbing the chart. The ones with a dash in the "last week's rank" column were the ones I got excited about, because it meant new music was on the way. Before I left for my route I made sure to cut the list out of my copy of the paper so I could follow along when Casey Kasem's American Top 40 came on later that day.

I mowed lawns for money then, too. (I really liked to work. I'd go to the ice cream packing plant in the Bronx with my dad and help guys stack cartons of ice cream for a dollar. To me, work looked like fun and it put me in the center of the action, or at least what that looked like to a ten-year-old kid.) After delivering the Sunday papers I'd get my lawn mower and my radio and hit up the neighbors. I'd put the radio on top of the mower handlebar and tune in. At 9 A.M. the American Top 40 with Kasem came on.

I calculated that four strips on a typical Uniondale lawn was a song. If I liked a song, I'd stop to quiet the motor and listen. If I didn't, I'd keep going. Four strips later I'd stop the lawn mower to see what the next song was. I always wanted to hear what Casey was going to say about each song. I dug the long-distance dedications. Though I wasn't raised in a corny and sentimental household, I love Norman Rockwell, I love Frank Capra, and I loved the sappy stories behind the long-distance dedications. (Alan the shrink would point out years later that at these moments I was yearning for a life I knew I was never going to have.)

Later on, I would report to my dad on everything I learned about each song from Casey. "Dad, did you know that Dionne Warwick and the Spinners got together to make a record?" I don't know if he cared or not, but he always pretended to listen.

To this day, when I know something about a song, Howard will say to me, "Who are you, Casey Kasem?" They make fun of Casey on the show a lot. One year a tape leaked out of Casey in the studio, recording his dedications. This one was about a listener's dog dying and, in the middle of reading the fan's letter, Casey screwed up and got really pissed. "You come out of these up-tempo numbers and it's impossible to make those transitions. Fucking up-tempo record every time I do a death dedication! Someone use their fucking brain and not come out of an up-tempo record when I gotta talk about a dog dying." The first time I heard those tapes I was shocked. I had bought into Casey's sincerity, hook, line, and sinker. I thought that clip must have been a fake that had been edited together, because Casey wouldn't talk like that about a dedication. Those things were sacred to him. Still, whenever Howard calls me Casey Kasem and he thinks he's ripping me, I take it as a compliment.

One time Corey Feldman came on the show and brought along his girlfriend at the time, Casey's daughter. She was pretty good-looking. When she was in the greenroom I snuck in to tell her how much I loved her dad. I was kind of embarrassed and didn't want anyone on the show to catch me fawning. I still think it would be cool to meet him.

Anyway, I used all the money I earned mowing lawns and delivering newspapers to buy records. It was an obsession that began when I was five years old. Anthony was ordering some albums from Columbia House record club and my mom said to him, "You gotta let your brother pick one." I had seen Gary Lewis and the Playboys on Ed Sullivan, and since his first name was Gary and mine was Gary, I decided I liked him. The record came to our house as part of a big package; everyone in the family got something from Columbia House. Since Anthony was the one who placed the order he handed the record to me. It was shrink-wrapped and I tore the plastic off and just stared at the cover, which was green and had the name of the band written in pink letters across it. I couldn't wait to play their big song, "Everybody Loves a Clown," but I had to wait; Anthony got to the record player first.

Gary Lewis was my first record, but the first 45 I bought was "Valeri" by the Monkees. It was during the summer of '68 and I was at my cousin Pat's in Bensonhurst. We went up to the big record store on Kings Highway and they were having a special: six 45s for one dollar. Pat told me I could choose one. So I did. The B-side of "Valeri" was "Tapioca Tundra." The stupid shit we remember . . .

I did my music scouting at Tom's Coffee Shop in Uniondale, a decrepit, decaying place. Tom was a miserable old fuck who had no business being in a service industry. Over the magazine rack hung a sign: *Free reading material can be obtained at the library.* But we kids never bought anything, magazines or otherwise. It was so dirty you wouldn't even want a doughnut. We went there because Tom had a killer pinball machine and a jukebox loaded with new music. That's where I first heard the song "Be My Baby" by the Ronettes, which even then I could tell was as close to a perfect pop song as possible.

I'd play Bally's Eight Ball on the pinball machine and listen to the jukebox, then go out to Korvette's and buy the 45s I liked best for ninety-nine cents a piece. When I came home I stacked all my 45s on a shelf in my room, right next to my bed, in alphabetical order. If I had two 45s by the same artist, they were placed chronologically.

If nothing else in my life could be orderly, at least my music would be.

Because my dad was an ice cream salesman, we took all of our family vacations in winter. (Summers I went to Brooklyn for six weeks to visit my mom's brothers and sisters. I may have been the only kid on Long Island who actually moved *into* the city when school ended.) It was ironic, since the most we could afford to do was drive to the Poconos for skiing—and no one in my family actually knew how to ski.

My dad didn't own a ski coat, ski gloves, or ski boots. He was never a suburban guy; he was just a guy from the city who happened to raise a family in the suburbs. If he could have, he would have skied in his brown double-knit pants and a pair of black leather shoes. He probably would have looked more comfortable.

The most memorable ski vacation we took was in the winter of 1970. It was a two-and-a-half-hour drive from Uniondale to the house we rented in the Poconos. To a nine-year-old kid it seemed like ten hours. We were piled in my dad's red Chevy Impala, a company car, and we listened to WABC on the radio.

Normally my dad liked listening to WOR talk radio in the car. That was my first education in radio. I still can recite the lineup for WOR: Bob Grant was the original angry, abrasive conservative guy. He was Glenn Beck before there was Glenn Beck. He would argue with the callers, yell at them, and tell them they were stupid. Then he'd invite them to come down for a fight. "I'll beat you on the head," he'd yell. My father would laugh. It was like professional wrestling. It was riveting. Long John Nebel would come on late at night. He'd tell insane stories about spaceships landing on the roof of the WOR building.

But on family road trips we'd listen to WABC, which was the station everyone in New York tuned into and everyone in the country followed. Programmers from Cleveland or Dallas would come to New York for a week, stay in a hotel, listen to WABC, copy the jingles and the station breaks and the pacing, and then take it all back home. Anywhere you went in the tri-state area and beyond, you could listen to WABC, which was a 50,000-watt AM station. We call stations with signals that powerful flamethrowers. Back then, with fewer channels, you could get WABC as far away as Boston. We definitely didn't have to change the channel on the way to the Poconos.

Every year, during the last two weeks of the year, WABC would do a Top 100 countdown, only it would play the songs all out of order. The DJ would play No. 50, then No. 72. That was the hook to make you listen. You could send in a self-addressed stamped envelope when the two weeks were up if you wanted the whole list in order. But in the Chevy Impala on the way to that vacation in 1970, the year the Carpenters' "Close to You" became a massive hit, Steven showed me a different way to keep track.

He bought a composition notebook and, before we left the house, listed the numbers 1–100 in the margins of the first few pages. For the next two and a half hours we listened to WABC intently, filling in all the songs as we went along. We never finished it (sorry, this isn't a Capra movie), but it did teach me new

ways to obsess over music. Soon after that vacation I was studying it and collecting it in a passionate way. First I'd put a record
on my parents' record player. Then, after a verse, I'd lift the needle and write down the lyrics in my composition notebook. I
repeated the process over and over, for hundreds of songs.

I also began to study liner notes. I liked knowing who
guested on which track. It was important to me to see that on
one of Linda Ronstadt's songs Andrew Gold did the claps in
the background. Amassing a record collection became my all-
consuming hobby. From an early age I thought of myself as a
collector. I even used my mowing money to buy rock-and-roll
trivia books and plastic sleeves for all my albums. Look, if you
wanted them to sound good, they had to be handled correctly.

When I was in seventh grade and Steven moved out of the
house, he gave me the collection of records he kept in orange
crates. I put every piece of music I owned into the crates—
alphabetically by artist, then chronologically. I can still picture
the cover for the Allman Brothers' *Eat a Peach,* because that
was always the first album in the pile.

Steven's gift left me with hundreds of new records to thumb
through and listen to and learn about. I sat on the floor at our
record player for hours listening to the most obscure stuff and
reading liner notes as if they were holy scripture. That era, the
early to mid-'70s, was the height of the storytelling songs, like
"The Night Chicago Died" and "Billy Don't Be a Hero." These
were bad songs with bad stories, but every verse advanced the
narrative. You had to listen to the whole song to figure out what
happened. The collection in the orange crates was the greatest
gift anyone had ever given me. (Until Steven topped it for
Christmas 1975 when he bought me all the records on my wish
list: Jefferson Starship's *Red Octopus,* Pink Floyd's *Wish You
Were Here,* and the record that changed my life, Springsteen's
Born to Run.)

I didn't realize how singular my passion was until late in seventh grade, after nearly a year of picking through Steven's collection. I was in an art class and it was close to the end of the 1974 school year. Our teacher was a hippie who had the windows open and music playing on a radio. I looked totally cool that day in a pair a flame red bell-bottoms, and I was about to prove I was so much cooler. As we were painting and listening to the music, the song "Band on the Run" came on. The cute girl at the easel next to me said, "Who sings this song?" Without hesitating I said, "Paul McCartney and Wings." Then "Benny and the Jets" came on and she asked the same question. "Elton John," I said. I wasn't showing off. I wasn't even all that nervous when I answered. The responses came as naturally as breathing. Finally, the song "Be Thankful for What You Got" came piping through. "Who's this?" she asked. "Oh, that's William DeVaughn," I said.

"Wow," she said. "You listen to a lot of radio." I don't know if she was impressed when she said that or if she meant something more like, *Wow, you loser, you must stay home and listen to the radio a lot.* But I took it as a compliment. I liked that I had a lot of knowledge about something and that someone recognized it. It made me proud. And it still does.

Sometime in 2004, we had Adam Duritz, the lead singer for Counting Crows, on the show and he was claiming to know everything about '80s music. We had just been sent a collection of twenty CDs loaded with '80s classics. So we started playing hits from those days and quizzing Duritz as well as a guy who called in and claimed to be an '80s music trivia whiz, too. The first song was "Jessie's Girl" by Rick Springfield. Duritz knew the performer and the song; the caller did not. Next was "867-5309" by Tommy Tutone. Same results. The third song was "Harden My Heart" by Quarterflash. Again, Adam got it and the caller didn't. Finally, for a challenge, we played "Believe It or Not," the theme song from the TV show *The Greatest American*

Hero. Adam knew the song title but not the performer—Joey Scarbury. But I did.

We had been looking for another fan-centered segment like "Win Fred's Money," in which listeners competed against Fred to answer rapid-fire trivia questions to try to separate him from his cash. During a break that day, I said to Howard, "I could do a music trivia game. We should make a bit about it on the show."

"Okay," he said. "Set it up."

We called it "Stump the Booey" and the premise was simple: Beat me in a five-question contest about '80s music trivia and you win ten thousand dollars. I rarely lost. One of the highlights was when a guy took me into four overtimes—nine questions—before it was finally settled. I won on the song "Lawn Chairs Are Everywhere" by Our Daughter's Wedding. My reaction when I won: "You'd know the song if you bothered to turn on the radio during the 1980s." Pretty soon I was getting hate mail for being such a jerk.

I love being "that guy" when it comes to music knowledge. I was once at one of my son Jackson's baseball games when a father from the opposing team approached me. He introduced himself and said he was a fan of the show, but that's not why he wanted to talk. He was working on a graduation video for a relative and wanted to know who sang the song "I Can See Clearly Now."

I told him, "It depends. Are you looking for the original version made famous by Johnny Nash in the seventies or are you looking for the Jimmy Cliff remake for the movie *Cool Runnings*?"

He walked away happy. For a moment I felt like I was back in seventh grade.

GREATEST AM RADIO
SINGLES OF THE '70S

"Alone Again (Naturally)," Gilbert O'Sullivan

"Bennie and the Jets," Elton John

"I Can See Clearly Now," Johnny Nash

"I Want You Back," Jackson 5

"Play That Funky Music," Wild Cherry

"Shining Star," Earth, Wind & Fire

"All Right Now," Free

"Stuck in the Middle with You," Stealers Wheel

"Spirit in the Sky," Norman Greenbaum

"Bad Luck," Harold Melvin & the Blue Notes

"Let's Get It On," Marvin Gaye

"Love Train," O'Jays

"Strawberry Letter #23," Brothers Johnson

"Band on the Run," Paul McCartney & Wings

"Smoke on the Water," Deep Purple

"A Horse with No Name," America

A Day That Will Live in Infamy

1990

Boy Gary.

That was my nickname for the first six years on the show. It wasn't even original. The guy I replaced had been "Boy Lee." Before that, Howard had called his college roommate "Boy." I was just another in a long line of boys. In 1989, the Rolling Stones held a press conference at Grand Central Terminal to announce their Steel Wheels tour. This was the early days of cable. Every network—from MTV to CNN—covered it live. With cameras rolling, I asked the first question. "Mick," I said, "Boy Gary from *The Howard Stern Show*."

I was getting too old to be called boy: I was pushing thirty. I was more than a decade older than our interns. I looked forward to shedding the tag. But I had no idea what would replace it. Until July 26, 1990.

The day began like any other—with me saying something that became fodder for the show. In the late '80s and early

'90s collecting animation art became popular. These were iconic cartoon cels—Bugs Bunny eating a carrot or Yosemite Sam sitting on a keg of dynamite—drawn by the original cartoonist, signed and then framed. They weren't mass-produced. Each picture was numbered, making them limited-edition, high-end pieces of art. Galleries began selling them for a few hundred bucks. A Mickey Mouse at the time sold for more than four hundred thousand dollars. I thought they would be a good investment. "They will never go down in value," I would say to Howard.

And he would make fun of me. I babbled about getting a Friz Freleng or a Chuck Jones, two of the big Warner Bros. artists back in the day. The truth was, I talked about the cels more than I collected them. After months of research and browsing, I owned exactly one, a picture of Bugs Bunny and Yosemite Sam.

But I had made a decision: I was going to buy a new one. And that morning, July 26, 1990, I mentioned my intention to Jackie before the show. It was a big deal for me—I was leaving the Warner Bros. family to purchase something from the Hanna-Barbera collection. I told Jackie the characters I wanted to buy and he shrugged, like he wasn't that interested. I was wrong. He was very interested.

A couple of minutes later, after we were on the air, Howard called me in. "Gary's into this weird thing, he collects cartoon art."

"Animated cels. Get it right," I said.

"My next purchase will be a Da Vinci or a Marmaduke," Howard said, imitating me in a dopey voice.

"I am strictly a Warner Bros. collector," I said. "But I am thinking about dabbling in the Hanna-Barbera stuff. I am thinking about getting a Quick Draw McGraw or a Baba Booey."

"Good, good," Howard said. "How do you make the final determination? How much does a Baba Looey go for?"

"Quick Draw and Baba Booey are about three hundred and twenty-five dollars."

"What do you call him?" Howard asked.

"Baba Booey," I answered, emphasizing the word *Booey* by raising my voice an octave.

"It's Baba Looey! You're going to hang a picture of a guy and you don't know his name. Baba Booey? Baba Booey!"

A resigned, disgusted silence descended, then Howard continued.

"Baba Booey . . . I didn't know what he was saying. A Baba Booey."

I was bored with the conversation. I figured they were done with me and they'd move on in a few minutes. This is what happened every day. I stood up and left the studio.

"He just walked out," Howard said. "He thinks we've exhausted this, but we haven't exhausted this." A pause. Then he yelled, "It's just the tip of the iceberg! Baba Booey!"

Then we went to a commercial and I said, "Okay, guys, joke's over."

I sat down at my desk and thought, *All right, it's 8:30. They'll be on to something else in an hour.*

But an hour passed, and they were still laughing at me. I'd hear *Baba Booey, Baba Booey,* followed by cackles. They sounded like monkeys who had been smoking dope all morning. The next morning it lingered and I realized it had a little bit of a shelf life. Maybe it would last a week or two. It just wasn't a nickname that was going to stick—it was like an Abba song that reached No. 1. It had two weeks, three tops. It's not that I hated the name. It was funny to say, but I just thought it was so silly. I didn't believe it would stand the test of time.

One day I came into work with a tape of Quick Draw McGraw saying the phrase "Baba Boy." If you listened closely it sounded like he was saying "Baba Booey." I even tried to bring it up, but Howard shot me down. "It's perfect," he said. "Why do you want to ruin it."

Every day, Baba Booey grew, leaving Boy Gary behind. Captain Janks, a fan from Philly who used to call talk shows like *Donahue* and scream, "Howard Stern rules!" started using Baba Booey instead. He realized that if he said it on the air, hosts weren't as quick to cut him off. They had no idea what he was saying. Larry King was his favorite target. Poor Larry. The worst thing he ever did was get an 800 number, because it meant Janks could call him nonstop without getting charged. Once, Janks got through the screeners and yelled, "Baba Booey, Baba Booey!" But Larry didn't hang up on him. He just stared into the screen, his eyes wide and confused behind those glasses, and said, "I don't understand."

Then, in February 1991, Howard released a CD called *Crucified by the FCC*, which was a compilation of all the moments that had gotten him in trouble over the years. It came with a booklet, and on the back cover was a list of the top phrases in the history of *The Howard Stern Show*. "That's not flab, honey, that's bulk" was No. 10; "It's too late, Soupy, I've already cut a string on the piano" was No. 5. And No. 1 was Baba Booey.

I thought, *Really?* It wasn't even the dumbest thing I had ever said on the show. Or the most embarrassing. I had once given such graphic details about my sex life that even my mom called to tell me I had taken it too far. And she beat people with shrubs!

But Baba Booey wasn't just about me acting stupid. It was something more visceral. The alliteration made it fun to say. It was a call to action. I used to spend a lot of weekends on the road making personal appearances. I'd hit strip clubs in Buffalo, mattress store openings in Cleveland, happy hours in Detroit—these were my specialties. A lot of times I'd bring one of my guys from Long Island with me. My first couple of times through each town I drew a lot of people. It's not as though I had a show. I'd just sign my autograph on my glossy head shots. By the third, fourth, or fifth time that I hit the same spot, the crowds grew smaller. The novelty wore off. It was just me, the guy from Howard Stern, signing my name on my face. That changed when I became Baba Booey.

Soon after the name entered the ether, the lines became longer wherever I went. It was as if Baba Booey gave people a reason to see me. "Hey," they could tell friends, "let's go see Baba Booey." Then they'd laugh—like they were stoned monkeys. I still signed autographs. But if I wrote, "To Jimmy, All my best, Gary," Jimmy would shove the picture back in my face and say, "No, just sign it Baba Booey." Pretty soon, that's all I signed.

It wasn't about me at all anymore. It had morphed into being a code for the show, like a battle cry.

Fans picked up on that idea, and followed in the steps of Captain Janks.

In 1997, a *Sports Illustrated* column mentioned Boston University and that it was Howard's alma mater. The piece ended, "Baba Booey!" It had nothing to do with me. There were the people who understood what it meant—the loyal listeners to the show; the members of the club—and the rest of the world who didn't.

The night of the O. J. Simpson slow-speed chase, in June 1994, we all learned that ABC News anchor Peter Jennings was a member of the latter group.

It was a Friday night and Mary and I were in Boston for a wedding that weekend. The Knicks were playing in Game Six of the NBA Finals. I really wanted to see this game. We were at Legal Sea Foods in Copley Square and I snuck away to the bar to get the score. I saw the white Bronco and said to the bartender, "Can you put on the game?" Earlier in the day there had been reports that O.J. had killed himself. I didn't know what was going on. Then some drunk leaned over and slurred, "O.J.'s in the car with a gun. Half of Los Angeles is chasing him."

I wasn't that interested. I wanted to find the game. So I dragged Mary, who was five months pregnant, all around Boston looking for a decent bar that showed sports. There wasn't a single one. All of them were tuned to O.J. I couldn't believe the people in Boston hated New York so much they would rather watch a freak show than the finals of an NBA game. I didn't sense the magnitude of the moment. Big deal. It's not like I didn't have a part in the night's drama. Kind of.

This was before the Internet was big, remember. I didn't care about the chase so Mary and I just went back to our hotel and went to bed. In the morning we drove twenty-five miles to the wedding in Salem. As soon as I walked through the door, I was barraged. "You were on TV last night!" "I can't believe you were in the middle of the O.J. chase!"

Well, I wasn't. I was asleep, next to my pregnant wife, completely ignoring the chase because I was pissed no one would show the Knicks game. But when a loyal and genius fan decided to call Peter Jennings, I instantly became a part of the biggest story of the decade. Here's how it went down:

"We have with us now Mr. Robert Higgins, who can see inside O.J.'s car. Mr. Higgins, Can you see him doing anything specific?" Jennings asked.

"He is just sitting there looking nervous."

"Can you hear anything?"

"There is too much commotion. But I can still see O.J. and he looks scared."

"Thank you, Mr. Higgins."

"And Baba Booey to y'all."

Jennings pulled a Larry King: confused silence. He had no idea what had just been said. If not for an explanation from Al Michaels, a fan of the show who happened to call in to Jennings after hearing the magic words, the anchor would have remained in the dark.

"Peter," Michaels began, "just for the record that was a totally farcical call. He said something in code at the end that is indicative of the name of a certain radio talk show host. So he was not there."

"Okay, Al," Jennings said. "Thank you very much. Not the first time or the last time we'll have been had."

We live by a rule on the show: Don't dissect the comedy. Do that and it's no longer funny. So we have never tried to break down why Baba Booey sticks with people. But we did analyze that prank call as much as possible. We wanted to make a Broadway musical about it. We even re-created the entire scene and had Al Michaels on to reenact his role. You could tell he had a hard time explaining to Jennings what had happened. He didn't really want to admit he had a foot in our world; it's like being at a party and admitting you know the slob who just walked through the door.

After that, it became so much more than just a catchphrase for fans. Mary and I have had this conversation a lot. It doesn't really mean what it meant anymore. It has morphed into something entirely different. Howard will sometimes say to me, "Can you believe it's lasted this long?" But it's not about me. It's just something said to make other people laugh, whether in sitcoms, songs, or in someone's living room.

Or airports. When Jackson was three years old we visited my brother Anthony, who had moved to Austin, Texas. The two of us were sitting at our gate waiting to go home when a man walked by and said, "Hey, Baby Booey." Jackson couldn't stop laughing. I asked him, "What's so funny?"

He looked at me with a big smile and said, "He thinks you are a Baba Booey."

Truth is, I am.

GREATEST ALL-TIME
BABA BOOEY SHOUT-OUTS

10. **David Letterman, Top 10 List:** Every once in a while, Letterman will randomly insert Baba Booey into his Top 10 lists. It's always 10 percent funnier when he says it.

9. **Dan Patrick on *ESPN SportsCenter:*** In 2003 the Cubs were five outs from going to the World Series when a fan named Steve Bartman interfered with a foul ball that would have been caught. They went on to lose the game, extending their World Series drought. On *SportsCenter,* anchor Dan Patrick takes a call he thinks is from Bartman. Instead it's Captain Janks, who screams, "Baba Booey!" just before he hangs up.

8. **Larry King:** In 1992, billionaire Ross Perot was running for president. During an appearance on *Larry King Live,* "Bob from Bowie" calls in and asks Perot if he can "mind meld with Howard Stern's penis."

7. ***30 Rock:*** Tina Fey tells Tracy Morgan that she's worried she may have said something inappropriate to a guy. Tracy replies, "I yelled out 'Baba Booey' at Cronkite's funeral."

6. ***King of Queens:*** Kevin James's wife comes home from work and finds him still in bed with a phone to his ear. He says, "I've been on hold with Baba Booey since six-thirty."

5. **Conan O'Brien:** Triumph the Insult Comic Dog, covering the 2008 presidential debates at Hofstra, says,

"Long Island is buzzing. I haven't seen this many people since a Baba Booey in-store appearance."

4. *Family Guy:* Peter is testifying before Congress. When he is at a loss for what to say, he yells, "Howard Stern's penis! Baba Booey, Baba Booey!" and then runs out.

3. *Survivor:* Five seasons ago the last challenge of the year was called Bob-on-a-Booey.

2. *Saturday Night Live:* The day after we left K-Rock, Tina Fey did a bit on "Weekend Update" about Iraq's presidential election. She mentioned Mahmoud Ali-abi and Muhammed Abibbi, and then said, "The winner was Baba Booey."

1. **ABC's *World News Tonight*:** "Baba Booey to y'all!"

Chapter 6

There Is Such a Thing as Being Overprotective

AS I SAID, MY parents briefly followed the Cotroneo tradition when they married: They moved into one of the apartments in my grandparents' building in Bensonhurst, close to the rest of my mom's family. That arrangement lasted for a little over two years, until the night Steven was born. That's when my grandfather kicked them out.

Everything was going smoothly when the night began. My mom had an easy delivery while my dad stood vigil in the waiting room, passing out cigars to celebrate the birth of his second son. Once my dad had seen his new baby boy and made sure my mom was comfortable, he headed back to the apartment to get a good night's sleep. As he lay in bed smoking a cigarette and reflecting on the day, he started to get tired. So he rolled over, snubbed the butt out in an ashtray on the nightstand, and fell asleep. Problem was, he didn't put the cigarette out completely. And he was a restless sleeper. At some point during the night he knocked the ashtray off the nightstand, and the smoldering cigarette rolled under the bed and lit the rug. Smoke started to fill the room and seep into the apartment upstairs, where my uncle lived with his wife. I told you, the Cotroneos were tight.

The smoke woke up my dad and he frantically tried to put out the fire. Meanwhile my aunt ran down and started banging on the door. She was screaming for my dad to get out and when he didn't answer she started yelling, "Oh my God, he's dead, he's dead, he's dead!"

"But I wasn't dead," my dad told me. "I was just too busy trying to put out the fire to answer her. When I finally did, there was smoke damage all over the room and in apartments above. And your grandparents never bothered insuring anything. So, well, they were mad and we had to move."

For the next several years my mom, dad, and brothers bounced around Bensonhurst, never straying too far from my mom's family. But in 1963, a couple of years after I was born, my mom and dad decided it was time to decamp for the suburbs. We settled in Uniondale, because my mom had a sister living there and it wasn't too far from the city for my dad to commute.

Now, there are plenty of really fancy, upscale places in Long Island, but Uniondale was a blue-collar town. Lots of my friends' dads wore uniforms to work with their names stitched on the front. I would say the town was about 60 percent Italian, German, and Irish, and 40 percent black.

There was a lot of white flight in the early 1970s. Our houses were on tiny lots and everyone's backyard fence touched to form four corners. I remember one time a black family moved into one of the houses that shared our four-corner zone. A few weeks later, another neighbor left town in the middle of the night. My mom got up at two in the morning to get a drink and saw the moving truck. Then she started panicking and launched into the whole "our house is going to go down in value" rap. But my father didn't want to move. That was another big bone of contention between them. She wound up living there for thirty-six years, until she moved to Florida in 1997.

Racial tension was a constant issue. Before I started Lawrence Road Junior High kids would say, "Watch your back," because the black kids were going to come after me. But those first few weeks I didn't notice anything unusual. Then, around the last week of September, I heard there was going to be a fight between the black kids and the white kids on the front lawn of the school after the final bell. I didn't know what was going on, but I went to the front lawn and there were about twenty-five white kids and twenty-five black kids facing off, yelling at one another. Then one kid from each group stepped out and started swinging, while everyone else screamed and cheered them on. Suddenly a car came screeching around the corner and two white kids jumped out swinging chains and tire irons. That's about when the cops showed up and everyone scattered. That scene went on every year until I graduated from high school.

The white guys in the middle of it were part of a group known as the Park Boys. They hung out at Uniondale Park, the site of my short-lived but magical journey to Woodstock with Anthony. He took me down there a lot when we were growing up, but he was always getting high while he was supposed to be watching me. Eventually, after Anthony moved out and I was in junior high, my parents let me walk down to the park by myself. If you went over there on a Saturday or a Sunday morning you'd take a seat on a bench and wait for someone to show up. Pretty soon there'd be two or three of you hanging out. By 10 A.M. around twenty-five kids would be loitering near this bench getting yelled at by the guy who worked for the town and managed the park. I started smoking cigarettes there. The

guys known as the Park Boys were tough by suburban stan-
dards. And, the truth was, I wasn't a tough guy, but I didn't
know where else to go. Hanging with them was kind of like our
version of hanging with Joe Pesci in *Goodfellas:* One second
he'd be laughing with you and the next he'd want to kill you for
no reason at all. In Queens they probably would have gotten
the crap kicked out of them, but in Uniondale they qualified as
badasses.

One of the guys, at sixteen, was already drinking a case of
beer a day. The older kids in the gang were getting into weird
shit like robbing houses. At first it was juvenile stuff—lawn
mowers and bicycles from someone's garage. Then it became
breaking into people's homes and stealing prescription pills like
Valium and Seconal.

One Saturday I got to the park early and one of these guys
was already there. He didn't like me and I was always too scared
to talk to him. But since no one else was around he asked me if
I wanted to go for a joyride. Someone who was playing tennis
at the park had left the keys in their convertible, which was
parked right by our bench, just out of sight of the courts. Being
an idiot, I just shrugged. I didn't want to look like a pussy. I
really just wanted to be accepted. So we got in and drove the
car around a bunch of local side streets for fifteen minutes. He
kept mouthing the words, "Be cool, be cool." He may have been
talking to himself. Other than that, we didn't speak. We were
both too scared.

The whole time I was thinking how stupid this was. The
dickhead didn't even let me drive. Plus, if we got caught and my
father found out he'd snap me in half. It would be much worse
than when I was thirteen and he and my mom caught me
sneaking a sip of a beer during a Jay and the Americans concert
in Eisenhower Park in East Meadow, which was Long Island's
version of Central Park. I wasn't even a drinker. A buddy of
mine was just about finished with his beer and asked if I

wanted to kill it. It wasn't even beer at that point, it was back-wash. As I put the bottle to my lips I saw my parents, staring right at me. They grounded me for two weeks on the spot. But since it was summer and I was always around, my mom let me loose after a week. She got sick of me. That was the only time I had ever been grounded. But stealing a car? The physical punishment I imagined was terrible, but the fact that my father would think I was beyond stupid was horrifying. I wasn't even stealing something that I could keep, or would make my life better, or would help me buy more records. He'd think his son was a moron and a bad thief. Thank God we were both shitting our pants, so the ride didn't last very long.

When we got back we parked the car a block away. For good measure he stole the tennis rackets in the backseat.

I knew that wasn't my scene. I wasn't a goody two-shoes, but I was never comfortable there. I'd see a kid shoplift something like a baseball glove, and then I'd have to go back with him to his house, where his mom would look at him, look at the glove with the tag still on it, and then ask him where he got it. "I found it," he'd say. Then his mom would roll her eyes and ignore it. I could never get away with that. If my mom saw me show up at home with a new baseball glove she'd grill me as if I'd shot Bobby Kennedy.

One afternoon we were hanging out at the park, playing a stupid game designed to hurt somebody. It goes like this: When a guy is standing up, someone sneaks up behind him on his hands and knees. Then someone else pushes the guy, who falls backward over the kid on his hands and knees. Well, I was the guy on my hands and knees, behind a heavy kid. When he fell he landed on my head, which smacked the concrete. I stood up and was acting spacey and weird and asking people strange questions, so they pointed me in the direction of my house and told me to go home.

When I stumbled through the front door and told my mom

what happened she freaked out and took me to the doctor, who diagnosed me with a mild concussion. That should be the end of the story. All I had to do was rest on our sheet-covered couches while my mom nursed me back to health.

But while I was half asleep on the couch, still woozy and feeling like I might puke, my mom bolted out of the house. I didn't have time to stop her, and couldn't have if I had managed to catch her. Her son had been injured; she wanted answers. Even if it meant leaving me disoriented with a concussion and alone.

When she got to Uniondale Park, instead of explaining who she was and asking what happened, she stormed into the middle of this street gang and raised hell. Of course she was right to want some answers. But she only provoked the park punks. They told her to fuck off. So she started yelling back even louder. "Fuck off" was her warm-up. She cleared her throat with "fuck off." These boys were amateurs. This wasn't her being depressed and acting out; this was her being Ellen, of the Fighting Cotroneos. It devolved into a shouting match, my petite mom and her dictionary of swears versus a bunch of hoods. I have no idea who won. When my mom got home she did what she always did: acted like nothing happened and made dinner.

But of course, I feared the worst. Every time my mom left the house I thought I'd end up having to explain her actions. A broken heel on top of the Empire State Building; using shrubs as weapons; firing Chuck Taylors at sales clerks. If my brain hadn't been scrambled maybe I could have stopped her. But I didn't.

The next day I quickly realized she had made an impression. People I didn't even know came up to me and said, "Man, your mom is nuts." It became a running gag for a while. If someone acted crazy some wise guy would always add, "Yeah, like Gary's mother."

I retreated when I heard the jokes, which were impossible to stop or to top. I thought, *If I don't say anything, people will get bored and let it go.* I wasn't being overly mature or intelligent; I was genuinely scared any response I had would result in a fight. I basically curled up in a ball and waited for it all to end. Eventually it would, and I could come back out of my shell.

Of course, my mom's instinct to protect me at all costs never changed. That was obvious to me once I was older, and it became obvious to the rest of the world on June 2, 1987.

I'd started working on *The Howard Stern Show* in 1984 on WNBC in New York. From the very first day, I had been a regular on the air and was often the butt of Howard's harshest jokes. I loved it. I had been taking abuse my entire life, so taking it on the show was no different. The gift of growing up in my house was learning to understand that someone could attack you and still love you. I knew how to separate the two. Sick, I know, but it's a skill that's served me well. It's when people ignore you that you have to start worrying. When the guys made fun of me it always felt like I was one of the gang.

While the show is on the air, I am usually in my office, doing several things at once. Nowadays I am checking email or confirming schedules or managing the staff. Back then I would have been opening actual letters in envelopes and cataloging tapes. But the constant is that I always have one ear on the show, in case I'm needed. No matter where we broadcast from, my office is just a few steps from the studio.

That June afternoon, Howard had called me in just before he started a segment about how he had recently been to the dentist. I didn't know where he was going with it and I wasn't particularly concerned. This was just another day at the office.

He said the dental assistant there had taught him how to brush his teeth—turns out he had been doing it wrong all these years. "A lot of people don't know how to brush," he said. "Gary, get in here." When I entered the studio he looked at me and said, "I look in Gary's mouth and see a disaster going on. Let me ask you something, when you eat spicy food does it bother your tongue?"

"My tongue?"

"Yeah, your gums, your tongue?"

"No," I answered.

"That's because he's burned everything out," Robin chimed in.

I smoked back then. A lot.

"But your gums don't ever burn and you don't get infections in your gums?" Howard asked.

"I haven't had that problem in a while."

"What happens is you get food caught in there and you start to smell," he continued.

"I've kissed women and never had anyone complain," I said.

"She must be in a coma, your girlfriend. She's unconscious from breathing in all those fumes. I don't mean to embarrass you or anything but you have to do something about those gums. Let me turn you on to my dentist."

"They are going to have to put on one of those astronaut suits to go in there," Robin said. Then she pretended to sound like an astronaut reporting over a static radio to earth, "We are going in now."

"Yeah, they are going to have to put on a space suit to get in Gary's mouth," Howard continued. "I mean everyone gets bad breath, but yours is unbelievable."

"That's not true," I said, meekly. I thought, *Why are they busting my balls? I get that it's for the good of the show but isn't it going pretty far?*

"Gary," Robin said, "I am over here wilting."

"Robin's eyes are watering," Howard said. "Come on, Gary, take a hint."

"No one in my life has ever told me I have bad breath," I said.

"Oh please, face it, man, you need a mouth transplant," Howard replied.

"I just can't believe you guys are having fun with this. I just can't believe it."

"Seriously, it's pretty damn bad when your mouth is your smelliest orifice," Howard said. Then the studio erupted with laughs and catcalls.

"Oh no, he's starting to cry," Howard said. "Listen, I'm going to make a dental appointment for you. But your bad breath is famous. I'm going to make it under a fake name. I don't want the dentist to know you are coming. Really, I've smelled *tuches* better than that. Gary's proctologist put his finger in Gary's mouth. He said 'Open up. Oh my God you have teeth in there. The man talks through his *tuches*.'"

"I just want the listeners to know I do not have bad breath," I said.

"Oh Gary, wake up and smell your breath," Howard said. "Look at Gary, he's getting all upset. Well, I'm going to get you an appointment with my gal Judy for your birthday," Howard said. "And you know her motto: When you see Judy, you don't smell like doody. I swear homosexuals smell Gary's breath and they go into heat. He thinks they are flirting with them, he is sending out a scent. Let's take a break."

I was moderately irritated during the commercial. But I told myself the same thing I always did: Deal with it, they're just busting your balls, move on. We have other stuff to do on the show.

"If you're just joining us we've been giving Gary a hard time about his breath," Howard said when he came back on the air. "So here is what we are going to do: We are going to bring people in and ask them to smell his breath."

"You know what," I said. "This is not a good morning for it.

I've been smoking a lot of cigarettes and I drank that Nutri-system shake and it coats your mouth. I'll lose."

"Get some of the workmen in the hallway. Bring them in here. Hi, how are you, sir? Are you a carpenter?"

"No, I am a painter," said a man with a thick Italian accent.

"We don't know you, right? Are you a fan of the show?" Howard asked.

"No," he said. "Not really."

"I want you to do me a favor. See that guy in the blue shirt? Gary Dell'Abate is his name."

"Oh that is my *paesano,*" he said.

"I want you to smell his breath."

"Oh my God."

"He's a good guy, but his mouth to me is smellier than his *tuches.*"

"Well, we put a little shellac in the mouth and polish it up."

"I don't think that will help. Now do you mind if he breathes in your face."

I did it. There was no reaction.

"Gary," Howard said. "Do me a favor, say, 'Hello, Boss.'"

"Hello, Boss." I knew the painter was going to say something mean. He had to. He was on the radio and wanted to be funny.

"Ooh he needs some mouthwash," the painter said.

"How bad is it one to ten, ten being the worst?" Howard asked.

"I go near the eight. But if he goes in the shower today he's a new man."

We took another break and I thought that would be the end of it. I was wrong. The next caller on the line was Howard's mom.

"I think, Howard, that you are really hitting the bottom of the barrel to do a show about Gary's breath. I think you have hit a new low. Gary is so devoted and sweet and wonderful. I have been near him and never smelled anything like what you are talking about. It's very unfair of you."

"Let me tell you something, Ma. We work with the guy every day."

"I know you do, and he is wonderful. And this is the way you show your love? If anyone did this to you, Howard, you would hit the ceiling."

"Mommy, they took a poll and four out of five dentists said he doesn't own a toothbrush. It's the worst-smelling orifice on his body, and if I don't tell him, who is going to tell him? Gary, don't you appreciate this?"

"No, I really don't, Boss, because I don't believe it."

"How could you do this to Gary?" Howard's mom said. "He is so devoted to you."

"I am doing this out of love."

"How do you think his mother is going to feel?"

We'd soon find out. Because when I got home later that day Howard called. I was watching *Jeopardy!*, which I watched every day. I am a trivia genius, after all.

"How you doing?" he said to me.

Howard didn't ever call to ask me how I was doing. I said, "Okay."

"Were you okay with today?"

"Yeah." Actually, I hadn't given it any thought. He had been making fun of me for years and never apologized.

"I'm sorry if I was too hard on you this morning."

"Howard, what is all this about?"

"Your mother called my mother. She was very upset. Then my mother called me and said I better call you and apologize. So I'm sorry."

I was mortified. Whose mother calls their boss's mother to complain about their son's treatment? All I wanted to do was get off the phone with him so I could call my mom and ask her what the fuck she was doing. Howard didn't know anything about how I grew up or my mom's tendency for outbursts and her history with depression. Suddenly I was ten years old again and remembering how anxious I got when she and I were out in public—would she lose it? Would someone be asking me the next day if she was crazy? Was Gary's crazy mom going to be a recurring bit on the show, just like she was in Uniondale Park? And then I realized there was something worse: my mom calling the office every day to yell at someone, like she used to do to my dad's secretary, co-workers, and boss. I decided I needed to show her I was a big boy, that I didn't need coddling. And, in a way, I wanted her to hear that calling my boss's mom made things worse for me, not better. So I said to Howard, "Listen, tomorrow I want you to hammer me as hard as you ever have."

He had no problem with that. After we hung up I called my mom. "Mom, you gotta be kidding me! You can't do that. I'm a grown-up, I have my own apartment! I live in Manhattan!"

"I know," she said. "But you sounded so upset."

"That is the show!" I was still yelling. "Why wouldn't you call me, not her?"

I was really angry, not just because of what she did, but because I wanted to be clear that she was never to call my office or anyone I worked with ever again. Maybe it was a singular moment of clarity for her, because I never once heard about her interfering again. But I still spent many months after that being wary whenever I got ripped on the show. I was never out of the woods. It reminded me of something my father always said about my mom: She does the right thing in the wrong way, and the way she does it pisses everyone off.

In junior high I first started exploring the idea of dating girls. There was one girl in particular I liked to flirt with and we began passing each other notes in class. I don't think we had ever been alone together or held hands, let alone kissed. But we joked about a lot of stuff. At the end of one of the notes she sent me she added, "PS, I'm pregnant and you did it and now you are going to pay."

If you were thirteen and read that note in context, you'd know it was a joke and think it was hilarious. I tucked it in my wallet and forgot about it.

The next day I accidentally left my wallet and my lunch money at home. I called my mom and asked her to bring it to school. Uh-oh. You had to be three steps ahead of her, and already I was a step behind. I hadn't remembered what was in my wallet until after I'd asked her to bring it to me. *Okay, she won't read it,* I thought, and then almost immediately realized, of course she would. I told myself, *If she reads that last line, she'll get that it was a joke.* Then I immediately thought to myself, *Of course she won't know it was a joke.*

I was sitting in English class when I got called to the office. When I walked in I found my mom, crying hysterically. "Mom, you read the note didn't you?"

She couldn't even speak; she just nodded her head yes. How could I have known she probably had visions of the night Steven came home and announced he had knocked up his girl-friend?

"It was a joke, Mom!"

Didn't matter. I should have known better. I should have run through the scenarios *before* I called her. In that way, it's no different than producing a radio show—it's all about being able to anticipate.

"Please leave now, Mom," I said, while she sat in the office sobbing. "You are making a scene. Go home."

That night, as soon as my father got home, I watched the two of them walk into their bedroom and close the door. A few minutes later my dad came back out, alone. "You shouldn't joke about stuff like that," he told me.

"Okay," I said.

To this day, I think what my dad really meant was, You shouldn't joke about stuff like that—because then I have to deal with your mother.

My Caps

1988

My mom had taken the antibiotic tetracycline when she was pregnant with me. Turns out, doctors later learned, that a common side effect for pregnant women who take the drug is that it can permanently stain their kids' teeth. No joke. My entire life, I had teeth that were stained in a strange, asymmetrical pattern. Kids made fun of me for it. They were merciless. Most of what I remember about fifth grade is being picked on for having a mouthful of yellow teeth. I asked a girl out once—who even knew what that meant at that age—and she turned me down because of my banana-colored chompers. I was crushed and told my mom about it, which you might think was a stupid move, but in moments like that my mom was at her best. She was absolutely convinced the girl was an idiot.

"You are the most handsome boy in that school," she told me. "That is her problem, not yours." I was thinking, *Ma, I've got a mirror, I know that's not true.* But if your mom isn't your biggest fan then you are kind of fucked.

Anyway, it didn't help matters that I was deathly afraid of the dentist. Sometimes I outright refused to go. If anyone put their hands in my mouth I would gag. But my freshman year in college, as I was gaining more confidence in school and working at the radio station and thinking about the life I might have once I escaped Long Island, I decided it was time to get my yellow teeth capped.

The experience was brutal. I thrashed and gagged and struggled. And that was just when they put the bib on me. When the dentist finally came in and saw what was happening he exhibited exactly the kind of empathy I'd become used to all my life: He told me to calm down and grow up. I was so shocked, I did.

After that dreadful, scary, painful experience, I swore off going to the dentist again. I couldn't do it. I was just too scared. A year went by, then two, and three. I might have gone once or twice before graduating from college, but when I started working I never bothered. It didn't matter how much Howard made fun of my teeth or my breath or any combination of how they worked together. I wasn't going. And it turned into an issue. My gums became badly infected and my teeth were in really bad shape. Underneath the caps my teeth were literally rotting, like something out of eighteenth-century England.

My teeth, how big they were, how bright they were, how much they resembled a horse's, became a constant topic of conversation on the show, along with my deathly fear of dentists. By the time I had been working with Howard for a couple of years, it had been close to six years since I had sat in a dentist's chair. My mouth was killing me, but I could not bring myself to make an appointment.

One afternoon in 1987, I went to a graduation party for one of our interns at her parents' house. One of the intern's uncles walked up to me and introduced himself. He said his name was Charles Randolph and that he was a big fan of the show. He also happened to be a dentist. "I know what you've said on the air about dentists," he said. "But you've got to see someone. Come by my office. I promise I will make you comfortable."

Of course that phrase—"I promise I'll make you comfortable"—sounds creepy now, but I immediately liked and trusted him. And even I knew caps didn't last forever, especially if you never bother going to the dentist. So I resolved to see Dr. Randolph and have them replaced.

But it wasn't that easy. After years of neglect, my gums were so bad I needed several appointments and treatments to clean them up. Naturally, when it was finally time to take care of the caps, it couldn't be a private moment between me and Dr. Randolph. It was a part of the show. Only this time, it was going to be videotaped.

It was the winter of 1988 and Howard had decided to do our first pay-per-view special, called *Howard Stern's Negligee and Underpants Party*. It was the early days of pay-per-view on cable. There were still plenty of places around the country that weren't wired for cable. People were getting excited and ordering the special. The numbers coming in were astounding. We started hearing about fans who had plans to drive for miles just to get to a town that was wired, so they could book motel rooms for viewing parties. It became one of the highest-grossing premium specials of the time.

We did a Lesbian Dial-a-Date segment and had Dweezil and Moon Unit Zappa on as guests. Vinnie Mazzeo lit his underwear on fire and then cooked an egg. And they filmed me at the dentist getting my teeth capped. Unfortunately, the show ran long, so most of Vinnie's bit and all of mine got cut from the special. That's when Howard had a brilliant idea: Let's sell a videotape of the show and include the stuff that was cut out, including my dental visit. Only instead of just slapping the segment onto the end of the show, Howard and I added a running play-by-play of my procedure. Basically it was the equivalent of the bonus commentary on a DVD, a decade before anyone was doing that.

Honestly, it's pretty gross to watch. I'm not sure how either of us made it through the analysis. In fact, while I'm sitting in the chair, I look into the camera and say, "You have no idea how disgusting this is going to get."

First there was a shot of Dr. Randolph sticking a needle several inches long into my gums, right above my two front teeth. Then he took a drill and sliced open my caps, a straight line down the middle. "There goes twelve hundred dollars' worth of caps," I said on the tape.

"Oh man, oh man!" Howard was screaming.

It was actually an excruciating experience all around. There was a camera inches from my mouth as Dr. Randolph took a pair of dental pliers and started tugging and pulling on my caps, jimmying them back and forth as if each one was a wedding ring that was on too tight. First you see the cap, which is split in two, moving my gum line and then all of a sudden, crack, it comes loose. What's beneath it is a yellow tooth that looks as small as a baby's because it had been shaved the very first time I had caps put in.

"Hey look," Howard said in the voice-over. "It's Eddie Munster."

After that, Randolph took a tiny drill the size of a pin and started creating a space at my gumline so the new cap could slide in easily. Blood was squirting out, making my already yellow, shaved teeth look even more discolored and grotesque.

"Look how green your teeth are there," Howard said.

"That's how bad they used to be," I said.

"You look like Linda Blair in *The Exorcist*."

Then there was a shot of the nurse, grimacing. Even she couldn't believe it.

Pretty soon all four of my caps were off, revealing a bleeding, oozing mess of a mouth. Between my jagged, misshapen teeth were spaces as wide as Alfred E. Neuman's.

"Ugh, I can't believe we are asking people to pay $24.95 for this," Howard exclaimed.

"I look like Michael Spinks," I said.

Toward the end of the procedure Howard said into the camera, "Okay, give them the money shot."

I smiled wide and showed off my brand-new teeth. They were better than ever. It had been worth the pain, physical and otherwise.

Chapter 7

The Mott Street Gambler Goes Broke

I RODE MY BIKE all over town when I was growing up. To Uniondale Park, to a friend's house. I had an itch to just hop on and go somewhere all the time. It used to drive me nuts sitting on that park bench, talking about what we were going to do all day. We'd start at ten in the morning and twelve hours later, we'd smoked, gotten yelled at, annoyed each other, and hit each other, but we hadn't actually gone anywhere. Even worse, I couldn't really drink or smoke as much as the other kids because my mom was like the Gestapo.

Whenever I came home—from anywhere—she'd grab me by both sides of my face and tilt my head down so she could give me a big kiss on the top of my head. While she was telling me how happy she was to see me and how much she'd missed me, because it had been nearly a whole day since I'd seen her, she'd take a big whiff to see if she could smell smoke or alcohol.

I hated that. But she did it with all of her kids. I blame Anthony.

Once he went to the Felt Forum, the theater next to Madison Square Garden, to see the Doors. He smoked a lot of pot that night and came home at around two in the morning. Everyone was asleep, but he was still seeing things. So he popped open his bedroom window and lit up another joint. Suddenly my mom jumped out of the closet and yelled, "Aha! I caught you!" Sadly, Anthony realized he wasn't tripping. He was slammed back into real life with our mom.

I would get antsy hanging around the park every day, not drinking that much, barely smoking, not going anywhere. Around this age I started to develop the wanderlust my brothers had. Once I was old enough to know better, being at home was the last place I wanted to be. One day, months before I entered middle school, I hopped on my bike and rode over to the junior high. I was curious to see what the school was really like.

I arrived after the final bell had rung. School was out, but the doors were open, so I walked in to get a drink and have a look around. That's when I had a *World According to Garp* moment. I heard a commotion down one of the hallways, turned a corner, and in front of me was the lunchroom. The double doors were wide open. The benches and tables were pushed against the walls, there were wrestling mats on the floor, and there was lots of yelling. The coach spotted me and yelled at me to get the hell out of there, but I stood transfixed. That was it for me. All I knew was pro wrestling and turnbuckles, but this just looked so cool. It looked hard. It looked like you had to be strong and very macho. I was none of these things, so that may have been the appeal.

When I finally got into seventh grade, I was absolutely the worst wrestler on the team. The older guys relished twisting me, pinning me, and just plain beating the shit out of me. I really didn't have any idea what I was doing. But I loved practice; I loved trying to get better and seeing the smallest hints of improvement, even if I was the only one who noticed them.

I was so committed I went to a weeklong wrestling camp at Hofstra University, in Uniondale, between seventh and eighth grades. I got better. I even allowed myself to think I was getting good. I wrestled at 136 pounds. There were two wrestlers in each weight class on our team. But local meets only allowed schools to enter one wrestler from each class. So my team had wrestle-offs, where the guys in each weight class went one-on-one to see who got the tourney spot. I didn't win a single wrestle-off in seventh grade. But in eighth I did. Again and again. Then I started to win matches, too. The coach loved me and I was seen as a rising star on the team.

Until, of course, I fucked up.

I was hanging out on the tennis courts at school one day toward the end of eighth grade when a teacher strolling by saw me smoking a cigarette. She told the wrestling coach.

The coach, Mr. Calabretta, was such a good, young, supportive guy. We could relate to him; we loved him. So it was crushing when he kicked me off the team with only two weeks left in the season. I couldn't bear to tell my parents. Instead I spent time hanging at a friend's whose mom was never home. I stayed there until dinner. When I got home I'd tell my parents, "Wow, practice was exhausting today."

My mom probably had no idea, until now. Sorry, Ma.

It wasn't a particularly good time for me to be fucking up. While her moods became less erratic over the years, my mom was never cured. Even when she wasn't depressed she was always ready for a fight.

One Saturday morning my buddy Steve was over and, as usual, she was railing at me. As I got older, I gave it right back. And on this particular morning the fight ended with me at the bottom of the stairs in our basement and her at the top of them, heaving an Electrolux vacuum cleaner at me. It landed with a thud in the middle of the steps and rolled down, stopping at my feet. Steve said, "What was that about?"

"Nothing. It's just Saturday morning," I answered.

The tension level in the house when I was in middle school was unusually high, because my father was out of work. My dad was stubborn and, well, he was the Mott Street Gambler, so he wasn't afraid to play a game of chicken. He was very good at selling ice cream. So good that, when his boss started his own company making a high-end premium brand of ice cream, my dad was recruited as one of the first salesmen. The company was called Häagen-Dazs, which looked nice but meant nothing. The guy who started the company, Reuben Mattus, grew up in the Bronx.

My father once explained the company's philosophy to me: Most other ice cream was selling for sixty-five cents a gallon. "But we sold it for a dollar twenty-five a pint. The idea was that if it sounded exotic and it was expensive, it must be good." And it was. There were nights my dad came home and his trunk was loaded with Häagen-Dazs. The pints used to come in sleeves of eight and his car would be weighed down with ice cream packed in dry ice. We had an extra freezer in our basement dedicated to rum raisin, strawberry, vanilla, and chocolate, my favorite. We had so much of it we didn't even use bowls. Instead we'd put the first letter of our first name in Magic Marker on the bottom of a pint, eat a little bit, and then put it away.

Häagen-Dazs started to do really well and the company was growing, but my dad thought Reuben wasn't delivering on some of the compensation promises he'd made when the company first started. So my dad just quit. He felt betrayed and for a while the Mattus name was a dirty word around our house. The real problem was that my father didn't have another job lined up. And he wasn't making all that much to begin with. The only savings I knew about were in an old water cooler jug in my parents' closet that was filled with coins, mostly pennies.

My family struggled for three years after my father quit his job, throughout my time in junior high. But he handled it the same way he did everything else: with old-school stoicism. He'd never say that he felt scared or ashamed. But I knew it was killing him, because no one I knew worked harder than my father. He could be puking on the side of the road on the way to work and not turn around to come home.

He refused to go on the dole. Instead, to make ends meet, he hustled to scrape together a few dollars, just like he had when my parents were first married. Only this time the stakes were higher. He got involved with a guy who had a start-up panty-hose business. Then he tried selling ladies' clothing and hand-bags at flea markets. We were barely paying the bills. My mom did the food demonstrations at department stores, but she could never keep a job for very long.

Before he quit, I knew we weren't rich, but if I wanted to go to Nathan's or if I asked my dad for a couple of bucks to go hang with my friends, it was never a big deal. Now when I asked, he couldn't give it to me. The man had never been out of work in his life, and I could feel the pressure mounting. I quickly learned not to ask for stuff.

I knew things were getting bad when, the summer before eighth grade, I didn't make that annual trek to the department store for new school clothes. My father was working in the clothing business at this point and all I wanted was a new pair of Levi's, but there was no way we could afford them. Instead my father had a box of a brand called Cheap Jeans at the ware-house. He brought those home and that's what I wore when school started. Of course I got made fun of; there was a big label on the back of the pants that read CHEAP JEANS. It was humiliating. But I never told my father, because I knew it was worse for him.

Once, our phone was turned off. That wasn't something that happened to people we knew. I remember a buddy telling me at school that he had tried calling me but he kept getting a strange message from the phone company and couldn't get through. I just told him I didn't know what was going on, even though I knew exactly why he couldn't reach me.

Another afternoon I came home from school and there was a man in a suit sitting in our living room. The sheets were off the couch. That meant someone important was over. The man in the suit was talking to my father, in the middle of the day, and as soon as I walked in I could see this wasn't a conversation for me, so I went straight to my room. The man left a few minutes later and I heard my father screaming, "I've been paying this mortgage for ten years and you come after me because we're a month late?" Then he swore like an army medic under fire.

It's not like I hadn't seen financial stress in the house. But before this it seemed like something out of an *I Love Lucy* episode. Once a month my dad would break out the checkbook to pay bills and he'd notice one was missing.

"Ellen! Ellen!" he'd shout. She would pretend not to hear him. "Ellen, there is a check missing."

"Yeah?" she'd say. She was half asking, as though she was surprised, and half telling him, "So what."

"What did you do with it?" He knew, she knew, even I knew, that she would take the check, spend it, and forget what she spent it on. She did it to me, too. I used to keep my money in an old Tropicana orange juice jar under my bed, and she'd borrow it but often forget to replace it. Plenty of times she just preemptively gave me money in the morning because she had no idea if she had taken any from me or not.

"Ellen," my dad would continue, getting angry. "How can I balance the checkbook if I don't know what you wrote a check for?"

Then she'd start to cry.

When my dad was out of work, though, there was actually less screaming, less crying. That's how much tension there was. It permeated every day. Nothing was being released. It was so bad that, when I asked for twenty dollars to go on a school ski trip, my dad told me, "I am really sorry, but we don't have the money." For him to say that out loud was a big deal. I knew it broke his heart.

But a couple of nights later my dad handed me a twenty-dollar bill and said I could go. I was ecstatic and didn't think about the money until a week later, when I was looking for some change in my parents' water cooler full of coins. It was missing all the silver. Pennies were all that remained.

All those years that my dad hustled flea markets he kept getting calls from other ice cream companies. He hated the industry, felt burned by it, and had so much pride he didn't want anything to do with it. But he was a great ice cream salesman. And nothing else was working. So he finally answered one of those calls and said yes. After that we didn't really worry about money again.

Here's why I loved my wrestling coach: After kicking me off the team in eighth grade, he welcomed me back in ninth. He acted like nothing had ever happened. In fact, he made me a team captain. And I went undefeated! And I played on the football team! And I was voted Most Popular! Seriously! Three years earlier I had been in grammar school and kids made fun of me for having yellow teeth. Now I was one of the school's more accomplished athletes and most popular kids. I know it's hard to believe this when Tracey the office manager is going after me or Howard is ripping me for playing solitaire on the wrap-up show. But it was true.

In fact, it taught me a great lesson about being a minor celebrity. I didn't campaign to be most popular; it was a random vote. I was chatty and played sports, so people knew me. Afterward my closest friends were like, *How cool, congratulations.* Other people who had never spoken to me suddenly wanted to be friends with me. And then there were the kids who were nasty. They said, "Oooh, there goes Mr. Popular," whenever I walked by and mocked me for everything. The reaction was completely surprising to me. Being picked on—at home, at school, in the park—I understood. Being picked on because too many people liked me? That was new to me.

When I started on the Stern show it was the same thing. The first time it happened was when we were working at NBC and I went to a party at an apartment in the city. Now, I knew guys who truly showed off what they did. There was a producer for Don Imus who wore a black and silver NBC jacket with the peacock on the back that he bought at the gift shop. He had it embroidered with "Producer, Imus in the Morning" in big letters. That has never been my style.

At this party I was talking to a girl who was really excited that I worked for the show. She grabbed her friend, who was really cute, and said, "Do you know who this is?" The friend wheeled around, gave me the once-over, and sneered, "You think you're a big shot?" It was like she was looking for a fight. I don't think I am anybody. I'm not looking to be the big wheel. Occasionally I'd walk into a bar in New York City and people would automatically say, "Oh, Mr. Big Shot." That anyone could think I'd get a big head after a day getting destroyed on the show is remarkable.

Here's the thing about that year in junior high: I still never felt like I belonged. Maybe it's because I was afraid we were going to lose our house. But I was always sure someone was going to say to me, "Okay, we caught you. You are a fake and phony. Get out." I hung with the jocks but I didn't really think I deserved to. I felt like a poser and assumed that eventually someone else would see that, too.

Chapter 8

These Are My Guys

I'VE GOT SO MANY great pictures in my office.

There's a framed ten-by-twelve shot Howard gave me as a birthday present, showing all of us from the show dressed up in drag at a photo shoot for his second book, *Miss America*. There's my younger son, Lucas, doing the Tricky Dick Nixon pose on his campaign poster when he ran for fifth grade class president. I've got a framed, limited-edition etching of Jay Leno sent to me by Helen Kushnick, his old agent, who was played by Kathy Bates in the movie *The Late Shift*. She mailed it to me one September as an early Christmas present because she knew she was about to get fired. Hanging above it is a letter from her, dated two days before she got canned.

Across from that is a framed cover of the free local Connecticut magazine, *County Kids,* of me, Mary, and Jackson when he was just a toddler. It was taken right before *Private*

Parts came out and we were doing any kind of promotion that came along. On my filing cabinet is a picture from a *Saturday Night Live* newscast with Tina Fey. She's pointing to a picture of me as the punchline for a joke about the new president of Iraq. She said the guys who ran were Mahmoud Aliabi, Muhammed Abibbi, and Baba Booey. One day she was on our show and signed it, "Gary, Congrats on becoming President of Iraq. Tina Fey."

In a red frame on my wraparound desk is a picture of Frances Bean Cobain when she was around four. Courtney Love gave it to me and I call it the Four-Hundred-Dollar Picture. One morning we called Courtney for an interview when she happened to be in New York. Howard asked her to come in and she said, "No, I'm in pajamas. I'm a mess." He told her we'd send a car for her and, next thing you know, she was in the studio in her nightgown, doing a segment. When it was over I was trying to get her back in the car, which wasn't easy, and she finally stopped me and said, "Gary, I am sending you a picture of Frances Bean. I want you to put it on Howard's console in the studio so he knows, whenever he talks badly about me or Kurt, he is hurting her." I said okay and sent her home.

A couple of hours later someone dropped off a package at my desk. It was a picture of Frances Bean. Later that week we got a bill for four hundred dollars from the car service. Turns out Courtney had asked the driver to wait when he dropped her off, then she went up to her apartment, found a picture, and sent him back with it. Now I look at it every day.

Frances Bean's photo is right in front of a picture of me and Mary walking the red carpet for *Private Parts*. Next to that is a picture of the sign outside a Burger King in southern New Jersey. To get there you had to exit the New Jersey Turnpike at exit 7, drive thirty minutes, and then scan the horizon. It was easy to spot—there was nothing else around for miles. Here's the picture:

But my favorite is a candid shot of Fred, Artie, Howard, Robin, and me on set while doing the show in Las Vegas. It's rare that we have photographers shooting the show and even rarer for us to be in a picture that isn't posed. It's just us, working, doing what we love, what we're pretty good at, with people we like hanging out with. I hung it right above my computer, in my line of sight whenever I am staring at my screen. These are my guys, my family.

They're the reasons I've spent more than twenty-five years doing the show. We were all just a bunch of radio nerds who found a gig that felt like we were hanging with our friends every day.

I knew how special it was early on, after Howard left NBC for K-Rock and I was just a year into working for him. When K-Rock hired him, Howard wasn't able to take me along. There wasn't a spot in the budget for more than one producer and that job title was technically Fred's. I was still working at NBC—all the people that worked for Howard were—and we were trying to figure out what to do with our lives as the execs who fired Howard put us on random shows. It kind of sucked. The day Howard had his press conference for K-Rock I went to it, just to say hello and wish him luck. But when it was over he pulled me aside and said, "I'm really sorry we can't bring you along. The folks at K-Rock don't really get how the show works. But I am working on them and I feel good that I can get you back with us in six months. I know it's a long time and you might have to find a new gig before then. I get it, I understand. But I'm trying and if within the next six months it works out and you're around, it'd be great if you could be with us."

Man, I was surprised. I was dying to be back with those guys and was crushed when I had to stay behind at NBC. The fact that Howard was working to get me back made me feel pretty good.

The day of his first show—this was back when he was on in the afternoons—it felt like my floor of NBC shut down. We weren't supposed to be listening to him, but as soon as he came on the air every office door closed. I had my radio on and it hurt not being there. A lot. Then, at the first break, my phone rang.

"Hello, is Gary there?" It was a nasal, high-pitched voice. I didn't recognize it at all.

"This is Gary," I answered.

"Gary, it's me, Howard."

I was shocked. He was in the middle of his first break on his first show and was calling me. Using a really bad voice in case I didn't answer my phone.

"Listen," he continued. "I got a spot for you. It won't take six months. I can get you in here tomorrow. Can you do it?"

I was there early. I knew I'd found a home.

Every kid needs his guys, the group he bonds with. These are the guys who do as much to keep him out of jail and teach him how to behave as his parents. These are the ones who, thirty years later, he can sit in a room with and rip about personality tics only they understand.

For me, my guys were Vinny, Frank, Steve, and Paul, who I finally found toward the end of ninth grade. Now stick with me, because this may get confusing.

Vinny was a co-captain of the wrestling team with me. He and I became buddies toward the end of that ninth-grade season. Paul was on the wrestling team, too, and hung with us every once in a while. Steve was the one guy I stayed tight with from playing football, who also happened to wrestle. And Frank, well, Frank was with Vinny. Frank looked like a man when he was fifteen, bigger than everybody in ninth grade and a year older. He was the only kid I knew who wore nice slacks and dress shoes to school every day. But that's because he had gone to Catholic school and never dropped the dress code. Even after he was kicked out for fist fighting with a nun.

In fact, that may have been the reason I liked him at first. I had had bad experiences with nuns. When I was preparing for First Communion the class was held in the basement of the church—girls on one side, boys on the other. The nuns told us to come up one at a time through the aisle, pick out a carnation and a pin, and fasten it to the lapels of our blue suits. I did as I was told and, when I got back to my seat and was about to sit down, John Hackett, who was sitting behind me and was a real troublemaker, stuck his pin under my ass. I jumped up and yelled, "Whoa!" Without asking what happened a nun named

Sister Barbara (we called her Sister Boogie because her finger was always knuckle deep in her nose) pointed at me and told me to come to the front of the room. When I did, she grabbed me close by the lapels and then hit me on the side of the head with her open palms ten times over both ears. My ears were literally ringing. Then we had to go to the Communion service.

I was crying so hard my mom thought it was an emotional experience for me, as though I had found God and my calling. Not so. I was just sad. And angry.

So I could appreciate Frank's disdain for organized religion.

Vinny and Frank hung out a lot. Then Vinny brought in me and Paul. Then I brought in Steve. Except for Steve, we were all Italian. And, unlike the guys at Uniondale Park, they wanted to do things and go places. I felt a real bond with them.

People were actually afraid of Frank when he first came to school. It might have been because he knocked the wind out of a nun. Or because he was so big he just commanded respect. But as people got to know him they realized that he wasn't aggressive at all. He had his own car, a beige Pontiac Bonneville that looked like a tank and had a backseat the size of a queen-size bed. At parties people asked him for the keys to his car so they could hook up in the backseat.

Vinny was like me: He was short and built and really Italian looking. He had an older brother and was really into music. Since Frank didn't care about music at all, Vinny and I used to trade off sitting in the front seat of the Bonneville screwing with the radio and popping eight-tracks in the deck. Vinny would borrow some freaky jazz fusion from his brother that we liked to listen to.

Steve was like our Tom Hagan, from *The Godfather*. He was blond and Irish and had come from Catholic school, too. Only he left the right way, not like Frank. He was quiet and, really, he was the good-looking one in the bunch. His house was completely different than mine in that no one talked back to adults and no one yelled at another in front of guests. Years later, Steve was always my plus-1 whenever I went to Cleveland or Buffalo for an appearance at a mattress store opening or a strip club.

Paul was the baby of the group. He was the youngest of all of us—last to drive, last to drink. And his family was full of overachievers. His brother was a lacrosse star, his sister was super popular, and his mom was president of the school board.

That summer between ninth and tenth grade was when it all came together. We really grew tight. Vinny's family owned a cabin in upstate New York and one day he said, "Let's just go." It took a week of phone calls between all of our parents to let a group of teenagers go up there alone for a couple of days. But all the moms got along really well. And, mostly, they loved Frank, just like the rest of us. Even they knew how trustworthy he was. If he was going, I could go. So the three of us—me, Vinny, and Frank—headed upstate.

The name of the town was Halcott Corners. It had two main streets and a blinking red light at the four corners. We went up right after the school year ended. On the front window of the hardware store there was a sign that read, CONGRATULATIONS TO THE GRADUATING CLASS OF HALCOTT CORNERS. And there were twenty-two pictures in the window. That was it, the entire senior class. My senior class was the smallest in the history of Uniondale High School and it had more than six hundred kids.

Our first night we decided to go out, and Vinny, who was always the instigator of stupid shit, saw a supermarket on one of the corners. There was a watermelon stand by the front door and Vinny decided it would be fun to steal one. Then he decided to steal another. So now we had two watermelons in the back of Frank's tank and we were driving back to Vinny's parents' cabin. We saw a bunch of locals hanging out on the side of the road, about our age and drinking. It was like a scene from the movie *Slackers*. Bright Idea Vinny said to Frank, "Speed up."

Frank did and, as we passed them, Vinny threw a water-melon out the window. It splattered at the feet of all these kids. We were laughing so hard Vinny told Frank, "Turn around."

Frank did and, as we passed them again, Vinny hit them with the second watermelon. Bad idea. This time everyone got in their car and started chasing us. We were speeding down a one-lane road, careening side to side because the kids behind us were throwing beer bottles that exploded against the Bonneville. There were more of them than us, and they were pissed. If they caught us they'd beat the crap out of us.

Frank was a really good driver but, as big as he is, he was pan-icking. So he pulled off the road onto a tiny dirt trail that led into the woods. Then he turned off the lights. Now we were driving blind. We couldn't see shit. After driving for several minutes I looked back and was sure no one was following us. Or the other cars were driving with their lights off, too. In which case they were just as stupid as we were. We stopped the car and it was eerily silent, except for the sound of our heavy breathing.

One of us said, "Oh my God, how dumb are we?" No one answered. We were just trying to figure out how to get out of there. We snaked our way through the woods on this dirt road until we found another highway. It was on the other side of the mountain from where the house was and it took us more than an hour to get back home. We were the three biggest dumb-asses ever.

Of course, if I had been with the guys from the park they would have said, "Let's turn around and get them." So our re-sponse was actually an improvement. Instead we spent the rest of the weekend drinking beer and shooting at the bottles with a .22-caliber rifle. A couple of times we just shot at the fins on the Bonneville. Left a lot of holes. Those were real *Stand by Me* moments. There weren't any girls wrecking everything yet. We were just three guys being assholes who knew we could count on each other forever.

The Nancy Chronicles

1984–88

Her name was Nancy. I met her at a club in Long Beach, Long Island, called Malibu—a New Wave dance place—in 1984. I had just started working for the Stern show at that point, but was still living at home in Uniondale. Vinny and I went out on a Saturday night and I saw her standing at the bar. She was cute, a brunette with big brown eyes and a big smile. She could have been on the cover of *Seventeen* magazine. It was late enough—probably close to three in the morning—that I had my courage poured in, so I walked up to her and before I could even say hello she stopped me with, "Oh look. It's John Oates." I had a mustache and long, black hair thick as steel wool. He and I were practically twins.

I brushed it off and we started talking. Then the nightclub closed and we moved it outside. I was still chatting Nancy up by my car when I looked across the hood and saw Vinny making out with her friend, so Nancy and I started making out, too. That was all we did. The sun was sneaking up on us and as it did she told me she had to work the next day. She was a salesgirl in housewares at Gimbels in the Roosevelt Field mall, and that Sunday was Mother's Day. I took her number, said I would call her, and chalked it up to a good night. I was pretty drunk.

Of course, when I got up at some point on Sunday I realized I hadn't bought my mom a Mother's Day present yet. Since I was so out of it the night before I decided to go to Gimbels, try to catch a glimpse of Nancy to see if she was still cute when I was sober, and pick up a gift for my mom. If I did it right, I'd be able to sneak in and out of the store without Nancy knowing I was checking her out.

I didn't do it right.

As I was riding down the escalator she happened to be standing at the bottom. There was no way out. The good news was that she was cute even without the beer goggles. We laughed and talked and decided to go out later that week. I forgot to buy my mom a gift.

That first date was fantastic. Nancy was laid-back, sarcastic, and loved music the way I did. At the end of the night we hit a local bar that I knew had a great jukebox. I took the first turn picking out songs and when I sat down she told me, "I love the jukebox here." *Nice,* I thought. She continued: "They have an obscure song that I'll play when your round is over."

"What is it?" I asked.

" 'Can We Still Be Friends' by Todd Rundgren."

"I already picked it!" I said.

You know how when you're young and first start seeing someone and have some odd thing in common, you immediately think you're the only two people in the world? Those are magical moments. So we started dating.

We listened to music together all the time. She bought me a Bob Dylan box set. I used my access to impress her as much as possible. We went to see Peter Gabriel at the Garden and stood on the mixing deck. When he played "In Your Eyes" she couldn't stop hitting me on the arm with excitement, telling me how much she loved that song.

But this was a strange time in my life. I was working on the show, getting some notoriety, and, as Chris Rock says, I wanted to check my options. Basically I was a dick. Nancy clearly liked me a lot and told me so. But I was the asshole who believed he was doing the right thing by telling her he wasn't ready to commit. We went on like this for months—seeing each other regularly but never saying we were exclusive.

After we had been dating about a year I moved into the city. I was on the radio. Meeting chicks was easy, and Nancy lived out on Long Island. I was twenty-five and, well, I have a million reasons why I acted the way I did. I cared about her—everyone on the show got to know her and loved her—but I had other opportunities, too. There was an opening for a bar or a premiere to go to every night. Nancy and I would see each other one night on the weekend and then on the other night I could go out and party with my friends. I didn't know if she knew what I was doing when we weren't together. But I always knew that the one thing that could sink me for sure was Howard. If he ever saw me out with another girl, it would be fodder for the show the next morning. Fortunately, Howard never went out. Well, almost never.

We had Mickey Mantle on the show one day and he invited everyone on staff to the grand opening of his new restaurant that Friday night. Jackie was there. Fred was there. And I showed up with a girl who wasn't Nancy. I felt pretty confident that Howard wouldn't be there. David Letterman was having a party that night, too, and Howard and his wife were going to that. No way he would hit two parties in one night.

Fred and Jackie and I were sitting in a booth. My date was next to me and our backs were to the door. We were all having a good time when Jackie called out, "Hey, there's Howard!" I swear to God I almost pushed the girl's head under the table. Howard stopped by for two minutes to talk. I didn't even introduce my date; I was hoping he wouldn't notice we were together. When he left I thought maybe I had dodged a bullet.

Then came Monday morning. We got on the air and Howard's first question for me was "Who was that girl you were with?"

"She was just a friend," I answered.

That was it. He didn't take it anywhere else. Wasn't interesting enough. It's one of the few times during my tenure on the show where I was able to avoid playing out a personal drama on the air. Too bad it happened to be the exact two minutes that Nancy was listening. After this exchange she called me and, without even saying hello, said, "Who was she?"

"She was just a friend." I parroted myself. But she wasn't convinced. After that we broke up. And then got back together. And then broke up again. It was a cycle that went on for months. Until the night we broke up for good.

Fred, his wife Allison, Nancy, and I had gone to see Springsteen at the Nassau Coliseum. I was feeling pretty good. The four of us went out after the show and then when Fred and Allison left, Nancy and I went to a local bar. But something was off. Nancy wasn't so into the music. We weren't talking the way we always had. Finally she said to me, "I don't think we should be together if you aren't into it."

It was odd phrasing. Like she wanted me to say, "No, I'm into it." But I didn't say anything.

"But if you are into it, we don't have to break up."

The truth was, I wasn't into it. At least I thought I wasn't into it. I was still running around, checking my options. Only I was too much of a coward to completely break it off with her. I didn't want to hurt her, for one. And I liked having something steady. In that bar, at that moment, after seeing my favorite act of all time, I decided to be the asshole who makes the girl break up with you so you don't have to break up with her. Honestly, I was thinking she would always be there for me, so I wasn't too worried about it.

I should have been. Because Nancy wasn't just breaking up with me to sample the single life. While we were dating she had gone to school to become a medical technologist and began working at a hospital. She had started seeing someone she met there. If I was going to be a schmuck, she wasn't going to bother with me while someone who treated her well waited on the sidelines.

It's such a cliché, but after Nancy dumped me I became interested again. I called her repeatedly. Sometimes she'd speak with me, but other times she'd cryptically say she had to go. I'd ask if her new boyfriend was there; she would say yeah, and then hang up. I was so bummed out I told Jackie. He got it right away. He said, "In your mind, when she says that, she is on the bed with the guy on top of her and she's telling you to hold on while she tells him, 'That's it, just a little bit to the left, yep, that's it. Oh, Gary, I have to go.'"

I kept calling, and we'd talk every once in a while. But she rebuffed all my efforts to see her. This went on for seven months. And I never stopped thinking about her. By this time my buddy Frank was married. His wife, Maryanne, and Nancy were good friends, so I got updates on how she was doing pretty regularly. I looked for clues in the smallest details as to how she felt. Just because she broke up with me it didn't mean she stopped loving me, right? That's what I was thinking the day Frank told me that Nancy still had me in her speed dial. Okay, I thought, I have a chance.

But then, one day, Frank drove me home from the city for the weekend. I was going to his house for a party later that night and planned on hanging there until it started. But when we pulled into his driveway, Nancy's car was there. I had just been telling him how much I missed her so I was excited to see her. I started to open the door when he stopped me. "It's better if you don't go in," he said.

I let go of the door and slumped low in the front seat. It really was over. Done. I had lost her because I was a dick. I was pretty beat up about it and happened to tell someone at the office. Naturally it got back to Howard, who called me into the studio while we were on the air. It was May 12, 1988, toward the end of the broadcast. This is the kind of thing that never happens at IBM.

"How you doing on the women front?" Howard asked.

"Umm, okay."

"If you ask me you never should have broken up with that girlfriend."

"Oh no, here we go, you knew it was coming," Robin, Fred, and Jackie chimed in.

"You're a loser," Howard said. "You're an imbecile. You finally meet a good-looking woman who is polite and knows how to deal with me and . . . She is probably dating someone else."

"Let's just end the show," I said.

"You lost her. Oh he's crying. Who are you, Patrick Swayze? How come you never told me about this?"

"I'm not going to tell you everything."

"Well, someone better get to the bottom of this story. I'll take this up tomorrow on the air."

"I haven't seen you this happy in weeks," I said.

"Because you are an idiot. I told you to stay with her. Are you kicking yourself in the head?"

"Can we just end the show?"

"Really, are you that bad about it?"

"Come on, let it ride, Boss."

"You were in love with her."

"Cut me a break."

After that he mercifully signed off. But it's the one time in my life on the air that I was genuinely upset. Before I left for the day I was in the bathroom, washing my hands, when Howard walked in. I asked him, "Hey man, can you lay off about this one a little bit?"

He looked at me and said, "Are you kidding? Grow up."

Chapter 9

Conspiracies, Roy Rogers, Tampons, and Finding My Calling

MY MOM WAS ALWAYS OVERLY PROTECTIVE. When it came to her three boys she was a tigress. That's why she ran to the park—and left me at home—to find out what happened when I got the concussion. And that's how she ended up calling Howard's mom to complain about his bullying me on air. You can't fault her for that.

I like to think that's why she sniffed my head every time I came home. I know that's why she jumped out of the closet when Anthony came back from the Doors concert. She worried about us obsessively in a way that couldn't have been good for someone who was battling so many demons.

When Anthony had his prom, my mom helped him pick out his suit. Before most proms, a bunch of couples get together at someone's house for pictures with their dates, and all the parents come, too.

But after he got dressed, Anthony decided he didn't want

my mom to follow him to his date's house for pictures. So when he left the house my mom recruited a neighbor and they followed him in the neighbor's car. Then she hid behind a tree across from Anthony's date's house and watched him take his prom pictures. I don't see that as her stalking him. It's just a mom who is proud of her boy, no matter how much he tries to push her away.

And I'm sure my mom isn't the only mother who did this: We had two telephones in our house. When it rang I'd often pick it up first and then hear my mom pick up the other phone after. If it was for me I'd say, "Mom, hang up please." But there'd be silence. She didn't answer and she didn't hang up. But I knew she was still on the phone. I'd say it again. Nothing: My mom wouldn't speak or hang up. Then I'd quickly sneak into her room and catch her putting down the phone just as I walked in. Moms are nosy. They want to know who their kids are talking to.

Except that my mom didn't take anything at face value. She saw conspiracies everywhere, even in the most mundane things. There were no accidents. Part of this was her illness finding its way to the surface even during her balanced moments. But I also think it was a function of her being Italian. A wrong number wasn't just a wrong number. It was a plot. I always knew when it happened, just by listening to my mom's side of the conversation.

"Hello," she'd say. Then, "Umm, Bob who? . . . How do you know Bob? . . . What's your business with Bob?" Then finally, "There's no Bob here, sorry."

Long before we ever had Jim Florentine on the show terrorizing telemarketers, I heard my mom doing the same thing to unsuspecting salespeople who called our house. They would be begging to get off the phone after she grilled them about what they were selling and why. I knew these calls could be mined for comedy just by sitting in my kitchen and listening to my mom destroy people on Long Island.

By the time I was in tenth grade, for the first time in my life I felt stable. I was out of the house so often—at Frank's, or Vinny's, or at practice for one team or another—that I was around my mom's mood swings less and less. Mostly I saw her act out during the holidays, when she was having family over.

She'd start shopping and cooking days in advance and always insisted on cooking large. Half the stuff, like stuffed artichokes and stuffed mushrooms, never made it to the dining room table. It was relegated to a folding table set up especially for the holidays where appetizers sat and were ignored. It was like the kids' table for food. On Thanksgiving the menu was always the same: manicotti with sauce and meatballs, followed by turkey, sweet potatoes with marshmallow sauce, and green beans with bread crumb topping. And, of course, stuffing. Years later, when it was just me, my parents, and Mary, we'd ask her if she wanted to go out to dinner, which to an Italian is an insult, and she'd still cook for eighteen people.

When I was growing up, one by one—my dad, my brothers, me—would go into the kitchen and ask if we could help and she'd just yell at us, "Get out of my kitchen!" We knew what was coming next. You could set your watch by her blowups. Soon she'd be screaming, "No one helps me!" Then she'd go into the bedroom and sulk for half an hour before coming out to finish cooking. No one dared ask what time we were eating.

But who doesn't get stressed during the holidays?

Meanwhile, my dad's work was steady. Anthony, impetuous and rebellious, married a local girl he met in Eisenhower Park when he was twenty. He's still married to the same girl. They lived nearby. If things got tense I could sneak off to their apartment and thumb through his massive record collection. Steven lived in the city and let me visit any weekend I wanted. And me and the guys were attached at the hip, spending most of our free time at one another's houses. Now Frank, Vinny, Paul, and Steve were my brothers. Especially Frank. At his house I didn't even bother asking for food anymore. I just walked in the back door, opened the fridge, and took what I wanted.

Here's how good Frank was to me: When I was a junior in high school I quit the wrestling team. The coach, who also happened to be my offensive line coach on the football team, had taken all the fun out of it. He was nothing like the guy I loved when I first started wrestling in junior high. Instead I joined the bowling team. No joke. Bowling was something my dad and Steven did well together. They played in a league on Sunday mornings and sometimes I went with them. I was pretty good. I once heard my biology teacher, who was also the bowling coach, talking about the team. I liked him, so I decided to join. From then on, whenever my wrestling coach saw me in the hallway, he mocked me by walking behind me and pretending to roll a bowling ball. Honestly, I was a little embarrassed. I left my ball in the trunk of Frank's Bonneville so I didn't have to carry it around school on days we had tournaments. Frank, who never said no to anyone who needed a ride, would drop me off at the bus that was taking us to the meet. I'd jump out of the front seat, scramble to the back, pull my bag out, and get onto the bus as fast as I could. I didn't want anyone to see me getting on that bus. I always felt like it was one of those things you have to defend, but you know what? Fuck it. I enjoyed it. And I had Frank and his car to keep me from looking like an idiot.

Years later, on the show, Howard asked me, "You come home one day and there's a dead body on the floor of your apartment. Who's the first guy you call?"

"It's Frank," I said. "It's a no-brainer."

"What would Frank say?" Howard asked.

"Every solution for Frank always starts with 'I'll be over in the van in five minutes.'"

That's how I'll always think of him.

My buddies and I prided ourselves on being able to hang with any other group of kids, avoiding the petty rivalries that come with different cliques. I got us in with the Park Boys. Then there were the black leather boys, who all wore black leather jackets; and the guys on Maple Street. I know, it sounds like something out of *West Side Story,* but it was the 1970s. Everyone knew us as the guys who drove around in Frank's tank.

The one thing we always needed—especially to fill up Frank's gas guzzler—was cash. None of us was rich. Our parents gave us the basics; everything extra was on us. One night Frank pulled up to my house holding a stack of fifty New York Nets tickets. This was the old ABA team starring Julius Erving that played at the Nassau Coliseum, right by our house. I asked him, "How did you get those tickets?"

"A friend of my brother's took them out of the back of a neighbor's convertible," he said. "Let's go scalp them."

"Great," I answered.

That night we went to the Coliseum and hustled like never before. Every time I sold some tickets I'd run around the arena looking for Frank. I'd give him the money; he'd give me more tickets. When we were sold out we hopped in his car and went to a secluded place, where we laid out all the money and divvied it up.

We made forty dollars each. Not a bad score. But I always needed more. Records were an expensive habit.

By high school I'd given up my paper route and mowing

lawns and moved up to more glamorous employment opportunities.

When I was sixteen I spent the summer working as a stock boy at a women's clothing store in Hempstead. I was making $2.20 an hour, but it was a big deal to work in Hempstead back then. Main Street in Hempstead was the retail heart of Nassau County. Billy Joel sang about getting a pair of matador boots in "Keeping the Faith" and the line was "Only Flagg Brothers had them." Well, Flagg Brothers was on Main Street, just three miles from my house.

The store I worked at was near Flagg Brothers and right next to Newmark and Lewis, where everyone bought their television sets. I remember watching Elvis Presley's funeral that August on the huge bank of TVs that were set up in the window. A buddy of mine worked there. He's the one who told me about the job at the clothing store, which had been run by an old Jewish family for generations.

By the time I started working there, the town of Hempstead had changed a lot from the place Billy Joel sang about. It had become predominantly black, but there were still a few stores run by old white people who hadn't moved out yet. The clothing store I worked at catered to middle-aged women and sold designer brands like Givenchy and Ralph Lauren, but the merchandise was discounted. It was a place where women could feel like they were shopping in a fancy store but not actually paying that much.

I either took the bus to work or rode my bike. It's not like I had to look nice. I was the stock boy, so I wore jeans and T-shirts. Mostly the job was simple: boxes came in, and I opened them, looked at the list to make sure everything on the list was in the box, hung the clothes on hangers, and then used the pricing gun on the labels. I got a real education in women's fashion. In the middle of the day I usually had to go get Izzy, the store manager, a brisket sandwich from a deli that was about eight blocks away. Sometimes I had to pick up his dry cleaning, too, or make a bet for him at the OTB. He was the only guy who worked on the massive sales floor who wasn't re-lated to the owners.

I spent most of my time in the back with one other person, a real pretty black woman who was in her early twenties. She was stick thin but had a huge Afro that reminded me of Angela Davis's. She liked me because I was the low man on the totem pole and, well, I didn't appear to be racist. Shortly after I started working there, Izzy told me about the security buzzer they had behind the counter, underneath the cash register. It was a round buzzer made of brass with a black button in the middle. It looked like a doorbell. You could see how poorly it was wired— under the counter, down the floor, up the wall. Whenever someone pressed it, a buzzer went off in the back room.

Izzy told me, "If we buzz once, we need you to come outside because there are people to keep an eye on, and we will tell you what we want you to do. If we buzz twice, we have a large group of people we need to keep an eye on. And if we buzz it three times, call the police."

No one ever told me explicitly that the buzzer was used when black people entered the store. But they used it a lot, so it became obvious pretty quickly. The store was very wide and faced Fulton Street but had a back entrance to a parking lot. The bosses never buzzed when white trash sauntered in. But if someone who happened to be black was passing through on the way to the parking lot and lingered for too long around a rack of clothes, they hit the buzzer. The woman who worked with me in the back cursed the owners under her breath all the time when this happened. As soon as I heard the buzzer I could see her body language change. I'd just look at her and feel awful.

I'd get to the front and Izzy would say to me something like "Don't let anyone leave the store with any clothes." It was so obvious, it was painful. Once I was standing at the front door and a guy I was supposed to be watching said to me, "What are you, security?"

"Something like that," I answered.

"What are you going to do if there's trouble?" he asked.

I hadn't really considered it. I wasn't looking to be confrontational. I just shrugged my shoulders and said, "I don't know." I really had no idea what they expected me to do.

When school started I quit the job. One day, years later, I was talking about it on the air with Howard. People liked the story and called in about it. The next day Howard came in and told us that when he mentioned it to Ronnie the Limo Driver, Ronnie knew exactly what he was talking about. "Oh yeah, a schvoogie buzzer," Ronnie said. Then Ronnie came into the studio and talked about it, as if it were some kind of well-known security device in the retail industry. From there, the term picked up a lot of traction. Eventually, it made it onto urbandictionary.com under this definition: "A device in a retail store that is rung to let all employees know that a black person has entered the store. Made famous by Jackie Martling formerly of the Howard Stern Show who admitted he worked at a store that used such a device."

They got the wrong Stern show guy, but hey, at least they got the purpose of the thing right.

Another job I loved: Roy Rogers. Practically everyone I knew worked there, at the franchise across the street from the Coliseum. That's where Frank met his wife. It's also where my buddy Tom (who'd become a member of our group) first met his eventual wife. Maybe there was something in the secret fried chicken recipe. Before I actually got the job I was always hanging out there because that's where all my friends were. I had no one to go out with until their shifts were over. I still crave Roy Rogers fried chicken.

I got a job flipping burgers. The rush on the counter always came after events at the Coliseum ended. Grateful Dead fans were the worst. They wouldn't order anything; they'd just come in and start picking the lettuce and tomato from the fixings bar. Eventually we wised up and stationed someone at the fixings bar whenever the Dead were in town and the shows let out. They also stole anything that wasn't nailed down—toilet paper, paper towels, and sugar packets.

I've always been hyperproductive. And while I worked at Roy Rogers, I also juggled a few other jobs. During one summer in high school I worked from 7 A.M. to 3:30 P.M. as a custodian for the school district—thanks to Paul's super-achieving mom, who worked on the school board. Then, on the days I didn't work at Roy Rogers, I worked at Fortunoff near the Roosevelt Field mall. Vinny worked there, and so did my mom, so they put me in the stockroom. I still have dreams of being overrun by luggage. It came into the store all zipped one into the other, like Russian nesting dolls, and I had to take out each piece and set it up on the floor.

My poultry experience was parlayed into a job delivering Chicken Delicious on Friday and Saturday nights to parts of Long Island like Roosevelt, where Dr. J and Howard were from, and Hempstead, the slum where Anthony lived after he moved out. Dumbest job ever. I was a small white kid driving around the worst parts of town with bags of chicken and cash. At two in the morning. I'm lucky I was never mugged.

I even worked as a stock boy at a women's clothing store called Ups and Downs. I was the token man. I had to run out to buy the ladies their lunch, carry stuff to their cars, walk them out to the parking lot at night, and even buy their tampons. Really, it was like being on the bottom rung of some Hollywood agency, only without the scenery, the stars, or the weather. All I had was middle-aged women on Long Island. But it wasn't the tampons that made me quit. One day the manager sent me to Woolworth's to buy a paint scraper. When I got back she wanted me to scrape gum off the floor. I thought, *Fuck this. I know I haven't done shit in life yet, but I ain't doing this.*

Working in radio wasn't even on my radar when I was in high school. To me, music was still a hobby. I checked the album charts in *Rolling Stone.* I still tuned in to Casey's American Top 40. And, on the way to school, if Frank was giving me a ride, I'd make him listen to WPLJ, which catered to high school kids like us.

I thought that when I grew up I might own a kennel supply store. Really. When I was a junior in high school I got a job selling dog food, pet toys, and anything else people needed for furry friends at a store near my house. The place was owned by two brothers who really liked me. Those guys were making a lot of money. They always talked about opening a second store somewhere else on Long Island. One brother had two daughters who were never going to go into the business, so he said to me, "If you want to open our second store, I will stake you." I always had that in the back of my mind.

My dream career choice, though, was to be a photographer. We had a subscription to *Life* magazine and I remember being moved by the pictures. I can still see those images of soldiers in Vietnam and of the fatal shooting of a protester at Kent State. My dad bought me an Instamatic camera with the flashbulbs that attached to the top of it. I took pictures of all our vacations and I was sure I would be a photojournalist. I wanted to work for *Life.*

In fact, I was so committed to that idea I went to a vocational school. BOCES, which stands for the Board of Cooperative Educational Services, is a Long Island trade school. It had a rep as being the idiot school because it was mostly for people who weren't headed to college. It was where you unloaded kids. I did well in high school and my guidance counselor begged me not to go there. Howard actually still makes fun of me on the show for going there. It offered refrigeration, HVAC, auto body, graphic arts, cosmetology, and photography courses. Most of the guys were in auto body and most of the girls were in cosmetology. In eleventh and twelfth grades I did a half day at my high school and, along with Steve, who also took photography, a half day at BOCES. I loved it.

That's what I planned on doing with my life. Frank's father ran a camera store and photo processing shop in Rockefeller Center and he would lend me cameras. When I graduated from high school my dad bought me a used Nikon FM from the Associated Press sports photographer for Long Island, who was a friend of his. I still have it in my closet.

During my senior year in high school, Anthony and his wife moved to Austin. They decided to settle there after passing through on a road trip to Central America. I applied to the University of Texas because it had a great photography program and I got in. I bought a plane ticket to visit that Easter and even had a check ready to hand over for a deposit. If I liked it, I was going.

But the weekend I was supposed to visit, Anthony's father-in-law got sick and died suddenly. Anthony and his wife came home and decided they had to stay in New York for a while; they couldn't leave her mother alone. I panicked. My plan was to go to Austin, move in with my brother, and by my sophomore year, get in-state tuition. Now that I didn't know when he'd be back, I canceled that trip and changed my plans.

It was April of my senior year and I had nowhere to go. I was scrambling big-time. My dad had seen Anthony blow off college and Steven simply decide it wasn't for him. He wasn't going to let me do the same thing. So he said to me, "Just go someplace locally for a semester or two and figure out your next move."

Growing up on Long Island, there were three universities and one junior college, Nassau Community College. Everyone called it the University of Uniondale or the thirteenth grade. No way I was going to go there. It was literally walking distance from my house. It was a longer walk for me to go to high school than to go to Nassau CC. Then there was Hofstra University, across the street from Nassau Community College, and a great school. My buddy Gary Bennett's father was the dean of admissions and I knew I could get in there no problem. But still, I couldn't go to college where I went to high school; I had to move a little bit. C.W. Post was another local option. But I just didn't like it. And then there was Adelphi, which was about twenty minutes away.

My father and I went to an open house at Adelphi. And we got so taken to the cleaners. I wanted to study photography. Adelphi had photography classes, but no photography major. We walked around the displays set up for potential students and I met the guy who eventually became the chairman of the communications department. We started talking and he told me, "Communications is just like photography. They have cameras, they have lights. It's the same thing." Umm, okay. That's how I became a communications major at Adelphi. I was going to live at home, take a few photography classes, and then figure out my next move. That plan changed before I even started school.

During orientation I went on a tour of the communications department and took a walk by the radio station. It was like seeing wrestling for the first time in junior high. There was a guy sitting at a radio console and the ON AIR sign was lit. He looked so cool, so fucking cool, and I just lost it. I thought to myself, *I am getting in there.*

My feelings were confirmed that first day of school. I took an elementary radio class and the professor brought in a boom box—this was 1979. It was the teacher's first year, too. She was a gay woman who lived in the Village. She was young and cutting-edge and carrying a boom box, and I was into it. Then she said, "We are going to do an exercise. I am going to turn on different stations and based on what you hear, tell me what you are listening to."

Are you kidding me? This was a college class?! I was nailing every station, every kind of music. I had a natural aptitude for this.

That first week I signed up to work with the radio station. There wasn't a lot of competition and it wasn't long before I was doing a newscast on the school's channel, which was broadcast by something called a carrier current. That meant only people on the Adelphi campus could hear it. So basically, no one. I didn't give a shit. A girl and I were co-anchors. We had to be in the studio by 4:30 in the afternoon to get ready for a 6 P.M. broadcast. We'd read through newswires, rip up stories, decide who was going to say what, and then flip the switch. God, it was awful, I mean really horrible. I don't know if a single person was listening. But I was on the radio, hanging with other people who liked doing exactly what I liked to do.

The next semester I got a gig working for 90.3 FM, which was still a school station, but at least it was one you could find on the local radio dial. One afternoon Vinny heard me reading the news and called to ask me, "How come you sound like Ronald McDonald?" I made my voice rise and fall while I did the broadcast because I thought it sounded professional. No one was teaching us to be ourselves. The point was to be in front of a microphone and get comfortable. Which I did, eventually.

I could tell my parents dug hearing me on the air. One Sunday night all my relatives were over for one of our weekly dinners. Even for occasions as casual as those, my mom spent the entire day cooking. We also broke out the appetizer table. I left to do a show when the Cotroneo ladies were in full-throated debate about life and sauce. I figured things would have quieted down by the time I got home. Instead, as I walked through the door, I heard an unfamiliar sound: clapping. My dad had made everyone stay and listen to me on the radio. He was psyched, just totally loved it. And he loved that I loved it.

Halfway through my first semester I was looking to sell my photo equipment. That was it for me. I was having a good time in radio and I knew I could be good at it. I was making plans in my head. I thought I was going to get into radio and be the next muckraking superstar.

Chapter 10

The Coolest Radio Station Ever and Sticking It to Rick Cerone (Go Mets!)

ONCE YOU GRADUATED FROM POP MUSIC—and high school—the coolest New York radio station to listen to was WLIR-FM. It was progressive, playing the Allman Brothers and the Grateful Dead, but also new acts like Steve Forbert. It was the laid-back, hippie spot on the dial. The whole vibe seemed to say, "We don't care about making money, we just care about the people." All the best concerts for music snobs were sponsored by WLIR.

LIR also had a left-leaning, aggressive news department. On air, the reporters didn't act like talking heads reading copy: They projected opinions, liberal ones, into every story they broadcast. They also had this great segment called News Blimps, where they mashed up a real news sound bite with bits of music and comedy. Today that stuff is commonplace, but back then it was cutting-edge.

The studio was located in the shittiest part of Hempstead. It was crap, really. But because it was WLIR, every kid studying radio on Long Island wanted an internship there, including me. I knew that when I was a junior and eligible for the program, I'd try to get it.

Luckily, I didn't have to wait that long.

Just before freshman year ended, my radio teacher—the woman who brought the boom box to class that first day of school—asked me to dub a TV program for her. It was a fifteen-hour special series about the history of rock and roll that she wanted to use in a class the following year. To her the job seemed like a pain in the ass. There's no way to speed up dubbing. You need to let the tape roll and keep an eye on it so you stop when one episode ends and you don't run out of tape in the middle of the next one. It was definitely tedious stuff. But I saw it as being asked to watch a TV show about the history of music. That was right up my alley. I didn't mind doing it at all. And when it was over she was so grateful she asked, "What can I do for you?"

"Well," I answered, "I'd love to have an internship at WLIR."

At the beginning of my sophomore year, in 1980, I showed up at the WLIR office for an interview. The fact that it was in the slum of Hempstead didn't deter me. I couldn't believe I was inside a professional radio studio, seeing it all firsthand. The guy I listened to every morning, Steve North, was just finishing a news report. He was only about six or seven years older than me, but he might as well have been Edward R. Murrow. We were in the same studio but the difference between us was immense. He was on air and getting paid; I was an amateur. He was comfortable; I was quivering behind a mustache. He had on a suit and a tie; I wore the nicest outfit I had: a loud, blue and red striped button-down shirt that I bought at Just Shirts in the Roosevelt Field mall, a skinny tie that looked like something I stole from the band the Knack, a pair of beige slacks I picked out at Sid's Pants (which was right next to Just Shirts), and a snazzy pair of Capezios.

The first question he asked me was "Do you smoke?" Did he smell my breath? This was a newsroom with young journalists. I thought everyone smoked. I did, so I told him. "Well, that will not be accepted."

I made a mental note. Right after that we started talking about news and its value and other high-minded philosophies of journalism. The conversation turned to Geraldo Rivera and his late-night news show, *Good Night America*. Steve had been a producer on the show. I told him my favorite segment was when Geraldo had had on Jack Ruby's sister and Lee Harvey Oswald's widow and they got into a knock-down, drag-out fight on the air. I couldn't get over that. Seeing people fighting like that on TV was crazy to me. Turned out, Steve produced that piece.

I was hired that day.

I had to be in the office twice a week by 6 A.M. Three weeks after starting, my car radio was jacked from the LIR lot. But that didn't slow me down. I'd get there before the sun came up. Initially my principal job was called "sledding." This was long before everyone had a computer, but slightly after stone tablets. Reporters couldn't Google to find information. They needed interns. That was me. The station subscribed to all the major local papers. Every day I had to go through the papers and clip the most important features. Along the wall were packets of the biggest stories happening at the time and each day we added the new articles. That way, if someone was working on a piece about, say, Agent Orange, they could go to the packet, flip through all the stories, and be up to speed.

Steve was very methodical and precise. When he told you how to do something he wanted you to do it his way from then on. I did the sledding job well. I also learned a valuable lesson: If you do shitty tasks well and without attitude, someone will give you better stuff to do.

I hung around Steve as much as I could, watching as he did interviews on the phone, pulled articles from the sledding files, edited his pieces, and read newscasts out loud to himself before going on the air. The politics of the place made me chuckle sometimes: All the stories my brother Anthony warned me about when he was rebelling against my father were being played out and reported on every day.

About a month into the gig, Steve sent me out on an assignment. Nassau Community College was holding a "handi-capable" day to raise awareness for handicapped people. It wasn't political intrigue, but it got me out of the office. He threw me a tape recorder and said, "Go."

"Umm, what do I do?" I asked.

"Talk to people, ask them why they are there, what they hope to achieve," he said.

So I went down there and walked around all the different booths and interviewed people. I would start off asking everyone, "Are you having a good time?" Then I'd launch into an interview. I thought I got some good stuff. People were really excited about "handi-capable" day. I got back to the studio and gave Steve the tape. He popped it into a deck, started listening, and, ten seconds in, paused it.

"First tip," he said to me. "Never ask a yes-or-no question."

He didn't have to do that. He didn't have to give me the assignment, listen to the tape with me, or give me any criticism at all. He didn't really have to acknowledge I existed for any reason other than cutting out newspaper articles and making his job easier. But he did all of that. And when we were done going through the interviews he cut ten seconds of tape, put it into his broadcast for the day, and introduced it this way: "WLIR's Gary Dell'Abate was there and asked people what they thought of the event."

Holy shit! That broadcast ran six times throughout the day. I went to work at the kennel the next day and people said to me, "Hey, I heard your name on the radio!" That was it: my first taste of countywide fame. I was a month into my internship and my name was already broadcast on the station all my friends listened to.

After that, Steve kept throwing me the recorder. He knew I was a huge sports fan—he couldn't have cared less—and not too long after my "handi-capable" success he asked me if I wanted to interview Rick Cerone, the Yankees catcher, who was doing an autograph session at a mall in Hicksville. It couldn't have been more perfect for me. While my fandom had expanded to the Jets and the Islanders, the Mets and baseball were still my true loves. They were everything the Yankees were not: upstarts, scrappy, abused, laughed at. Clearly, I could identify with this team. Plus, my dad loved the Mets and I idolized my dad. Every year he'd take my brothers and me to a game for a Dell'Abate boys day out. At night he and I would watch the Mets together. He used to joke that on his third try, he got it right and had a boy who was a sports fan. It was something only he and I could share.

In 1980, the Mets were in the midst of a particularly bad run. They won the World Series in 1969. But during a stint from the mid- to late seventies, they finished above .500 just twice. And in 1980 they were in the middle of seven straight seasons with fewer than seventy wins. They were easily the worst team in baseball.

Meanwhile, those damn Yankees were the best. In 1980 they had won 103 games. But the good news for me was that right before my interview with Cerone, the Yankees had lost the pennant to the Royals. In fact they didn't just lose, they were swept by a team that had won six fewer games. By all accounts their season was a failure, no matter how many games the team won during the regular season. Now their catcher was signing autographs and our news director asked me if I wanted to go talk to him. *Hell yeah*, I wanted to talk to him! The Met fan in me couldn't wait to rub his nose in it.

At first I thought it would be an easy gig. I figured since Steve asked me it had all been set up and I would just arrive, interview Cerone, and then come back with the tape. Cerone was famous, and the Yankees were important. He wouldn't leave something like this to chance with an intern. Actually, he would. Steve told me to find out who was in charge when I arrived at the mall, show them the tape recorder, explain that I worked with WLIR, and ask if Cerone would talk to me. It would be just that easy.

As I approached the autograph stand I saw, of course, that Cerone was surrounded by hundreds of people. I fought my way through the crowd with a microphone in one hand and the tape recorder dangling from a strap that hung around my neck. It was mid-October and the equipment, paired with my fledgling mustache and John Oates hair, made me look like someone who was trying out a Halloween costume as an early '80s rocker.

As I was pleading my case with the woman running the event, Cerone caught a couple of sentences of our exchange and said, "Sure, I'll talk to you. As soon as this is over."

So I stepped off to the side to wait my turn. I started testing my tape recorder to make sure it worked. I did it half a dozen times, "Testing one-two-three, testing one-two-three." Then I'd stop, rewind, play it back, and do it again. I didn't want to blow this opportunity. I wasn't going to ask yes-or-no questions and I wasn't going to let a technical snafu get in the way, either.

I did, however, miss Cerone.

After all the triple-checking and psyching myself up, I looked over to the autograph stand and Cerone was gone. The crowd was gone. The person running the event was gone, too. What the fuck? The only guy still there was a security guard. "Excuse me," I asked him, panicked. "Do you know where Rick

Cerone is? I'm with WLIR and we are supposed to do an interview."

"He left," the guard said.

"I know. But he agreed to do an interview with me ten minutes ago and now he's not here. Where did he go?"

"I don't know."

"Come on, man, look at me. I need to get this interview. He said he would do it!"

Maybe he pitied me. Maybe he was already bored with the conversation. Maybe he was a Hall and Oates fan. In any case, he told me, "Check the mall office."

I sprinted up an escalator to the mall offices and banged on the door. It opened about an inch. The guy behind it put his face in the crack and said, "What do you want?"

"I want to interview Rick," I said. "He agreed to talk to me after the autograph session."

"He's busy," the guy answered and started to shut the door. But before he could close it, I wedged my foot in the crack. I literally had my foot in the door.

To this day, where on earth I got the balls to do that I have no idea. It was Rick Cerone, not Rick James.

"What are you doing?" he asked me. He was not happy.

"I was supposed to interview Rick Cerone," I answered.

Before it escalated I heard a voice from behind the door. It was Cerone. "It's okay, let him in, let's do it."

I turned on my tape recorder—it worked—and then fired out this question: "Do you guys see it as a failure that you lost the pennant?"

His eyes burned with anger, and not because it was a yes-or-no question. "We won a hundred and three games this year. How is that a failure?"

The interview ended shortly after that. But I got it done. And it aired all weekend long. I considered it a victory for Met fans everywhere.

BABA BOOEY'S TOP 7 CONCERTS

(You Don't Sully a List Like This Just to Get to 10)

1. **Led Zeppelin, *Physical Graffiti* tour, 1975, Nassau Coliseum:** I went with a friend and we paid four dollars a piece for scalped tickets. This was the first concert I ever went to. Zeppelin opened with "Rock and Roll." For the final encore Robert Plant said, "This is a song we recorded that has become popular beyond our wildest dreams." Then they did "Stairway to Heaven."

2. **Bruce Springsteen, *The River* tour, 1980, Nassau Coliseum:** My buddy Steve and I were in the second to last row directly across from the stage, but Springsteen made us feel like we were in his living room.

3. **Clash, 1981, Bonds:** The Clash were supposed to play ten shows in an old Times Square men's clothing store that had been converted into a club. But the first night the fire marshal shut them down. Since they were, after all, the band of the people, Mick Jones said they would honor every ticket that was bought. So they played for twenty-seven straight nights. I saw them on night twenty-five. They were losing their voices, but their energy was amazing.

4. **Talking Heads, *Speaking in Tongues* tour, 1983, West Side Tennis Club Stadium, Forest Hills, Queens:** This concert took place in the old stadium that was home to the U.S. Open in the late '70s. It was the middle of summer, hot and humid. The show progressed chronologically, starting

with David Byrne alone, carrying a boom box and singing "Psycho Killer." By "Burning Down the House" the stage was full of band members, percussionists, and dancers.

5. **U2, *The Joshua Tree* tour, 1987, Madison Square Garden:** I had never seen this band live before. It's the only other time I had that feeling I got when I saw Bruce: They turned a giant arena into an intimate room.

6. **Frank Sinatra, 1983, Nassau Coliseum:** I took my parents to see him. I was not a huge fan but realized he was a legend and wanted to catch his show before he died. Nothing better than watching sixty-year-old women act like twenty-year-olds. Before he'd start to sing you'd hear a woman yell, "We love you, Frankie!" He'd say, "I love you too, baby."

7. **Bruce Springsteen, 2005, Two River Theater, Red Bank, New Jersey:** It was just me and four hundred other people for a VH1 *Storytellers* performance. There was Bruce, a piano, an acoustic guitar, and his stories about every song he played. Unreal.

Chapter 11

I Own Nassau Coliseum

THE INTERNSHIP WITH WLIR went so well, they asked me back for a second semester. I was working nearly every day with Steve, doing grunt work like sledding, and he kept rewarding me with more assignments. This was when the New York Islanders started their run of winning four straight Stanley Cups. Steve sent me out to the victory parades, where I interviewed all the players, talked to people along the route, and then brought back a mess of tape for him to decipher, edit, and graciously credit me for on air. It ran for days.

I even got to cover some hard news. When John Lennon was killed in December 1980, grieving fans held vigils all over New York. All the good reporters were sent to Central Park. But I did get to cover the one at Eisenhower Park and file live reports from the scene.

The same thing happened after Ronald Reagan made some federal budget cuts almost as soon as he took office in January

1981, including taking out a huge slice of student aid. There were protests at colleges all over the country and, eventually, there was a march on Washington during my spring break. So what if it wasn't for peace or equal rights, my brother Anthony's issues. It was a cause I could get behind: I needed cash to go to school.

After my WLIR experience I went internship crazy. My parents were incredibly supportive. They could see how happy I was and knew I was killing myself at school and with week-end jobs—at the kennel, at the gas station—so my dad offered to pay for my car insurance. That meant I could work more gigs for free and not have to pick up hours during the week. In the second semester of my sophomore year, while I was interning at WLIR, I applied for an internship at SportsChannel on Long Island, which carried the Islanders and covered a lot of high school sports.

On my first day there my boss handed me a notebook and told me to go up to master control and log tapes. I didn't know where master control was, because it wasn't in SportsChannel's main headquarters. In fact, it was on top of Long Island Medical Center, the tallest building in the area, which meant it got the best reception. You took the elevator to the roof, then climbed a ladder up to a trailer that was filled with high-end video equipment.

The other problem: I didn't know what it meant to log tapes, or what I was logging tapes for. This is when it turned into a scene out of *The Karate Kid*. My boss explained that log-ging meant watching tapes of thirty different high school sporting events—soccer, lacrosse, football, basketball—and writing down the time on the video deck whenever a great play happened. Good kick, log it. Good save, log it. I did that for a week, then I carried the notebook with me whenever I came to work, waiting for him to tell me what we needed it for. It wasn't until the end of the internship that he sat me down and showed me how to cut up my logged highlights to create a highlight reel.

Meanwhile, here was the real perk: They gave me a press pass for all the Islanders home games at the Nassau Coliseum, which was walking distance from my house. I showed up for every game at 3:30 and ran through a litany of duties, all grunt work that anyone getting paid would be irritated doing. But I couldn't wait to get there. There were not enough hours in the week for me to learn what I wanted to learn. When I walked into the Coliseum I never wanted to leave.

The first thing I did when I showed up for work was check the pagers all the refs wore that alerted them when they needed to take a TV time-out. I walked around every spot on the ice checking for dead spots. Then I would dig out the Sports-Channel banner from the bowels of stadium storage and unfurl it in front of the booth where the announcers sat during the game.

After that, I spent hours making copies and gophering between the production truck and the stadium and the press room. I got to know everyone from the camera guys to the directors to the Zamboni driver. There wasn't a part of the job I didn't see. My favorite guy was Stan Fischler, a legendary hockey reporter who did player interviews on TV and wrote for *The Hockey News*. Between every period, players from both teams would stop by Stan's booth near the locker room and give him five minutes. Then, after the game, he picked a "Star of the Game" to interview. I was Stan's set decorator and wrangler.

Before the games I had to gather extra team jerseys to hang in Stan's cubbyhole as backdrops for his interview. The Islander equipment managers just handed the unis over. But the road team's managers always gave me the once-over—my hair, my mustache—and said the same thing: "You better fucking bring them back."

When the game ended Stan would make his Star of the Game picks. But the criterion wasn't who had a hat trick or the most assists; it was above all who would talk to Stan. I'd head into the locker room—Islanders or visitors—with a list of three or four guys Stan voted as that night's MVP. I'd ask the first guy, "Can you do an interview?" If he said no, I went to the next guy. On and on, until I found a guy who would do the interview. It wasn't always easy.

One time Stan had written an article for *The Hockey News* about which player he would take first if he were starting a team. This was the early 1980s. Wayne Gretzky was emerging as the greatest player in NHL history and one of the biggest stars in all of sports. He was young, handsome, well spoken. Forget hockey—if people were starting a pro basketball team at the time they would have taken Gretzky. But Stan wrote that his first choice would be the Islanders' Bryan Trottier. It had become a running joke, with Stan and the Islanders' lead broadcaster always saying Trottier was the best player in hockey. Truth was, he was scoring fifty goals a season and was the glue that held together an Islanders team that was in the middle of a dynasty. But Stan wrote the story in such a way that it was not so much about why Trottier was great; it gave all the reasons Gretzky wasn't.

Well, Gretzky happened to read this article. And when he and the Edmonton Oilers came to the Nassau Coliseum and beat up on the Isles, he was named Star of the Game by Stan. It was my job to get him to the interview booth. I walked in shaking at the prospect of having to bother him. When I asked him he said, "Fuck that guy. He wrote an article trashing me."

I moved down the line to Stan's second choice for Star of the Game. But as I was asking for an interview Gretzky overheard me and said, "Hold on. Tell him I'll be there in a few minutes."

When Gretzky sat down, Stan said, "So Wayne, another brilliant performance; congrats on being the Star of the Game." Then he pushed the microphone toward Gretzky's mouth. The Great One responded: "I'm just glad to get it, since you told everyone I was no good." Stan hemmed and hawed and stuttered until Gretzky finally smiled. He was a young Canadian kid. He didn't have it in him to go for the kill.

Gretzky was about my age and he was one of those guys who, because I saw him up close a couple of times, made me think I was just standing around picking my nose, even though I was working so hard. He was as thin as a hockey stick, had shaggy hair, and a boyish face. The way he skated was inspiring. I was once hanging near the players' locker rooms another time he was in town. Not too far from me was a board for a game that fans played between periods called ScoreO. This was a huge piece of wood with a mousehole-size opening at the bottom. During intermissions fans came onto the ice and tried to shoot the puck into the hole to win a car. Players on the road had—and still have—a lot of time to kill before games. They usually wound up at the locker room, playing cards and goofing around. Gretzky wandered out into the hallway, saw the board, saw me loitering, and asked me to prop it up. Then I just watched him practice getting it into that tiny hole. There was no one else around, just me and the greatest hockey player ever. He never made it, but he didn't care. He was just fucking around and had a great time trying.

I have one more memory of the Nassau Coliseum, and it might be the greatest athletic achievement of my entire life.

Back in 1989, Howard and I once got into a discussion on the show about how he believed he was a better athlete than me. He had a tennis court at his house and every once in a while he'd invite me out there and we'd play. He always beat me, but he was taking lessons every week while I played once every three or four years. Truly, I thought we were pretty evenly matched.

Still he kept saying on the air that he was a much better player and that he could actually kick my ass. He laid down the challenge, so we decided we were going to play one more time, once and for all, to settle the matter.

This conversation took place first thing in the morning, as soon as the show went on the air. By seven o'clock someone had called in and said, "I'd like to see you play."

Good idea, we decided. So then we talked about going to a public court where people could watch. But it continued to evolve. Another listener called and said, "I live in Jersey and there's a public court out here that has bleachers." Fantastic, we thought, let's go there. Next a guy who worked for the Trump Plaza in Atlantic City offered to let us use his four-thousand-seat arena. We could sell tickets! It had morphed from Howard giving me shit to a for-pay exhibition in less than two hours. Then it got so much bigger.

My buddy Ross was working for Ron Delsener, a concert promoter. He said he could get us the Nassau Coliseum, a sixteen-thousand-seat arena, if we were interested. It took a day for the deal to come together. The next morning we announced that the match would be held there. Within four hours the entire joint was sold out. We called it the "U.S. Open Sores" tournament.

This was a place that meant the world to me. I had had my internships there and had gone to Islanders and Nets games there. I'd seen every concert of importance there. Now I was going to be the main event.

When we arrived at the Coliseum the day of the tournament we wanted to warm up. I had on a bright pink warm-up jacket and jeans; Howard wore a bright turquoise shirt and never took off his sunglasses. We hit the ball for a few minutes, then Grandpa from *The Munsters*, Al Lewis, showed up, chomping on a cigar and wearing a fedora. Al, Robin, and Fred the Elephant Boy, one of the original Wack Packers, were going to be the announcers. While having his makeup applied, Howard piled it on again, telling the camera, "I'm going to kick his ass." Then they cut to me in my bright pink warm-up jacket and blue tennis shorts.

Finally, we played. Howard was introduced as the mentally fit, empty-jocked radio god. I was the oafish and dim-witted Gary "Beaver Teeth" Dell'Abate. The ball girls, dressed in G-strings, pasties, and sneakers, were lined up along the baseline and at the net. We had screened them in the studio on the air one day, all of them topless and seated around Howard's desk in the studio. As backup to the ball girls we hired a guy in a wheelchair, who was ready to roll into action if the girls were too slow. I ripped off my pink warm-up jacket—carefully, so I didn't dislodge the headband I had on to keep my hair out of my face—and revealed a sky-bright turquoise top.

I was ready. The match was best out of seven games, like the World Series. Immediately I took a lead off Howard's serve. He hit one into the net, the next one out, and soon I was up 1 game to nothing. But the next two games, I struggled and suddenly found myself down 2–1. That's when fate—and Fred the Elephant Boy—stepped in.

In the fourth game, Howard and I were tied 15 all. Howard won the next point, but Elephant Boy wasn't paying attention or had become confused by all the crowd noise, and so awarded it to me. He announced that I was now up 30–15. I quickly won the next two as well, before anyone realized what was happening. Not Grandpa Al or Robin or Howard tried correcting him. Now we were tied 2–2. And I was shuffling on the court and pumping my fists like I was a real athlete.

When I won the next game, the crowd started chanting, "Gary sucks! Gary sucks!" They had no idea how little I cared. That weekend was my moment. The night before was my ten-year high school reunion. Now I was on Long Island, five minutes from my house, winning an athletic event in front of sixteen thousand people. I was so psyched I started pointing my finger at the crowd and yelling back at them. I felt like I was back in my living room.

Midway through the sixth game, with me ahead 30–15, it got even wilder. The half-naked girls were running back and forth whether there were balls to grab or not. The guy in the wheel-chair was spinning around. There was a stadium full of people taunting me and I couldn't stop giving it back to the crowd whenever I won a point. Somewhere in the audience my mom and dad were watching, perhaps the only two people cheering me on. Finally I served the ball and Howard hit a forehand that nearly landed in the stands. It was wide. I won the match, 4–2. I was so excited I sprinted to the other side of the court, shook Howard's hand, and then threw my arms into the air. Everyone booed. Pretty soon I was surrounded by all the ball girls in their G-strings and pasties. I also won three thousand dollars.

After I accepted the trophy, Howard and I sat down at the broadcasting tables we had set up before the match. I said, "You played a good game. You are not a sports wimp and you probably can beat me. But this week I am going to buy a full-length leather coat with your fucking money."

I was obsessed with owning a full-length black leather coat that I had seen in a store on Eighth Street in the Village. It had big buttons and a giant leather belt. I had seen Sam Kinison wearing one. Rockers like Dee Snider wore them, too. I thought they were cool. It cost four hundred dollars and I never could have afforded it without that prize money. One day after the show, I took a subway down to Eighth Street, plunked down the money, and walked out with that coat. I looked like an idiot. I wasn't a rocker. I wasn't even Kinison. I wore it twice and put it in my closet.

It's still there. It might work for a costume party one day.

Chapter 12

Champale and Intimate Companions

I COULDN'T STOP with the internships, actually. One summer I worked at a recording studio in the city. It was a jingle house and I was the token gentile. They had no idea how to handle an intern, which is to assign them the crappy work and then show them how to do cool stuff. All I did for them was empty garbage; none of the bosses talked to me. But it did teach me about making your own opportunities and building skills as you go.

I befriended a young sound engineer who taught me how to set up microphones in the studio. I saw how to deal with clients. I learned how talent can fix anything. We were once doing an ad for Champale, a lowbrow alcoholic drink, and the corporate suits kept poking their heads in, complaining that the jingle wasn't working. Our engineer reassured them, saying, "Don't worry, it'll be fine when Grady gets here. He'll bring it to life." I didn't know who Grady was, but I knew the jingle sounded like crap. Finally, at four in the afternoon, after we had been there seven hours, Grady Tate showed up. He was an old black guy, a well-known club jazz singer, who swaggered in looking as cool as could be. He had a gravelly voice, but it turned the jingle from ridiculous to radio-worthy.

I also learned how talent controlled a room, no matter how minuscule the talent. At night the jingle shop transformed into a second-rate recording studio for would-be artists. Once, they handed the keys to a guy named Meco, who recorded a million-selling disco remix of the *Star Wars* theme. When he came around everyone kissed his ass and I couldn't figure out why. Sure, he wore nice wide collars and kept his shirt unbuttoned, but with his side part, high forehead, and oversize wire-rimmed glasses, he looked like an accountant doing karaoke. Besides, all he did was put a disco beat to someone else's song. But it made the studio some money, so he was the big shot.

Even the last internship I had, in the Adelphi film department, proved invaluable. The film teachers there had started a business shooting educational movies and used the students as free labor. One of the movies, commissioned by the ASPCA in New York, was called *Sam*. It was fifteen minutes of point-of-view shots in which you never see the subject of the film, just the world from his perspective. Here's Sam being abandoned on Fire Island. Here is Sam finding his way to the mainland. And here he is walking the streets, looking for food. The way it's written you'd think Sam was a boy, then comes the big reveal: Sam is a dog.

I worked on another film called *Intimate Companions*, which was about the human/animal bond. We interviewed this tough truck driver who was a real fuck-you kind of guy with the voice of someone who spent his life smoking cigarettes in the cab of his truck. Then we handed him his dog, a tiny toy poodle, and he started cooing, in his gruff voice, "Baby, hey baby, how you doing?"

The teachers tried selling all these films to schools around the country, so I was put in charge of the distribution department at Adelphi. That meant writing letters to schools, asking if they wanted to rent the film and, if they did, instructing them to send me a check. I realized that you can make the best movie in the world, but if no one distributes it you are screwed. When the check came in I sent out the movie and kept track of where it went. It sounds boring on the surface, but it showed me a different aspect of the business.

Being on the air wasn't the only option.

No, this is not Bettie Page. It's my mom! Ellen Cotroneo, circa 1946.

Papa Booey, Sal Dell'Abate, from his army days.

My mom and dad on their way to a
PTA meeting.

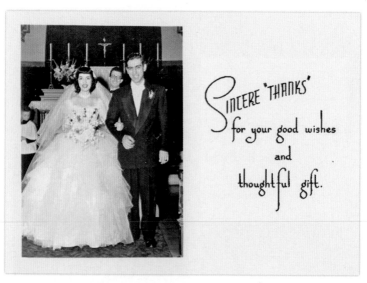

$\mathcal{S}$ince ̊e ˚"THANKS"
for your good wishes
and
thoughtful gift.

My parents' wedding photo, 1951.

My personal life was at a nine when
this photo was taken.

On the roof of the Empire State Building just before
my mom had a meltdown.

High school yearbook photo. I may have been a little influenced by *Saturday Night Fever*.

Steven, Dad, Anthony, and me. Mom made sure our shirts were just as tacky as the tree.

Me with Pacino and Scorsese during the filming of *Serpico*. Oh, wait, that's me, my brother Tony, and my dad.

Gary Dell'Abate

is a member of

WBAU

Adelphi University

Garden City, N. Y. 11530

Joseph C. Busch

(STATION MANAGER)

November 7, 1979

(SIGNATURE)

(EXP. DATE)

On my way to greatness at Adelphi.

I was severely towel-snapped right after this photo was taken.

In tenth-grade history class. That was the cutest girl in the school sitting behind me. I'm sure she was impressed!

With Mom and Dad after I won an award from the custodians . . .
a $50 savings bond. I went through a phase where I thought if I
didn't smile, no one would notice my teeth.

The closest I've ever
come to having abs!

I promise, my brother was the gay one. What the fuck was I thinking?

Me, Steve, Vinnie, and Frank—my guys—trying to look tough.

Read the shirt. I was such a guido. This was the last time I ever wore a Yankee hat.

Camping with the boys in 1980. Alcohol, cigarettes, crappy haircuts, crossed arms, and cheesy mustaches. See what happens when you leave five guys in the woods with no girls?

One of our "guys" vacations. I can't even comment on how odd this photo looks.

My girlfriend Nancy and me with Phil Collins and Genesis. Nancy was the recipient of my infamous "I Want You Back" video, which, unfortunately, has lasted longer than Genesis's career.

I had the look to be in Hall and Oates . . . just not the talent.

Me and Robin Quivers during one of our shows.

Me and my brother Steven.

Gilbert Gottfried, Stuttering John, me, Sting, and Jackie. John hired me to book celebrities for his music video.

Just when you thought my teeth couldn't get any bigger. Booey on Broadway!

Jackie, Fred, and me dancing on the bar to "Hands Up" at my wedding, 1992.

My first pitch went great in 2004. I shouldn't have pressed my luck five years later.

They get the best seats and the best pieces of chicken, but I get the best kids in the world!

The greatest family a man could ask for.

Still together after all these years.

Doing karaoke at one of our Vegas shows in 2004. Train was the backing band. I was so drunk I almost fell off the stage.

On the set in Vegas. These are my guys, my radio family.

My Brother Steven

1991

Over Christmas of 1988 my roommate Greg and I decided to have a blowout of a party at my apartment on Amsterdam Avenue in Manhattan. The place was packed all night. I don't think the last person left until about five in the morning. I went to bed wasted and, when the phone rang around nine the next morning, I was still pretty drunk.

It was Anthony. Before I could yell at him for calling so early he said, "Listen, I have something to tell you."

"What?"

"Steven has AIDS."

Anthony knew a lot more about the way Steven lived than I did. He had heard from mutual friends that Steven liked to party a lot, and he worried about him. We all understood that AIDS existed and that it was decimating the gay population. A guy I worked with at WNBC told everyone he had AIDS at Halloween and by Thanksgiving he was dead. In my heart I knew Steven was at risk, but like everyone else I was in complete denial. It certainly didn't cross my parents' minds. That's not how it was with Anthony, though; he's too smart. Anthony harped on Steven to get tested every month and call him with the results.

It started to feel like a game of Russian roulette. Anthony would beg Steven to get tested, then he'd wait for Steven's call. When Anthony heard Steven was negative, he would breathe easy for a few weeks, then he'd wait for the call again the next month. This went on for several years. I had no idea. Until I got that call.

There was no preamble. Anthony didn't tell me to take a seat or that he had bad news. It was just, "Steven has AIDS." So matter-of-fact. When Steven called him to deliver the same news there was nothing ceremonial about it, either. Steven just said, "I'm positive."

I was stunned. I couldn't speak. The conversation didn't last more than a minute after he told me. I just hung up and spent the next several hours trying to absorb the news. I didn't know if I should call Steven. Instead I called Anthony back and tried to talk through the shock. "I don't understand," I said. "He looks healthy. How could he possibly be sick?"

Anthony and I didn't really know what to do with the information, or even how to process it. And worse, we were sad for our parents, who had no idea. When Steven told Anthony he was sick, Anthony's first response was "You have to tell Mom and Dad." But Steven couldn't do it. At least not yet. He didn't know how.

It was a couple of days before Steven and I spoke. I had decided not to call him, probably because he was a private person and had always let me know when he was ready to talk about stuff. When we finally did connect it wasn't one of those Hallmark moments, full of emotion, where everything that had always been left unsaid is finally shared. He never actually told me he was sick. He just said, "You spoke to Anthony?"

"Yes."

"Did he tell you?"

"Yes." I didn't want to say any more than was necessary.

"Then I need your advice," he said. "How should I tell Mom and Dad?"

The first thing that came out of my mouth was "I don't think you should. I don't think you should tell them until you have absolutely no choice."

To this day, when I tell that story, some people jump all over me. They think I was wrong and that my parents had a right to know their son was dying. But my reasoning was that there was nothing they could do. Steven didn't look sick. He wasn't showing any symptoms. He was living his life. Their only option was to freak out and worry. That would not make Steven better; it would only make them more miserable. Why should they have an extra year of that kind of pain? Their son had been given a death sentence, but they didn't need to spend the rest of his life thinking about when he was going to die. I also worried about how my mom would take it. She was fragile when life was going well. Just thinking about Steven telling her conjured visions of her falling to the ground in agony, kicking and screaming and crying. It would have been the most natural reaction for her to have.

Steven agreed with me. No one else would know he was sick until it was obvious. Anthony and I told Steven we would help him decide when it was time.

Before Steven was sick we'd occasionally get together for a steak dinner or to go to a Knicks game. But I was young, working hard and then partying on weekends. When I had free time, I went back to Long Island to see my parents and hang out with my guys. Steven was driving a cab on the overnight shift, from 4 P.M. to 4 A.M. We were just living two very different lives. But after I learned he had AIDS, I made an effort to see him regularly. That turned out to be pretty weird.

When someone is terminally ill, the last thing they want is for you to change your behavior and pity them or act differently around them. The more I made an effort to see Steven, the more obviously my behavior changed.

I tried not to ask him how he was feeling. He didn't talk about it much, either, other than to tell me he was going to different doctors and trying different things. One had him on an all-vegetable diet for a while. But in those early days, even doctors weren't sure how to make people better; they were trying solutions and tonics and cocktails. When my grandmother was dying of cancer in the 1950s, she paid a lot of money to a doctor who put her on an all-steamed-vegetables diet. People get desperate for miracles.

That first year Steven didn't look any different. He had always been trim and athletic-looking, and he still maintained his weight. I wanted so badly to believe he had figured out a way to beat the disease. If he avoided talking about how he felt it was because he was feeling fine. If I checked him out and he didn't look any worse, maybe he'd been cured. The whole year went by like that. I guess I was in denial.

Soon enough I became painfully aware of reality. Over Christmas of 1989 we were all at my parents' house on Long Island. I broke out my video camera and was getting shots of the whole family doing their thing. At one point I went over to Steven and started interviewing him. I knew I was doing it because he was going to die and I wanted to remember him, what he looked like and sounded like. I wanted to be able to see him twenty years from now, so that when I told my kids about their uncle Steven they'd know who I was talking about. He knew why I was videotaping him, too. Which is why he told me to get the camera out of his face.

That spring, though, we could see that the disease was progressing. Steven didn't look healthy and fit anymore; he started looking sickly. By Easter he looked especially hollow. I wasn't sure if my parents noticed—they didn't mention anything—but Anthony and I both told Steven it was time to tell them. A week went by, and he didn't do it. Another week went by. He still hadn't done it. Finally Steven admitted he couldn't tell our parents. He asked Anthony to do it, just as he had asked Anthony to tell them he was gay.

This was a huge burden to put on someone, but Anthony didn't balk. A couple of weeks after Easter he drove over to my parents' house to tell them. Dad broke down crying, freaking out with sadness. Mom turned out to be the strong one. She was like a rock. I guess as long as she had other people's problems to focus on she could handle anything.

We had planned to get together on Memorial Day. My father called me early in the week to let me know he'd be picking me and Steven up in the city on Saturday morning. He casually mentioned that he had tried calling Steven, too, but no one had answered. By Saturday morning, before he left Long Island, my father called me again to tell me that he still hadn't been able to reach Steven. "I'm coming to get you first," he told me. "So we can go check on him together."

My father was a brave and strong man who had earned medals in World War II, but he feared the worst when he didn't hear from Steven. He had been in this situation before.

When I was very young, too young to remember, my grandfather developed throat cancer and had to have his larynx removed. But he refused to break old habits, like chewing tobacco. He'd walk around his apartment on the Lower East Side with a wad of chew in his mouth while carrying a real glass spittoon, like something out of the Wild West.

For years my dad would drive into the city on weekends to pick up his parents and bring them out to our house for a weekly visit. But as my grandfather grew ill, he became too tired and uncomfortable to make the trip. He'd stay home while my grandmother came out. One Sunday afternoon, while dropping my grandma back at home, they realized they didn't have the key, but they couldn't get my grandfather to open the door. They banged, they rang the doorbell, but there was no answer. My father walked downstairs, walked up the fire escape, and climbed in through a window. His father was lying facedown in the living room. There was blood everywhere. He had fallen. His glass spittoon had shattered. His neck had been cut and he'd bled to death. This was one of those strange family secrets that I didn't know of until many years later. I always thought my grandfather had just died of cancer.

We didn't know why Steven wasn't answering his phone. But my dad didn't want to be alone when we found out. When we arrived at his building in Chelsea, I rang the buzzer downstairs, but there was no answer. We waited and then we tried it again, but there was still no answer. We stood there wondering what we should do when, finally, we heard Steven yelling from his window, "I am sick! I can't buzz you in!"

My brother lived alone in an old building and often the buzzer to let people in didn't work. When that happened, Steven would put the front door key in a sock and toss the sock out the window. I yelled back to him, "Throw down the sock."

"I can't," he said. My only option was to climb up an old, rusty fire escape to his fourth-floor window.

I slowly pulled myself up, with my dad eyeballing me from the street. As I reached Steven's window, I stopped. There was Steven, naked and curled up in a ball on his comforter in the middle of the living room. There was vomit all around him.

He had been there for nearly two days, too weak to move or even to answer the phone.

I threw down the sock with the key to my father and he raced upstairs. We lifted Steven and put him in the shower to clean him up, holding him the whole time. We took him to a diner to get some food in his system, but he threw up all over his plate. Then we rushed him into the car and, for some reason, decided to take him to a hospital in Long Island rather than in Manhattan. To this day I don't know why we thought that was a good idea; the hospital didn't know what to do with him. Steven was given fluids, and the doctors told us that he'd be more comfortable at home. That night he slept in my old bed in the room we used to share.

My mom became his nurse, twenty-four hours a day. This was her greatest trait: mustering energy for tragedy. She had the strength of an ox. Steven was incontinent so she changed him. He was too weak to eat so she fed him. A routine was established and they existed in a kind of AIDS purgatory: He was too ill to take care of himself, but hadn't deteriorated to the point that being in a hospital was better than being at home. This went on for several weeks.

Then I came home one weekend to visit and found Steven looking especially bad. As he and I were talking, his eyes rolled back into his head. His body went limp. We panicked and called 911. A part of me was thinking, *Okay this is it. This is where he is going to die.* The ambulance arrived while he was still conscious and my parents jumped into the back with the paramedics. As they raced off to the hospital with my brother, I was alone in the house. I walked out to the backyard and began to cry.

At that moment, believe it or not, the person I was mad at was Nancy. She had been a good friend after I found out Steven was sick. She was a medical technologist who worked in hospitals. She understood how AIDS patients were treated and had seen how the disease progressed. We had just had a fight and stopped talking a few weeks before they took my brother away. Now I wanted to call her so badly and tell her what was happening. I was in the yard talking to myself. "I fucking need you for this and you are fucking me over," I said. But I couldn't bring myself to reach out. What was there to say? I believed that was the last time I'd ever see my brother.

Somehow, Steven survived that day. When he was admitted to Nassau County Medical Center it was as though he had the plague. The building had a floor designated for people with AIDS, but he had mistakenly been taken to a different unit where no one wanted anything to do with him. The disease carried such a stigma; there was great fear and ignorance about how it was spread. For a week my mom railed against doctors, nurses, and administrators to have him transferred to the AIDS floor. God bless her for being so tenacious. As soon as Steven was moved, his life got better. All of the attitude he had been getting disappeared. The nurses on that floor were there because they wanted to be. They knew how his life was going to end and they treated him with dignity.

When I went back to work that week I sat down with Howard, Fred, and Robin individually and told them, "My brother has AIDS. He's in very bad shape and was admitted to the hospital this weekend." That's when I realized: *No one yet knew my brother was gay.* They all tried to figure out how Steven had become sick without bluntly asking, "Is he gay?" I sat with Robin for an especially long time. She told me she had a relative who was gay and their biggest fear was getting this kind of news.

I didn't say this to anyone, but I worried what kind of impact my situation might have on the show. We made gay jokes on the air all the time, and I didn't want the others to stop or feel uncomfortable because of me. It would have been patronizing. We received so many hate letters that began "I was always a fan of the show until you made fun of people with cancer, because my sister had cancer and ..." My attitude was, if a bit was funny before it became personal, it should still be funny.

But once everyone knew, their support was comforting. Shortly after I told Howard, he rushed into my office. He had been reading a cover story in the *Daily News* about a guy who had just appeared on Joan Rivers's late-night talk show who claimed he had beaten AIDS. Howard said, "We have to get a hold of this guy; maybe he can help your brother." So he called Joan and asked her to make the introduction for us.

Another day, Howard had me call a well-known local doctor with a show on public radio in New York. This guy had potions and powders and preached healthy living. We spoke for more than half an hour about how to cure my brother of AIDS.

The problem was, nobody knew anything. The guy on the Joan Rivers show was full of shit. We never heard from him. The doctor's advice: Take massive doses of vitamin C to destroy the virus. All there was was fear and ignorance. One afternoon I was on the subway coming home from work. The train was packed and I leaned against a pole. At this point I always had reading material about AIDS with me. I pulled out a pamphlet and, as I read, I noticed a teenaged girl leaning against the pole, too. She was dressed in a gray sweater and black skirt, a typical New York Catholic school outfit. When I looked up I realized half the train was filled with girls who went to this school. I didn't think about it, but after I put my head back down I could see over the edge of the pamphlet that she was reading the other side of it. Her eyes moved back and forth quickly.

Then she screamed. "He's got AIDS!" She was pointing at me.

Everyone stopped and stared at me. What do I say? *No, I don't!* Inside the car all activity seemed to come to a halt. I dropped my arms and let them hang at my sides. A small circle of space cleared around me. A guy in a suit gave me the eye. A businesswoman, too. In a packed subway car, just for that second, it felt incredibly lonely.

The people who understood the alienating effect the disease had were the ones who helped my brother the most. As much as medicine, he needed comfort. My mom was at the hospital every day, from eight in the morning until eight at night. As the months went by and my brother's condition deteriorated, she became more ornery, fighting with doctors and nurses who were powerless to do anything. Finally a social worker told her she was going to lose her mind. She had to pick an hour or two to come, not twelve hours every day.

I would go to the hospital by myself. Once I got there, Steven and I had a ritual: I'd fill a basin with warm water, pull on a pair of rubber gloves, lather his face with shaving cream, and then give him a shave. I didn't know how else to help him.

One afternoon Richard Simmons called me at home and told me he was going to be in New York the following Sunday morning and he wanted to visit my brother. "I'll pick you up at seven-thirty and we will be in Long Island by nine," he told me.

Richard and I had grown close over his many appearances on the show and we talked regularly. I remember one afternoon, after Howard had been particularly rough on him, he appeared in the lobby of my building on the Upper West Side, crying. He was wearing his usual outrageous outfit—red and white striped shorts, a red tank top, white gym socks, and white sneakers—and I sat on a couch with him for half an hour, my arm draped around his shoulder, as he sobbed. We were sitting right in front of the elevator, and every time the door opened someone started to walk out and then stopped short, looking at me cradling Richard Simmons, probably wondering what the hell was going on.

The truth is, Richard is one of the most generous people I've ever met. He has a list of hundreds of people he calls regularly to check in on as they struggle with their weight or difficult times. There was a receptionist in our office who was overweight and really sad. Richard made a point of talking to her and sent her all of his videotapes. One day when he came in to do the show he asked her how she was doing and if she was watching the tapes, and she started crying. She said, "I can't afford a VCR!" He wrote her a check for three hundred dollars on the spot.

So I wasn't surprised he wanted to visit my brother. He pulled up to my building in a stretch limo. He was in the backseat, wearing his striped shorts, tank top, and sneakers, eating half a bagel with cream cheese and drinking orange juice. When he finished he flipped over the cards in his Deal-A-Meal book, because he was keeping track of his calories.

He clearly knew what he was doing when he picked early Sunday morning as his visiting time. The hospital was quiet, and he was there to bring it to life. As we walked to my brother's room we passed a black nurse in a too-tight white uniform wearing bright red underwear you could see from down the hallway. The woman weighed close to three hundred pounds, and as Richard got close to her he said, "Girl, I know you are wearing your special red underwear today." And she just started cracking up. He was carrying laughter with him. As he walked into my brother's room, Steven's face lit up.

Richard talked with him for an hour. He had a way of bringing levity to the most dire situations. For once, it didn't feel like we were just there waiting for Steven to die. Richard took pictures with everyone, and a nurse asked if he would visit the half-dozen other patients on the floor. He tore the place up, saying hello, teasing, encouraging, laughing. After we left that day he put my mom in his rotation of people that he called every few weeks, just to check on her. He didn't have to do any of that, but he did.

That was just a couple of months before Steven died. Every week he was more out of it and less able to communicate. At Christmas we were all at my parents' house while Steven was in the hospital. We all knew it would be the last holiday that he was alive. Howard would say, "Science is changing; the cure could be right around the corner." But we realized that even if they found a cure for AIDS tomorrow, Steven was too far gone.

He died on a Monday night. I had just gone to bed when the phone rang. I didn't feel like answering it. When the machine picked up I heard my father's voice. "Hello, Gary, it's your dad. I wanted to let you know that Steven passed." When I called him back he told me that my mom had felt the end was near. She had cut her routine down to visiting once a day, in the mornings. But that night after dinner she decided she needed to go back. She was sitting by Steven's bed when his life ended.

He was thirty-four years old. People always talk about funerals being celebrations of life, but this was no fucking celebration. His life hadn't even happened yet. He was one of the good guys, the kid who managed to stay above the fray in family dramas, the one who didn't fight with anyone but had a tack-sharp sense of humor. So many people came for the funeral—Howard, Robin, Fred. All my guys from Long Island. Mary, who was then my girlfriend, was there, Nancy, too. We were all shell-shocked.

Anthony and I were both to deliver eulogies. But when it was time for us to speak, Anthony looked at me and said, "I can't do it. You have to do it alone." I talked about how Steven had given me his record collection when he moved out. I told everyone that it was Steven who taught me to love New York; he actually made me a New Yorker—taking me to concerts and dinner whenever I visited from Long Island—because he loved the city so much.

Mary says I spent that day in producer mode. We had just started dating when Steven went into the hospital and she stayed close by my side, gently rubbing my back in case I broke down. I just tried to keep things moving. I wanted the funeral to be organized and made sure everyone was in the right place at the right time. That was my way of dealing with it.

I held it together at the funeral, but I'd break down when I'd see a TV show or a movie or heard a song that reminded me of him. Elton John's "Last Song" always brought me to tears; it's about a man dying of AIDS who didn't share a lot with his family because he was always afraid of what their reaction would be. There's a line that goes, "I guess I misjudged love between a father and a son." In the video for the song the dying man's father visits him in the hospital and he holds his hand. They're shot in silhouette and I thought, *That could be them, that could be my brother and my dad.* I had gone to visit and seen them looking just like that. My dad was devastated when Steven died. The Christmas after we buried Steven I went to visit his grave in Queens, where he lies next to my grandmother. When I got back in the car and headed for home, "Last Song" was playing on the radio. I lost it. I had to pull over. Every time I hear that song the visual of the father and the son is in my head.

A year later we were talking on the show about what makes us cry and I was dumb enough to mention this experience. They played the song and I started bawling midway through the first verse. Years later, at Sirius, someone recalled that conversation and they played the song again, to the same effect. They told me if I ever needed to make a movie and had to cry on cue, I had this song in my back pocket.

It wasn't just that song, though. The movie *My Life*, where Michael Keaton is dying of cancer and his father shaves him while he's sick, leveled me. The parallels are uncanny and yet, whenever it's on, I can't ignore it.

The *NYPD Blue* where Jimmy Smits died crushed me when I saw that, too. At Steven's funeral I cried, but I never really let go. I never had that moment people always talk about in grief where you completely break down and it all comes rushing out. In this episode, everyone in the cast comes to visit Smits as he lies dying in the hospital. I couldn't stop thinking of Steven. And not just because a young man was dying too soon. Jimmy Smits had been healthy on the show a month earlier. Now he was on his deathbed. I watched that episode in the fetal position on the couch and completely let go. Mary and I agreed that it wasn't because I was so attached to the Jimmy Smits character. Years after my brother died I was finally, truly grieving.

I always knew that I wanted to get involved with a cause that would honor Steven's memory, but it wasn't until I saw the movie *Philadelphia* that I was finally moved to act. My friend Peggy and I were both blown away by the movie and went out for coffee after. We decided we were going to do something; we were going to call places dedicated to helping gay men who were sick and in need. There were only two in the city: Gay Men's Health Crisis and LIFEbeat.

GMHC was a prominent organization, well funded with lots of volunteers. But LIFEbeat was smaller. It reminded me of a scene from *The Mary Tyler Moore Show* where Mary asks a candidate's campaign director why she is helping that candidate. "Well," the director answers, "I got letters from all the candidates. But his was the only one in crayon. So I went where I was needed." At LIFEbeat, I felt I was going where help was needed; it was an all-hands-on-deck situation.

I read PSAs for them on K-Rock. One year I raised two hundred thousand dollars on the TV show *Don't Forget the Lyrics*. The reason I was doing this, I soon realized, wasn't to help me heal. It was to honor my brother. That became clear to me one afternoon when I spoke at a LIFEbeat event in Manhattan. Mary and our infant son, Jackson Steven, were in the audience. I wanted him to know that he had an uncle. And that he had been loved.

Chapter 13

My Fellow Music Nerds

BETWEEN THE RADIO STATION, school, and my internships I didn't have much spare time. What little I did I spent at the Roosevelt Field mall. There was a great head shop there, with black lights and Pink Floyd T-shirts. And it also happened to be home to the greatest record store in the history of the world. Or at least Hempstead.

Record World was where my brothers bought all my Christmas gifts. It's where I bought all the albums that filled the orange crates Steven left behind. In my junior year at college, a girlfriend gave me a two-hundred-dollar Record World gift certificate—an unheard-of amount of money. To the people that worked there I became the guy who had the gift certificate. I never spent it all at once; I slowly chipped away at it, being very selective about my choices. I didn't want to waste a penny on stuff I'd listen to once and scrap. I bought Hall and Oates's *Private Eyes* and the Cars' first album. I was spending a lot of time there.

By my senior year, my internships had ended and I was rich with experience. I was also broke. My buddy Steve's older brother worked at Record World and I asked if he could get me a part-time job there. Really, I just wanted to make a few more bucks to buy beer and even more records. A gig at Record World would let me do that while feeding my musical jones. None of my boys cared about music the way I did. But everyone who worked at Record World had that bug. They loved listening, talking, debating, and learning about records and musicians and sound. They were just like me. It was one more group of surrogates I could count on. Plus I got a 30 percent employee discount.

We were the quintessential record snobs, or nerds, depending on which side of the counter you stood. Think of the movie *High Fidelity* and that was my life at Record World. There was Ken, who only cared about the Beatles. As far as he was concerned, they were the greatest group of all time and any group that wasn't them was automatically inferior. If you started talking about Earth, Wind & Fire you couldn't finish a sentence before Ken would come sprinting across the store to say, "They recorded a version of 'Got to Get You into My Life,' you know?"

There was a woman named Mary McCann, but we used to call her Mary McTapes, because she worked in the tapes department. There was a cute girl, a quintessential JAP, who loved all the dance music.

Rob was a buddy of mine who was a little bit younger. We tried to be less judgmental of music and instead acknowledge the brilliance in all of it. Our philosophy—and we had one— was that a good song was a good song, whether it was rock or pop. He's remained a great friend and we still have debates about music.

Karen Rait, who worked there, is still a close friend. She became a bigwig at Interscope, dealing with artists like Eminem.

When she brings guests to the show we'll sit in the greenroom saying to each other, "Can you believe we get to do the shit we dreamed about doing all those years ago?" We joke about how when we were at Record World, we used to think that the people who had the coolest jobs were the guys who worked for record companies putting together in-store displays.

Then there was Leslie, whose brother Elliot Easton was the lead guitarist in the Cars. Leslie talked about the Cars all the time, dropping the fact that his brother was in the band at every opportunity. Most of us working there were college students making a little extra cash, but Leslie was older, so we gave him a hard time. One day we got so sick of him talking about the Cars that someone said to him, "Leslie, can't your brother get you a job sharpening pencils for the Cars?"

Believe me, it hurt at the time.

We all had our specialties. Mine was that I was a wiz at '70s pop music, especially the singles. It became like a game show in the store. Somebody, a grandmother, would come in asking for a record and she'd give you nothing, no hints at all. "My son said there's a band . . ." Or somebody would come in tunelessly humming a song and having only a few lyrics, like, "Free, on my own is the way I used to be." Inevitably, the other staff would call me over, repeat the lyrics or hum a bit of the tune, and I'd identify the song and artist. ("Fooled Around and Fell in Love" by Elvin Bishop, by the way.) There was no Internet; you didn't go to play.it. There was a big book in the back of the store that listed every song ever made by title and artist. We were constantly adding pages, and replacing the ones that fell out because we thumbed through it so much.

We felt like we owned the place. And customers weren't immune from our snark, either. People would come in and stare at me because they thought I was John Oates. I wore a blue vest and had a name tag with "Gary" written on it clearly. But once a guy came up to me, looked me up down and side to side, and said, "Are you John Oates?" I said, "Yeah, that's why I work at a record store making minimum wage."

The store was long and narrow, with a cash register on either side of the aisle. The walls were lined with album covers, seventy to eighty on each side. Up front on the right were the 45s, in the back left was classical, which no one ever bought, and in the way back were cassettes. Down in the basement was the stockroom where we had lunch every day. We went to Woolworth's and bought chicken salad sandwiches.

The front of the store was where all the action happened. That's where the "boat" with the bestselling records was set up. If a new record came out and no one had heard of it then we'd get sent three copies from the label. If a band was well-known you might get twenty-five copies. With really well-known bands we got fifty. And with a supergroup like Bruce we were sent a hundred. I wasn't there when Barbra Streisand released *Guilty* in 1980, but I'm told the response was insane. That had gone down as the single most harried day in the history of Record World.

Until December 12, 1983: the day *Thriller* was released.

Records came in boxes of a hundred. Before we could put them on the floor we had to unpack them all, make sure we received the right amount of copies, and then label them with the sticker price. We must have gotten a thousand copies of *Thriller* that day. I remember coming up one afternoon carrying a box full of albums—a hundred albums are heavy—and there was a crowd waiting for me at the entrance to the basement. They'd heard I was down there with new *Thriller*s. People started pulling them off the pile before I could get to the boat. By the time I got there I had two albums left. This was a narrow fucking store. I didn't know it could hold a mob a hundred people wide. When the day ended, out of the thousand *Thriller* albums we started with, we had just six left, enough to last the first hour or so of the next morning, until we got the next shipment.

When the new music came out we were all over it, loving something when no more than three other people in the country were into it. That was part of why we liked it so much. No one else knew as much as we did. But as soon as a group became popular, we dropped them. European New Wave was big back then and I was responsible for ordering all those records. I was the guy who imported "99 Luftballons" to Record World.

We fought about what record would get played over the instore loudspeakers (we'd let the album play through full length). This is back when albums told stories, as movies do. Pete Townshend's *All the Best Cowboys Have Chinese Eyes*. Joe Jackson's *Night and Day*. Rush's *Signals*. We didn't skimp on a single track. Then we'd have to play some Top 40 hits—store policy—before the fight started all over again about who had next. Some nights we put on the strangest records we could find, hoping to entice browsing customers into buying it. When they did, we'd say to one another, "Chalk it up to instore play." And when we closed the store at the end of the day we drove around Long Island to see the local bands we loved.

The great thing about Record World was that if you worked there and you owned an album that was in good condition, you could trade it in for one of equal value. When I started working there I had two full orange crates of records. But a lot of them were Steven's that I wanted to get rid of. I was constantly trading out funky crap for classics. It took eighteen months before I ran out of records to trade in and got my collection to a state of perfection.

I was on my way to graduating with a 3.79 grade-point average. And because I was always hanging around the Adelphi communications department, I won the award for most outstanding student in my class. They called it the Richard C. Clemo Award. I actually had no idea what it meant until years later when Steve Langford, one of our Howard 100 News reporters, did some digging. Turns out this guy Clemo founded our department. If not for him, I'd be a photographer.

Naturally, with the internships, a high GPA, and the Clemo Award in my arsenal, I was thinking I'd kill it in the real world. But I wasn't quite ready to get a real job. I'd spent so much time working in college. When I was a junior I took a class called The Italian-American Experience, taught by Sal Primeggia. Honestly, I don't remember a thing about the course, but Sal was a very animated speaker, always waving his arms and doling out grand pieces of advice during his lessons. The one thing he said that stuck with me: "After you graduate, go do what you always wanted to do. Go to Europe. Because when you get that first job you will be working for the rest of your life."

A real pick-me-up. But it had a profound effect on me. My senior year, when I saw an offer on one of the bulletin boards at Adelphi for an all-inclusive, monthlong trip to Italy after graduation, at a cost of eight hundred dollars, I jumped at it. My parents gave it to me as a graduation present and then threw me a party, too, where relatives handed me envelopes stuffed with cash to take on my trip. So Italian. (It took me years to get someone a real gift for their wedding or graduation, rather than just handing them a wad of cash.)

These parties were always tough on my mom. She'd spend a month cleaning and getting ready. You couldn't go near her or offer any help, just like when she was cooking a holiday dinner. It was real manic behavior. Then when it was over, she would feel blue for days, as if coming down from the event was hard. In this case, it probably didn't help that her baby was graduating from college and heading off to Italy.

I saw Perugia. I saw Rome. Halfway through the tour, a few of us decided to ditch the program and travel on our own. We spent a couple of days in Bologna, then we hit Venice, and went on to Switzerland. We stayed in cheap hostels and pensiones and partied. The trip was exactly what I wanted it to be. And then it was time to go home. On the plane back I was thinking about my future. I wasn't arrogant, but I told myself I had more work experience than most kids my age, I had great grades, and, while it might be hard to get a great job, I thought I'd be able to land a decent one before the summer was over. I figured I'd hit the beach for a few days and then throw myself into the search.

While I was in college I had bought a cheap, beaten-up Firebird that did exactly what it needed to do: shuttle me from job to job. Before I left for Italy, Frank told me he and Vinny would clean it up a little bit while I was away. On the day I got home, the two of them picked me up at the airport and, as we walked out to the curb, Frank headed for this souped-up Firebird. It had a fin and an emblem and fancy seats. When he stopped in front of it, I said to him, "Why are you stopping here? Where's the car?"

"You don't recognize it?" he said.

"Recognize what? Where's my car?"

He tossed me the keys. "This is it. I told you we'd clean it up. Happy graduation."

It was the nicest gift anyone got me. Now I had my kick-ass car—and nothing but my adult life ahead.

RECORD WORLD PLAYLIST, CIRCA 1982–83

"Only Time Will Tell," Asia

"Every Breath You Take," Police

"Billie Jean," Michael Jackson

"Flashdance . . . What a Feeling," Irene Cara

"Down Under," Men at Work

"Sweet Dreams (Are Made of This)," Eurythmics

"Do You Really Want to Hurt Me," Culture Club

"Come On Eileen," Dexys Midnight Runners

"Hungry Like the Wolf," Duran Duran

"Let's Dance," David Bowie

"Electric Avenue," Eddy Grant

"She Blinded Me with Science," Thomas Dolby

"Africa," Toto

"Der Kommissar," After the Fire

"Puttin' on the Ritz," Taco

"The Safety Dance," Men Without Hats

"Mickey," Toni Basil

"Rock This Town," Stray Cats

"Our House," Madness

"Rock the Casbah," Clash

"Photograph," Def Leppard

"Pass the Dutchie," Musical Youth

"Don't You Want Me," Human League

"Abracadabra," Steve Miller Band

"867-5309 (Jenny)," Tommy Tutone

"We Got the Beat," Go-Go's

"Caught Up in You," .38 Special

"I Ran," A Flock of Seagulls

"Kids in America," Kim Wilde

"Edge of Seventeen," Stevie Nicks

"Sunday Bloody Sunday," U2

"Girls Just Want to Have Fun," Cyndi Lauper

"Owner of a Lonely Heart," Yes

"Steppin' Out," Joe Jackson

"Uptown Girl," Billy Joel

"Family Man," Hall and Oates

"Cum On Feel the Noise," Quiet Riot

"Harden My Heart," Quarterflash

"Burning Down the House," Talking Heads

Chapter 14

I Am a Clemo
Winner, Dammit!

A WEEK AFTER I GOT HOME from Italy, I typed up my résumé.

All the important stuff was on there, with a line or two about my responsibilities: the WLIR internships, reporting from D.C., covering the Islanders and Rick Cerone, and sledding newspaper articles. The SportsChannel gig where I hauled banners and hustled interviews for Stan Fischler, the recording studio where I set up microphones, my job as a production assistant on *Intimate Companions*, and running the distribution center for the Adelphi Film School PSA movies. I had a 3.79 and the Clemo Award.

It was a fine-looking résumé. I congratulated myself on being so well-rounded.

The next morning I woke up early and opened up *The New York Times* to the classifieds. I sat at the kitchen table with a pencil and circled all the help-wanteds that read RADIO AND TV EXECUTIVE ASSISTANT. That sounded professional, like it

would pay well, and since I had so much success with internships, it might be the kind of job I could learn from. I'd be as-
sisting an executive, and executives know a lot of shit.

After breakfast I took a shower and threw on my gray pin-
striped suit. It was the middle of July, a little hot for wool. But
it's all I had, and I wanted to look professional. No one hires assistants that look like John Oates. I put my résumé in a folder
and put that in a leather briefcase one of my relatives had given
me for graduation. Then I hopped in my tricked-out Firebird
and drove to the Long Island Rail Road station. Everyone else
on the platform looked like a more grown-up version of me:
briefcase, suit, empty stare, not sure what the day was going to
bring. Professor Primeggia was right about getting away before
getting a job. The rest of our lives was going to last a long time.
Is this what it looked like?

On the train I prepared, writing down the addresses of the
offices I wanted to hit and the interview times, and then map-
ping out my path. I was methodical.

I arrived at my first interview, already starting to sweat in my
suit, and began to pull my impressive résumé from my new
leather briefcase for the woman behind the front desk. She
wasn't interested. Instead she pointed to an empty chair in the
waiting room, the only one available in a space packed with as-
piring executive assistants. Pretty soon they called my name
and sent me to another room filled with even more people and
rows and rows of typewriters. Everyone was clanging away.

I had to take a typing test. I didn't learn typing at the Adelphi School of Communications! None of my internships fo-
cused on that, either. In fact, I was and still am a terrible typist
(one more thing I get mocked for on the show) who uses the
hunt-and-peck method. They weren't looking for Clemo
Award winners; they wanted 80–100-words-per-minute typ-
ists who didn't make any mistakes. Everywhere I went, it was
the same story. All the executive assistant jobs were for people

with experience and skills I didn't have. What the hell was I learning in college? Clearly, despite my brilliant planning, I was looking in all the wrong places and circling all the wrong jobs.

It was the middle of July and it was sweltering as I trudged across Midtown, from one glass skyscraper to another, waiting in the same rooms to fail the same typing tests. My wool suit was getting heavier every time I stepped outside.

Finally, toward the end of the day, I had had enough. I found myself walking by the New York Public Library, where people were lounging all over the steps out front. It was late, after five in the afternoon. They all looked like they were taking a break at the end of their workday, undoing their ties, loosening their collars. Who knows if they were successful or just shlubs like me, looking for work. I assumed it was the former, and that I was the only loser in town at that particular moment.

I sat down in an empty spot on the steps, slung my jacket over my shoulder, and loosened my tie. Then I rested my elbows on my knees and dropped my head to my chest. That's when I saw them: pit stains under each of my arms big enough to block out the sun.

It was the perfect way to end the day.

The Videotape

1988/1999

The workday was almost over. We were done with guests. No more breaks. A couple of minutes and I'd be on the way back to Connecticut to spend a beautiful summer afternoon with Mary and the boys. It was 1999. Jackson was a little more than three. Lucas was still a baby. It would have been a great day, a sweet spot in life.

Until that call came in.

"Hey, Howard," the caller said. I was half listening while returning emails and planning out the next day's show. But I noticed the guy had an accent, a thick Long Island one, like he could have grown up in or spent time in Nassau County. "I'm the guy Gary's old girlfriend dumped him for."

Here we go again, I thought. Ever since Nancy dumped me and the guys went after me on the show for it, people still called in to talk about it. They'd call me a pussy or make fun of me for having been so heartbroken. That segment aired on the *Best of Stern* shows we reran every few years, so a lot of people were just discovering it for the first time.

But by 1999, eleven years after Nancy and I broke up, even Howard was getting tired of the story. He quickly lost interest in these calls because it meant explaining the situation to everyone all over again. And he was just about to drop this douche bag on the phone—he had his finger on the button to cut him off—when the guy pulled this comment out of his bag: "Howard, there's a tape."

I gasped at my desk. The hairs on the back of my neck stood up. I thought back to the days after Nancy dumped me. I was desperate. And when that happens your mind takes off in new directions. You find clarity that wasn't possible when more logical options were still available. And in that state of mind, I came up with a brilliant idea: I'd make Nancy a videotape.

It was the summer of '88. I had just bought a video camera. I thought I would film myself and show Nancy how much I missed her. It would explain everything, with a lot more impact than a letter. If she could see the pain in my face and hear the regret in my voice she would take me back. For sure.

I lived with a roommate in an apartment at 105th and Amsterdam. I came home early one afternoon. My roommate wasn't home. I set up the tripod and the camera in the kitchen, jotted down a few points I wanted to make, and threw on my Atlantic Records 40th Anniversary Concert T-shirt. I had the sleeves rolled up tightly around my arms. Even wearing the T-shirt was a strategic move: The concert had taken place just a month earlier. Since we were both so into music, if she saw it she'd think it was cool I was there, and maybe even subliminally, she'd regret that she wasn't with a guy like me.

"What do you mean there's a tape?" Howard asked the caller.

"There's a tape of Gary begging Nancy to take him back," he said.

Howard called me into the studio.

"Is this true?" he asked me.

I am not a good liar. I can't think the five steps ahead to

successfully dodge the truth. I love the show *Survivor,* but I know I would be the second one voted off because I'm not conniving enough.

"Yes," I said. I didn't even think about saying no.

"We gotta see that tape," Howard said. "Do you have a copy of it?"

"I think so," I answered. "I'm not sure. I'd have to look. But let me tell you something. There is not enough money in the world for me to show you that tape even if I find it."

"I'll give you five grand," Howard said.

"So will I," Robin followed up.

Jackie and Fred chimed in with offers of one thousand dollars apiece.

And that's when things spiraled out of control. Howard offered to do a screening for fans. Anyone who wanted to pay could come to the studio and watch the tape on the air. Highest bidder would win. A guy from Miami offered ten thousand dollars if he could bring two friends.

Suddenly, there was a lot of money on the table. We were sitting at twenty-two thousand dollars. And here's the truth: I was in the middle of finishing a remodel of the kitchen in my house. That money would come in handy and help me breathe a little bit. I decided to do it.

But first, I had to do some explaining. Now, my wife is a very understanding woman. It's practically a requirement for anyone who gets involved with a guy on the show. They perfect the shrug and the eye roll. When I work the Sybian machine, Mary doesn't say a word. "Well," she says to me, "it's not like you're touching anyone." She's immune to these things and knows they are harmless. Besides, she'd much rather I be doing this job than working one hundred hours a week at a law firm or trying to close M&A deals. She always tells me that she appreciates that I am different and have a sense of humor.

In fact, only twice in the early days of our marriage did she get annoyed by my antics. The first time, we were playing Butt Bongo Fiesta on the show, and well, for a second I guess I forgot I was married, because I got into the act. I didn't think twice about it. Until I got home and Mary reminded me that we were married, so maybe I better knock it off with the slapping of girls' asses.

The second time was after the videotape conversation on the show. As I sat down at my desk I decided I should call her and make sure everything was cool. "Hey," I said.

"Hi," she said. That was it. An abrupt *hi.*

"What's going on? Did you hear the show today?"

"Yeah." Hmm, that was a short answer.

"So what do you think?"

"What should I think? Do you think I should be happy about this?"

"I didn't think you would mind. In the grand scheme of things it's pretty harmless."

"Oh, you think so?"

"What are we talking about here?"

"The tape."

"What kind of tape do you think this is?"

She paused for a very long time. "A sex tape."

Turns out a friend who had heard only snippets of the show called her and said they were discussing my sex tape.

I laughed and said, "Do you think I would call you up so calmly if we were talking about a sex tape on the air?"

She was relieved. Later that night saw me digging through a box of videotapes I had hauled out to Connecticut when we moved. To this day, people still ask me why I saved that tape. I had dubbed a lot of stuff from that video camera onto VHS, and it happened that some of the last footage I had of my brother was on the same tape as my ode to Nancy. That's why I saved it, and that's why it was so easy to find.

As I held the tape in my hand, I told myself, *I made this a long time ago. It is now worth a lot of money.* Then I popped it into the VCR and watched a couple minutes of it. It was really embarrassing. I asked Mary to come in and take a look. She said, "Oh, who cares? It's no big deal." I thought that Mary wouldn't want the world to think she was married to an idiot, so how bad could it be? Right?

The answer: really, really bad. Mary's fatal flaw is that she is too sweet to have recognized the opportunity for money in the tape. I'm not. I had to bring the tape in early so the TV people could dub it into the right format for the show. As they were watching it I immediately was sorry I found it. I could tell by their reaction that it was bad.

Then one of our supervising producers gave it a look. Her reaction was sobering. "It was all about you," she said. "You never say you're sorry or how you will make it up to her. It's all about you and what you expect and what you want."

This had never occurred to me. I felt like a dick. But it was too late to turn back. The guys from Miami were already in the studio, waiting for the 7 A.M. screening. Howard said into the microphone, "You guys ready in the audience?" Then he hit Play.

Hello, hello, guess who? Umm, I think you're a little surprised by this, and you'll have to excuse me because I lost my voice on Friday. It is Tuesday at 12:28 in the afternoon, and I came home from work early because I wasn't feeling that good. I wanted to get this out to you.

First of all, as you might have noticed I bought a new video camera, and I wanted to try it out. So that is what this is all about. I have had a lot of things I wanted to say to you, which I think I should be saying in person, but getting an audience with you seems to be difficult. I could have wrote this to you in a letter, but these are things I don't want to say to you over the telephone because I think you need to hear my voice and you need to see me to understand some of these things.

This may get a little bit boring because when you don't have someone to talk to you kind of have to do it all by yourself, which is why I am sending you this videotape. But, hey, guess what? You haven't seen me in seven months, and this is what I look like now. I've got my Atlantic Records T-shirt, my hair is a lot longer, but I just came in out of the rain.

I took some notes down. I had a lot of things I wanted to say, and like I said when you don't have someone to talk to on the telephone to remind you stuff, so don't think I am cheating, but I had a lot of things I wanted to say and wanted to get them all in.

Let's start with the thing that prompted this whole thing. Last Friday night I felt like the biggest idiot in the history of the world and I was pretty hurt. I was pretty hurt. I'm sure that wasn't your intention. If you don't know what I'm talking about let me tell you what I am talking about. I came home from the city and Frank drove me over to his house and he told me to sit in the car while you were upstairs. And I felt like a schmuck, Nance. I felt like a real dick. Frank was like, "I will drop you off at Vinny's because Nancy really doesn't want to see you, and Maryanne said it's not a good idea if I bring you back here. She really doesn't want to see you."

We're civilized here, don't you think? What is this all about? It kind of hurt a lot. You know I told Frank the whole way there how I missed you and spoke to you early in the week. There have been a lot of op-portunities where I could have seen you and set something up and I didn't. I respect your wishes that you don't want to see me. And I haven't been doing it, and this was one of those purely coincidental things and I would have been nice to you. I would have said hello. So I gotta tell you I was really hurt by that.

But in a way it makes me feel good because it tells me something: If you didn't still care about me you'd see me, and I think you still do care about me. You care about me a lot. And I was telling Frank how the last seven months have been and how I knew I was wrong, and I started to tell him a lot of things and he said, "Do you think she knows that?" and I said, "Yeah, I think she knows it." And he said, "Are you sure she knows it?" And I said, "I don't know."

So I am going to try and put them down on video-tape for you. These are forever, man. You'll always have these to hold against me one way or the other.

Let me start out, I feel like I'm asking your father for permission to marry you. I want to lay out my in-tentions. I want to lay out what I want, what I want from you. Obviously, I want to go back out with you again, that goes without saying, but I want more than that. The first thing that I want is I want a com-mitment. I want to give a commitment and I want to get a commitment. I want to be your boyfriend and I want you to be my girlfriend. I would dump every-one I was going out with in a second if it meant you'd be back with me. And it would be just me and you. I want to be clear. I want to do things for you. I know I was kind of insensitive before, and ah, there is not much I can do about it. I can say I'm sorry, but I am not going to sit here and make excuses. What's done is done. I can't change what's behind me; there are a lot of excuses why I acted that way, but there are no reasons and that is behind me.

I want to do a lot of the things we said we were going to do but never got to do. I wrote so much stuff down, a lot of it had to do with the fact that I was afraid of commitment. I know you think I was insensitive. I was afraid that anything I did for you, any kind of love I showed you or any kind of stuff like that, would lead you more down the way that I didn't feel at the time. Let me try to explain. Let's say I gave you roses for no reason at all. I felt in my mind how could I do that if I didn't love her because in your mind you were going to think that I did.

But I'm romantic. A lot of people find that hard to believe. I could be if I was up for a commitment, but I wasn't at that time so that's that. The other part of the intention here is that I've been saying I'm a marriage martyr for a long time. And I am not asking you to marry me on videotape and certainly not tomorrow, either, but I would like to think if we got back together and became a couple again and it was working, somewhere off in the distance would be the possibility of mmmmmmm. I'm trying to make light of a serious subject. I don't want to be running around anymore. I do want to get married, and yeah, I could see myself marrying you, especially if you were interested in marrying me back.

I have something like that in mind, and I am not just bullshitting. I miss you. I miss you. I miss you. I am not even trying to hide that. None of my other relationships have worked because of you. I am not even trying to hide that. I miss you, man, don't know how else to say it. I lost my lover and I lost my best friend. And you lost your lover and you lost your best friend. You gained a lover and a best friend: I gained a couple lovers, I mean one lover, but I gained no friends. There is no one there to come home to call or tell all the great stuff. Right now I feel like my professional life is at a nine and my personal life is at a two. Now I feel great about the way work is going and the curse with that is that I have no one to share it with. That sucks.

I can tell you that going back out with me would solve a lot of problems. Because your friends are my friends and mine are yours, and I have to sometimes feel uncomfortable around my friends when it comes to you and it sometimes feels weird. I don't know if you are happy where you are right now. I mean I hear stuff through the grapevine. I gotta tell you the people I hear from think that you are happy and that you are content, but they don't know if you are really, really happy. And I think I can make you that happy. I thought you and I were really happy when we were happy. I want to do all the things we said we were going to do and never did like going to the Metropolitan Museum of Art and the Philharmonic. Things that I promised we would do and never did because I was afraid of the c-word, the commitment word.

Here's my final statement. I know that sending you this tape is very unfair. I realize that. But I don't give a shit because all is fair in love and war. I'm playing a little dirty and quite frankly I am trying to get any edge I can to get you to listen to me. If you want me to leave you alone, I'll leave you alone. I'll stop with the phone calls. I'll stop sending you T-shirts in the mail and, you know, this videotape. I'll put it all to an end.

But I am not going to let you off the hook that easy if you want me gone. I want to take about ten minutes of your time. If you want me gone you have to tell me face-to-face: you have to look me in the eyes and tell me you don't care about me anymore. I think you owe that to me. Well quite frankly you don't owe me anything, but for the time we spent together I think you do owe me that and if you could do that you would really make me believe it. I don't know if you can do that.

I am trying to figure out if I made some sense. I am in a very confused state. I miss you. I not only miss the things we did I miss the shit that we should have been doing and never got to do. I just want to be part of your life again, and I want you to be part of my life again. And, um, you know, I don't know what else to say. Think about it please. I am not begging now. I am not the begging type, but I am close to begging as I can get. I really want you to think about this whole tape, and the great thing about videotape is you can rewind it and watch it all over again, make sure you didn't miss any important parts.

I think we could be good together. Please think about it. Thanks.

When I was done making the tape that day I took it out of the camera and dubbed it onto a VHS tape. Then I wrote a short note that read, "Watch this tape. Everything I need to say is on here." After mailing it off I felt good. I felt successful, actually. I knew I had made the tape that would make Nancy break up with her boyfriend and come running back to me.

Eleven years later, I didn't feel quite so successful. I sat there during the showing with a yellow legal pad over my face the entire time so the camera couldn't see me. I felt exposed and naked. This was something that I never expected anyone to see except the person I made it for. I was brutally honest and the world got to see that. Even the interns looked at me funny. I was supposed to be their boss, and it turned out I was an embarrassing, sniveling dick.

"And so ends our journey," Howard said when it was all over. "You guys didn't pay enough. Our audience is stunned and can't really speak."

"Did it live up to the hype?" I asked.

"Better than a Barbara Walters special," said one of the audience members.

What killed me was that, at the time, I couldn't convince Nancy to come on the show and tell everyone how she felt when she actually got the tape. The truth was, she didn't think I was a stalker and she didn't call 911 after watching it. In fact, when I decided to do this book I reached out to her again—we've kept in touch over the years—and this time she was ready to share what she was thinking. Finally, here's what Nancy has to say about the tape, twenty-two years later:

"People I know who listen to the show say to me, 'Did you listen today? They mentioned it again.' It's like infamy.

"But no one had done that for me before. I was living at home at that time, on Long Island, and I watched it by myself, although I did tell my best girlfriend about it. And I told the guy I was dating, too.

"To be honest, I thought the tape was a romantic gesture. If you asked any woman what she thought of something like that she would be like, 'Wow, I wish a guy would sit down and do that for me.'

"We were in our twenties at that point and I had just gotten out of college and we had a pretty tight relationship. After I watched it, I was crushed and cried. I showed it to my friend, and she was like, 'So what are you going to do?' But there was nothing to do. That's one reason why it was hard to see it, because everything that was said about being together came too late, after I had decided to break up and move on. We had a close relationship and I did lose my best friend. I remember not wanting to get together after we broke up because I knew you were not going to let me off the hook. You were going to do what it took to get me back; there was no doubting what you wanted. You were saying, 'I realized I was a jerk and want to do the right thing.'

"But it was also upsetting, hearing it on the show all those years later, because it was like someone ripped a page out of my diary from ten years earlier and then played it over and over.

"I don't know which emotion came first: I felt embarrassed, angry, mortified, and extremely apologetic. That tape was buried in a box somewhere with letters that go with it. I just watched it for the first time in twenty-two years. And I am sorry for ever sharing its existence with anyone. I will say this though: I didn't even notice you were wearing the Atlantic Records T-shirt. It didn't make a single lasting impression on me."

To be honest, if you asked me whether or not it was worth it, my first answer used to be yes. It helped pay for my kitchen. But now I'd immediately change my answer to no. I just didn't know there would ever be such a thing as YouTube and this tape would live in perpetuity. Even today, people still react to it. It's the brawniest guys who usually stop and whisper under their breath to tell me they did something just like that once. But it's the women's reaction that is most surprising. A lot of them are like the callers that day, telling me I'm a pussy and that I should have manned the fuck up.

At the time that twenty-two thousand dollars seemed like a lot of money. Now, it's been played so much on the show and on YouTube, I feel it's down to a nickel a play.

Chapter 15

Fridays and Sally Foo

AFTER THE DREADFUL DAY of executive assistant interviews, I had to regroup. I didn't have a job. And I wasn't going to the city to look for jobs, because I couldn't type. I needed a plan, so I decided the plan was going to be: Don't have a plan.

Instead of moping on the couch, I went back to work at Record World. Summer was a great time to work there. The mall was always buzzing and hot girls were always in the store looking for records. I liked the action. I put in thirty hours a week, listened to great new music every day, hung with Frank, Vinny, and the boys or friends from the store at night, got in some good beach time. I decided to give myself the rest of the summer to relax and then, come September, I was going to figure out my life. My parents weren't bothering me to get out of the house and most of my friends hadn't lit it up in the job market yet, so I didn't feel too bad hanging around. Then, right before the summer ended, the manager at Record World asked me if I had a job lined up for the fall. When I said my calendar was wide open, she offered me a full-time job there. Fantastic, I thought. I'd make money while I looked for a career.

That first Monday in September I showed up for work at 10 A.M. I had never been there that early during the week. My shifts had always been nights and weekends. It was strangely quiet, in the store and in the mall. Everyone I was used to seeing had gone back to school. And the people working at the store were actually people who didn't have any other options. They were adults, pushing thirty, and this was how they paid rent and bought food and filled their gas tanks. It dawned on me that my future was being shoved in my face like a shaving cream pie, and I didn't even see it coming. It's one thing to be hanging at the store on the weekends and fighting with your friends about which records to play. But it's another to be there early in the morning during the week, with no chicks looking for music and a feather duster in your hand to clean the tops of the cabinets.

I freaked a little bit. I didn't want to be a Record World lifer. I had to find a job.

First I called Steve North, my old boss at WLIR. He had moved on and was now working at WNBC radio in New York. He said he'd keep his eyes open for me. Then I reached out to fellow communications majors from Adelphi and kids I had done internships with. I quickly found out that a lot of these people didn't have the passion for working in radio that I did. They had spent a few months looking for those kinds of jobs, had struck out, and started getting real work. They had given up and gone into retail, or became travel agents, or did pharmaceutical sales. This was discouraging. Once you do that, that's what you do. Forever.

Here was the rub: I was working at the record store during the day. And that was the only time to interview for jobs that could lead to a real career. I was in a dead-end job that was keeping me from getting a new job. I had to quit the store.

Believe it or not, the best option I could find for work was as a host at T.G.I. Friday's. An ex-girlfriend hooked me up. It was the perfect scenario, in theory. I worked as a host from five in the afternoon until eleven at night. On Saturdays it was packed, with people bribing me to get them to the front of the line so they could sit down and order overstuffed potato skins as soon as possible. And then I had all day to hunt for my dream job.

Except T.G.I.F. was like entering the abyss. It offered employees a free drink and half off food after work. When I clocked out at eleven I went over to the bar and joined the rest of the people whose shifts had just ended to have our free beer. While we were sitting there we thought, *Let's get some food, it's half off.* Then we got more to drink. Then more to eat. Pretty soon it was closing time and everyone would decide to head somewhere else. Then when that place closed we went to someone's house to hang out. Suddenly I was getting home at six in the morning. Not only could I not get up for any interviews, I could barely get up in time for my 5 P.M. shift.

Not that it mattered how available I was during the day. I couldn't even find jobs to interview for. In fact, between September and Christmas, I had one job interview. That was in October. Steve North called me and said that the NBA needed someone with entry-level TV production experience. If I wanted to interview, he could get me in.

I drove from Long Island to the NBA production office in Secaucus, New Jersey, and I was exactly what they needed: a sports-crazed kid who knew how to work professional TV equipment, log tapes, and cut promos. I killed it. The guy I interviewed with told me he was working on a piece about George Mikan, the NBA's original superstar back in the 1940s. I shook my head up and down like it was a great idea, but I had no clue who George Mikan was. I was a sports nut, still am, but I was a Mets/Jets/Islanders guy. The NBA wasn't ever my thing. Clearly I fooled him because he asked me to come back the next day to discuss it with some more people.

That night I went to the library and looked through every book I could find about basketball, writing it all down on a fact sheet. Then I went home and studied. Overnight I became a George Mikan expert, to the point that at the interview the next morning I was spewing stats that even he didn't know. "You are perfect for the job," he told me. "Now you have to go to the corporate office on Park Avenue in Manhattan and meet my bosses."

"Fantastic," I said. I could see T.G.I.F. in the rearview mirror.

"But I'm warning you," he added. "You are the tenth person I'm sending over there. They haven't hired anyone yet."

Whatever, I thought. *Those guys don't have what I have. I won the Clemo.* They *don't want it like I want it.*

I woke up the next morning, put on my best (and only) pin-striped suit, and rode the LIRR into the city. I had my résumé packed in my black briefcase. My internships were lined up on the page like well-behaved kids, each one announcing what I had accomplished as a dutiful employee. I sat down with a man and woman in a fancy office on Park Avenue and they started asking me about my experience. I explained how I kept a log of highlights and learned how to cut promos and highlights at SportsChannel. Then one of them stopped me and asked, "Are all the jobs listed on here internships?"

"Well, yeah," I said.

Then they just looked at each other and nodded. That was the end of the interview. I didn't get the job.

My dad had dropped me off at the train that morning and wished me good luck. He was on his way to New Jersey for some ice cream sales calls and then headed to the office. If I was done early, he said, I should call him. He'd swing through the city and pick me up.

"You'll meet me in the neighborhood," he said. That's what he called the area where he grew up, on the corner of Mott and Hester streets in Little Italy. He never said we were going to the city on Sundays; we were going to the neighborhood. I liked it down there, right on the border of Chinatown. Turn one way and you'd walk onto a street lined with Italian restaurants with cannoli displayed in the front window. Turn the other way and you were face-to-face with roasted ducks hanging from hooks.

The two parts of town were so intertwined, Dad's buddies had nicknamed him Sally Foo because it sounded Chinese. Even my mom called him that. After my mom and dad were first married and living with her parents, someone came to the door and asked for Sal Dell'Abate. My grandfather had no idea who that was. He thought his son-in-law's name was Sally Foo.

Whenever we visited the neighborhood we stopped by a place on Hester called Mo's, a hole in the wall that wasn't open to the public. It was a social club, one that wasn't all that friendly if you didn't belong. Inside you'd find a bunch of old Italian guys drinking, with one jukebox in the corner. It actually always freaked me out whenever we stopped by there. The old-timers sort of smirked when they saw me, then patted me on the head and slipped me money or Hershey bars. Once, I told my dad I had to go to the bathroom and he pointed to a long hallway and said it was the door on the right.

But I was little and scared and by the time I got to the end of the hallway I couldn't remember if it was right or left, so I picked the door on the left. When I opened it I saw a bunch of guys sitting around a table with stacks and stacks of money on it. One of them screamed at me, "Shut the fucking door, kid!"

What? No candy?

Clearly something weird was going on here. As I got older and realized this I asked my dad how come he never joined the mafia. He was a gambler. He was tough and he lived in the right neighborhood. He told me he always had chances, but it just wasn't the way he wanted to go. Not that he didn't know people who did. He and my mom used to talk about this one guy he grew up with who had a cockeyed look about him. He scared her. In fact, they thought, it was the look that may have gotten him killed.

Once, after my dad had lost his job, we were at one of the big flea markets in Oakdale, Long Island, where he was selling crap to make ends meet. This was out in the middle of nowhere, a real rural area. We were sitting together and it was pretty busy, but my dad suddenly stopped talking and just stared at someone, an older guy, who was walking around the racks of clothes. Wherever the guy went, my dad's eyes tracked him, until he had to get up and follow him to keep him in his sights. When my dad confronted him, the guy turned white and quickly walked away.

"Who was that?" I asked my dad when he came back.

"I thought it was a guy from the neighborhood," my dad said. "But he said I had the wrong fella."

A couple of years later my dad showed me the guy's picture in the paper. He'd been killed. The mob had been looking for him for years.

After I was rejected by the NBA, I went down to the neighborhood, found a pay phone, and called my dad. He told me to meet him at Mo's.

I walked into the bar looking like some kind of FBI agent. I was carrying my black leather briefcase and had on my gray pin-striped suit, a starched white shirt, and a tie. As I walked through the door a bartender dropped his rag and jumped over the bar. He stood in front of me and said, "This is a private club." Before I could say anything, he was pushing me. "What are you doing here?"

"I'm here to meet my dad!" I screamed. "Sal Dell'Abate."

"Never heard of him," the guy yelled back, pushing me harder.

"Sal Dell'Abate, Sal Dell'Abate, he used to live on Mott Street, he comes here all the time."

"I don't know him," the guy answered back.

I really thought the guy was going to kill me. He was angry and pushing hard. As I was about to fall ass backward onto Hester Street I yelled, "Sally Foo."

"Hold it!" a voice in the dark yelled out. "What did you say?"

"Sally Foo," I answered. "That's my dad."

Then he looked at me and said, "You Sally Foo's kid?"

"Yeah," I said.

Then he looked at the bartender, said, "He's okay," and bought me a club soda. I sat at a table by myself, sweating through my suit, until my dad finally showed up. He laughed at that story all the way back to Long Island.

GREATEST BAD STORYTELLING SONGS OF THE '70S

"The Night the Lights Went Out in Georgia," Vicki Lawrence

"Billy Don't Be a Hero," Bo Donaldson and the Heywoods

"Gypsys, Tramps & Thieves," Cher

"Seasons in the Sun," Terry Jacks

"I Shot the Sheriff," Eric Clapton

"Angie," Helen Reddy

"Brandy (You're a Fine Girl)," Looking Glass

"Me and Mrs. Jones," Billy Paul

"Patches," Clarence Carter

"Ride Captain Ride," Blues Image

"Run Joey Run," David Geddes

"Daddy Don't You Walk So Fast," Wayne Newton

"The Wreck of the Edmund Fitzgerald," Gordon Lightfoot

"Bad, Bad Leroy Brown," Jim Croce

"Cat's in the Cradle," Harry Chapin

Chapter 16

The Birthday Pact

FOR A COUPLE OF MONTHS following the NBA fiasco, I fell headlong into the T.G.I.F. abyss. I was partying nonstop, letting that one free beer and a plate of half-price skins turn into full-on benders. It got so bad that one night, one of the bartenders yelled at me for treating the job and the restaurant with such casual disregard. "I know a lot of you are using this to get through college or as a job till you get the one you really want," he said. "But for some of us this is our livelihood." I felt like an ass.

Finally, around Christmas, I got a real job in radio. Kind of. I took a once-a-week midnight to 8 A.M. shift at an all-automated station called WCTO that played an easy-listening format. I did this on one of my off nights from Fridays. WCTO played elevator music. Every fifth song had vocals. In the radio business the demographic for this format is called sixty-five to dead. It turned out to be the worst job I ever had, including cleaning the grease traps at my cousin's pork store.

I would start my shift by going to the deli across from the station—which was in Farmingdale, about twenty-five minutes from my house—and buying anything that would keep me up all night. Iced tea, cupcakes, Hershey bars. I'd have a snack and a drink whenever I felt myself nodding off. Which happened often. Because the station was automated it had no DJs. The music, the teases, the commercials—all of it ran on reels and tapes. My job was to make sure the right reels and right tapes went on at the right time. Each reel was fifteen minutes, and when it ended, I needed to shove a tape into the deck and play an intro or a commercial. It was mind-numbing work that went on for eight hours. And if you were late changing a reel, leaving dead air, an alarm started beeping after fifteen seconds. I never understood why it mattered. Anyone who listened to us was either dead or asleep after midnight.

At least that's what I thought. One morning at around 4 A.M., the phone started ringing. It startled me, because I had fallen fast asleep. When I picked it up an old man at the other end started yelling, "You're off the air! You're off the air!" I had passed out and left the station silent for twenty-five minutes.

When I first interviewed for the gig they asked me if I was committed to staying longer than three months. I said of course. After three months I realized why they asked. No one could stick it out longer than that.

I was so depressed about my plight, I made a pact with myself: If I didn't get a real job in radio by my birthday in March, just a couple of months away, I was going to bag it. I had decided I would become a pharmaceutical salesman. That's what I was suited for and I kept seeing those jobs available in *The New York Times* classifieds. I was a convincing talker, had my own car, and it seemed like you could make a lot of money. Best of all, I didn't need to type.

The pact was a stupid idea. What difference did it make if I had a career path at twenty-three or not? Obviously I know that now. But back then I just got more and more upset as it drew closer and loomed larger. I worked at T.G.I.F. four nights a week, and every time I walked through those doors I realized I was headed nowhere. By February, six weeks before my birthday, I had gone four months without an interview, had no leads, and was working the graveyard shift at an automated station for minimum wage. I was in a sorry state.

That's when Steve North saved me again. It was a slow night at Friday's. I had my chin propped in my hands and my elbows on the host stand when the phone rang. "Hello, T.G.I. Friday's, how can I help you?" I said.

"Hey Gary, it's Steve. I think I have something for you."

He had seen a posting at WNBC for a desk assistant in the news department. It was part-time, he told me, but he said he could help get my résumé to the people who were doing the hiring. I sent in my résumé with a cover letter in which Steve's name was featured prominently, and then started planning for my first day. Of course they were going to hire me.

But after a couple of days, I hadn't had a callback. So I called. They said I was on their list but they hadn't gotten to me yet. A week went by, still no interview. So I called again. Still on the list. The next week I called a few times, trying to be persistent without being a stalker. I wanted to show how interested I was in the job but didn't want to seem so annoying they'd never want to hire me. It got to the point where I just called at 2 P.M. every few days for a couple of weeks, but the answer was always the same: They hadn't forgotten about me, they wanted to interview me, they hadn't gotten to me yet. My hopes evaporated.

On March 1, two weeks before my birthday, I called at my

usual time and spoke to the same woman. "Oh hi," she said. "I am so sorry, but we are filling the position from within."

"Okay, sorry for bothering you, thanks for telling me," I said. It was soul-crushing news. I wanted to cry. I felt like I had run out of options. My birthday was just up ahead and if I kept this stupid pact with myself I'd have to get a real job. I worried that whatever I did next would be what I did for the rest of my life. I lay down on the couch in my parents' living room and stared at the ceiling.

Twenty minutes later the phone rang.

"Hello," I answered.

"Gary?" said the voice on the other end. It sounded familiar. Then I realized it was the woman from WNBC.

"Yes."

"We've decided to rethink the process and we are going to interview. Can you come in tomorrow?"

I had gone from being dead to getting a lifeline. I called Steve to say thanks and told him I'd be going in the next day. He mentioned that one of his best friends, Nell Bassett, worked as the public affairs director on the floor where my interview was. If I saw her, I should say hi. The next morning I got on the elevator at the WNBC offices at the same time as another woman. Someone next to me greeted her, "Hi, Nell." So I asked, "Are you Nell Bassett?" We started talking and then she walked me to my interview, introduced me, and said if Steve North sent me I must be great.

My interview was with Meredith Hollis, who ran the news desk. She explained to me that the position was just a part-time gig as assistant to the traffic reporter, Roz Frank, who flew around the city in a helicopter giving reports every ten minutes. There was a morning spot open and an afternoon spot. The job entailed sitting in a cubicle all day and feeding information to Roz.

Meredith didn't ask questions. She made statements, such as

"We have a large news department here." Then she stared at me and leaned in real close, just waiting for a response. She also presented me with some strange hypotheticals: If you are working on deadline and someone yells at you, how do you handle that? If you get something right but are yelled at for being wrong, what's your response? The whole process struck me as odd.

But it worked out okay, because when it was over she told me to come back the next day. I had to meet Roz. And she warned me: I better know my stuff. That meant understanding every highway, byway, roadway, bridge, and tunnel that connected all five boroughs and the rest of the tri-state area—New York, Connecticut, and New Jersey.

When my dad drove us around the city I paid attention. I knew the Long Island Expressway and Grand Central Parkway and the Queens–Midtown Tunnel. But I knew nothing about New Jersey. All of New Jersey—and all the ways to get to New Jersey—was an enigma to me. I needed to study up.

On the way home I bought a map of the tri-state area, memorized all the highways going north, south, east, and west and circled all the bridges and tunnels. For hours that afternoon, I memorized them, starting with the northernmost Hudson River crossings, moving around the tip of lower Manhattan, and coming back up the East River: George Washington Bridge, Lincoln Tunnel, Holland Tunnel, Brooklyn–Battery Tunnel, Brooklyn Bridge, Manhattan Bridge, Williamsburg Bridge, Queens–Midtown Tunnel, 59th Street Bridge, and Triboro Bridge. By the time my dad got home from work, I had them down.

As soon as I sat down the next morning Roz barely said hello. She just hit me with a question: Name the Hudson River crossings. I rattled them off. Then she wanted the five East River crossings. I hit those, too, almost. From south to north, I said the Williamsburg Bridge came before the Manhattan

Bridge. When she was done she looked at Meredith, looked at me, and, without smiling, said, "All right. You're hired. Start to-morrow."

My first day at WNBC was March 5, 1984. Nine days before I turned twenty-three. I was working the morning shift.

Marrying Mary

1992

A month after Steven went into the hospital, I was still struggling to make sense of it all. I had tremendous support from Howard, Robin, Fred, and everyone on the show. And the outpouring from my Long Island guys made me wonder why I was ever afraid to tell them Steven was gay.

But I wasn't going out much. After work I'd usually come home, watch *Jeopardy!*, and go to sleep. I wasn't depressed, or blue, as my mom had always put it. I could function. I was just sad all the time.

One night a publicist friend was having a party in Manhattan to celebrate the opening of his firm. I had asked my friend Patty to join me, but when she was busy I contemplated blowing it off. "Just go by yourself," Patty urged me. "You need to get out."

I took her advice. I was strolling through the scene when I met these two girls. One of them was tall and cute and blond. The other one started talking to me.

"Hey, I recognize you," she said.

"Hi, I'm Gary."

"I know. My brother listens to your show. I hate it. I think it's disgusting."

I heard this a lot. And normally it would send me running. But I wanted to talk to the cute chick so I stuck around and tried to charm them. The good news was that the one I liked, whose name was Mary, almost never listened to the show. The one time she had heard it she was in the car and happened to hear a bit where Howard was talking about the size of some guy's penis, so she changed the channel. Mary was a graphic designer at an investment bank on Wall Street and had no idea who I was. After a while, we all decided to leave the party and grab a drink nearby. It turned out to be a really fun night and, when it was time to go, we all exchanged numbers and said we should do it again sometime.

I shared a cab home with the girl who said she hated the show. I didn't know if she was into me, but I was into Mary, and I didn't want it to be awkward when the cab dropped us off. So when we pulled away from the bar I asked the friend, "Does Mary date guys that are shorter than her?" Mary is five ten; I am five eight—just tall enough not to be short. I got the green light.

The next morning I called Mary at nine. Mary still jokes that she was amazed I called so early. She didn't know that nine o'clock was my lunchtime.

The truth was, we were two people in our late twenties who dated a lot and none of whose relationships had worked out. Her previous boyfriends were usually tall investment bankers. My type was short girls with dark hair. We probably both saw each other as a change-of-pace date.

Before our first date I asked Patty for advice. I could get tickets to a concert or go to a Broadway show. Patty told me, "Don't try to impress her with stuff like that. Just go to dinner. Have a conversation." A great idea! So we went to a restaurant called Ernie's. After dinner we went to shoot pool. The date was over by 8:30 because of my work schedule. Mary thought I didn't like her because I sent her home at the time when most people headed out.

I did most of the talking that night. And I said enough of the right things that we went out again the next weekend. And the weekend after that. We were getting together at least once on a Saturday or Sunday, just for a few hours, so we weren't in each other's face constantly. It was casual and comfortable. But things were going well enough that I thought it was a good time to put her to the test.

I happened to have an appearance at Madison Square Garden just a couple of months after we started dating. It was a truck show, and I invited Mary to come with me. Before we left I told her, "It's a white-trashy event but it will be done by nine and then we'll get a bite to eat."

It wasn't just a truck show, though. It was a mud bog truck show, in which they filled the middle of the arena with dirt and then used industrial fire hoses to spray it down until it was a muddy mess. And I wasn't the only one making an appearance. I was sharing the stage with four Penthouse Pets, two of whom I knew from the show.

These types of appearances never have a grand plan. You just show up and hang around until someone tells you what you're doing. On this night, I happened to be having a nice conversation with Mary backstage when they called my name. I was handed one of the fire hoses and dragged to the center of the bog. In front of me were the four Pets, ready to be hosed down. I did what any man would do: I hosed them down. When it was over I dropped the hose and, as casually as possible, asked Mary if she wanted to go get something to eat.

I could tell she was kind of freaked out. Even though she had begun to listen to the show since we started dating, she wasn't prepared for this. I tried to ease the tension. "Look," I said, "I know it's goofy but I get paid a lot of money to do stupid stuff like this." That made her feel better. For the moment.

We continued seeing each other every weekend, but we still hadn't declared ourselves as boyfriend and girlfriend. I loved that it was low-key, no pressure. But I also knew we were starting to dig each other, so I decided to take her to Uniondale. It was time for her to meet my family.

We went out there on a Sunday afternoon, classic Italian dinner day at my house. My mom knew I liked this girl; I had warned her that Mary could be someone special. But I didn't tell her to be nice. I knew it didn't work like that. She was who she was when she woke up. There was no telling her how to act.

I never told Mary that my mom had had mental health issues. I told her she was a little quirky and funny and that sometimes she got mad at people—far from full disclosure. I said, "My mom can be a little nutty." Those were the exact words. I didn't want to scare her off.

We walked into the house and we could smell the manicotti and sauce cooking on the stove. My parents were sitting in folding chairs at an aluminum table that was awkwardly placed in the middle of a small path from our living room to our den. Mary thought the table was there because my parents had a lot of guests coming through on their way to see Steven in the hospital. Eventually I told her the table had been there my entire life. I had no idea why. Maybe it was a blockade, since no one was allowed to sit on the living room couch.

Mary took a seat next to my mom in one of the aluminum chairs and my mom took Mary's hand and held it in her lap. She looked her up and down and then looked in her eyes. Finally, in a thick accent born in Brooklyn and cured in Long Island, she said, "Alllriiight." None of us knew if that was good or bad. But I was the baby of a fiercely protective, confrontational woman, so she was especially sensitive to any other female relationships in my life. It was your typical, dysfunctional mother-son stuff. But it wasn't easy for Mary in the early days of our courtship.

Since Mary and I wanted to spend as much time together as possible, she'd come with me to Long Island on the days I visited Steven in the hospital. She knew he had AIDS and that he was gravely ill. But I didn't share the details of his disintegration, and I didn't want her to see Steven the way he was. She actually never met him. Normally I'd drop her at Frank and Maryanne's for an hour or two, which was awkward for her. Or she'd get stuck at my house, sitting with my parents. Which was even more awkward.

On their first visit alone, my mom broke down crying in the kitchen. Thinking she was distraught about Steven, Mary put her arm around her and tried to comfort her. But my mom recoiled, telling her it had nothing to do with Steven. It happened again a few weeks later but this time Mary asked my mother, from a safe distance, if she was okay. After another couple of weekends she realized that sort of thing happened all the time. If Steven were healthy and sitting on an aluminum chair in the living room, my mom would still be crying.

In small ways, my mom tried to assert her superiority over Mary. At holidays she'd tell Mary to bring a salad, even though she knew no one would eat it. The random gifts she'd give Mary were usually a size too big or a size too small. When they had conversations my mom talked about her family in a possessive way, as if to say, "Not so fast . . ."

If Mary tried to discuss the little slights she felt from my mother, I'd get defensive and we'd argue. A lot of the fights we had, right up until the one that led me to Alan, could have been avoided if I had told Mary how nuts my mom was from the beginning. Instead I kept it to myself as long as I could.

Mary had to deal with my other family, too. I hadn't told anyone on the show I was dating someone. That September, Mary and I scheduled a trip to Puerto Rico, when the show was going to be on break. But at the last minute there was a change of plans and the show stayed on the air. I had already bought plane tickets and Howard told me not to change my plans, so we went. It's one of the rare times the show has been broadcast and I wasn't there.

One night in Puerto Rico, Mary and I went out drinking and we were really skunk drunk. The next morning, at 6:30, the phone rang. I could barely find it because my head was still spinning. When I finally picked it up I heard someone saying, in a heavy Puerto Rican accent, "Hello, this is Manuel."

"Huh?" I said.

"Um, yes, this is Manuel."

"Who?"

Finally I realized it was Howard, calling me while the show was live.

"So who are you there with?" he asked.

"A friend," I answered.

"Is it a girl? Put her on the phone."

"She doesn't want to be on the phone."

"How's it going with her?" he asked.

"It's good," I said. I was trying to be coy so Mary didn't know what I was talking about.

"Are you in love?"

"No," I yelled. Then I whispered, "But we really like each other. I have to go." Mercifully, he hung up.

By the time I got back from the trip, everyone was asking about Mary. She had a long Italian last name and they all wanted to know if she was a gorilla girl with lots of hair. I tried to tell them she was everything I was not: classy, demure, polite.

I spent that Thanksgiving at Mary's. By then I knew I was in love with her. And I think she loved me. But I hadn't won her father over yet. He hated every tall, good-looking, perfect-for-her banker that he had ever met. He was Italian, ready to intimidate. I had long hair and three earrings. Mary begged her dad to keep an open mind when he first met me months earlier.

He had, but we still hadn't found much common ground. Then, that Thanksgiving, we realized we were both Knicks fans. The conversation swung around to the jobs he'd had over the years and he mentioned he worked for RCA. This was another bond for us, since RCA had owned NBC when I was working there. I told him about the battles the show had with management and censors and how, eventually, the chairman of RCA, a guy named Thornton Bradshaw, ordered that Howard be fired after hearing a raunchy Dial-a-Date.

"Thornton Bradshaw, huh?" Mary's dad asked.

"Yeah," I said.

"I hate that guy. He fired me from RCA, too."

We had both been canned by the same guy. After that we became fast friends.

When I was ready to propose I decided to do it at the '21' Club. It had such a romantic, old-time New York flavor. I should have known, after living in the city for so long, that it had seen better days. I also didn't know, until we got there, that the tables inside were placed in a horseshoe pattern around the room. It didn't feel like you were eating just with your date, but with everyone in the restaurant. When I proposed, everyone in the place would be able to see it.

At this point, though, there was nothing I could do. This was the night. I had spent twelve thousand dollars on the ring—a ridiculous amount of money for me—and had become a nervous wreck about it. I was terrified of losing it. When Mary got up from the table to use the bathroom I gave the ring to the waiter and asked him to bring it out on a silver tray covered by a silver top. Classy. I was so anxious I felt like dry heaving the entire time she was in the ladies' room.

When she came out the waiters were on her in a flash, setting the tray down on the table and lifting the top with a flourish. Mary looked down and said, "Oh my God!" I was smiling nervously and everyone around the horseshoe was now looking at us. All I could say was, "So?"

"Well," she answered. "Ask me."

"Will you marry me?"

"Yes!"

All our new friends in the restaurant applauded.

"I'm getting married," I announced to the gang during a commercial for the jewelers who sold me the ring. Everyone was excited about it. They had all met Mary by then, and I had been the single guy on the show for so long, it felt a little bit like the end of an era.

Then Howard started giving me the business. "Why are you marrying her?"

"I love her," I said.

"But you're in such a good spot; there are so many women out there. Can't you just live with her? Tell me exactly why you love her."

"Elegance and class. That is what I love about her."

Then he looked me in the eye and with great seriousness

said, "That is exactly what you are going to come to hate about her."

I laughed. It was a risk I was willing to take.

We chose a catering hall in Glen Cove, Long Island, for the wedding. Scott the engineer, who also owned a DJ company and DJ'd himself on the weekends, offered to give us a DJ for the wedding as his gift. We thought this was totally generous. Then, a month before the wedding, Mike Gange had a graduation party at which Scott was the DJ. We were horrified. He did everything we didn't want at our wedding: throwing sunglasses to the crowd, displaying a scrolling electronic ad for his company on the DJ table, organizing a cha-cha line. Mary and I were freaking out. The music was horrible. "Celebration" by Kool and the Gang, "The Electric Slide," and, worst of all, the cheesy Club Med song, "Hands Up."

Of course, I mentioned this to Howard on Monday. The show is a great way to face up to uncomfortable conversations you'd otherwise never have the balls to have. Howard brought Scott into the studio and explained the problem I was having, on the air. Scott calmed me down, telling me that whatever Mary and I wanted—or not—is what he would do. Great. I requested that he not play cheesy songs like "Celebration" or "Hands Up." "No problem," he said. "You will not hear those songs."

Midway through the wedding, everything was going great. The music was fantastic. Everyone was drinking and eating and having a good time. All the practical jokes I was afraid the guys were going to play on me—yelling "Baba Booey" during the ceremony, for example—didn't happen. Until . . . I heard the opening riffs to "Hands Up." Jackie, always the master prankster, told Scott I had changed my mind and really wanted to hear it. Scott shrugged and figured,

Okay. Before the song was half over, Fred and Jackie were standing on the bar dancing. I was laughing so hard I couldn't get mad at Scott. I jumped on the bar and started dancing, too.

I still have a picture of the three of us up there, laughing and dancing and having a great time. I know it sounds corny but that was a fantastic day in my life, because my two families—the Stern show and the Dell'Abates—celebrated together.

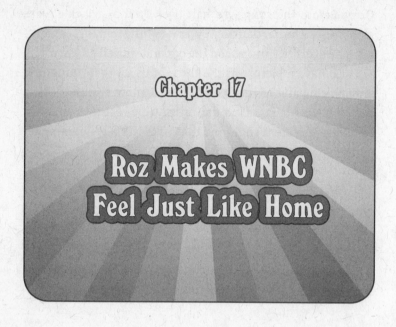

Chapter 17

Roz Makes WNBC Feel Just Like Home

I HAD MY NBC ID and I was psyched. I may have only been working three hours a day, I may have been a traffic boy instead of an assistant on the news desk, but I had my fucking NBC ID. And every single day I was going to work in that building.

On my first day, the producer for *Imus*—the show that aired while Roz was doing her traffic reports—opened the door for me. His opening line when he saw me: "What do you want?"

"I'm Gary," I said. "I'm the new traffic assistant."

He didn't say another word. He just turned his back. So I followed him, and he led me to a shitty cubicle that faced a wall. To my right was an aisle that led to the studio and to my left was a window into the studio, where Don Imus did his show every day. The producer could barely bring himself to acknowledge me as he took me through the tools on my desk. "There is your two-way radio, that is your ticker, and that is your phone. Good luck." Then, as he was walking away, he told me, "Oh yeah, don't make eye contact with Imus. Ever."

Well, that wasn't going to be easy. If I moved my head to the left even a little, I could stare right at him as he did his show. I made a note of this and recognized that it might be a challenge.

I had to be at my desk every day at 6:15. Other than not looking at Imus, this was the hardest part of the job. I am my mother's son in that I like to do everything at night. In college I wrote all my papers after midnight. I'd clean my room or do my laundry or just listen to music in my room long after the rest of the world was sleeping. I'm a night crawler, and at that point in my life, a year out of college and having just come from the T.G.I.F. party patrol, I was used to going to bed at 4:20 in the morning. Now that was when my alarm went off so I could make the 5:11 train into the city. I had to be in bed by 8:30 p.m.

Five minutes after I sat down at my desk every morning, Roz got in the chopper. I knew she was in there when I heard her clear her throat. It was a series of hacks, like she was coughing up quarts of oil. It never seemed like she got everything out. Then, if she was in a good mood, she would say, "Good morning, Gary," in a southern accent that was sweeter than butterscotch candy. But usually she was pretty ornery and just said, "You there?" Then she was off, into the air, an accent yelling at me over twirling blades.

My responsibilities were pretty simple. As Roz flew over the tri-state area, she reported back to me when there were accidents. For example, if she hovered over the Grand Central Parkway and saw a tractor-trailer stalled in the left lane at Francis Lewis Boulevard, she'd radio to me over the two-way, "Got a tractor-trailer stopped on the GCP at Frankie Lewis."

At the time, each mile-long stretch of highway in the New York area was patrolled by different towing companies. And I had a list of all of them, as well as the area they controlled, hanging on the wall of my cubicle. When Roz told me of a breakdown, I called the tow truck company responsible for that part of the road to let the drivers know something needed clearing.

I wasn't just being a Good Samaritan. Once Roz flew over the Grand Central Parkway, she was on to other spots in Staten Island, then New Jersey and into Manhattan. It was going to be forty-five minutes before she got back to that scene, but we had traffic reports every ten minutes. It was my job to let her know if the accident had been cleared. And the only way to know for sure was by keeping in touch with the towing companies.

Problem was, towing companies aren't exactly known for customer service. Depending on the day and who picked up the phone, getting an answer was a crapshoot. Some days they told me, "Yeah, we got that one." Then I'd find out a few minutes later, usually at the next traffic report, that they hadn't. Other times they just said to me, "Fuck off, we're busy." Occasionally I'd get a sympathetic ear and they'd give me the real scoop.

Not that it mattered. Roz was a petite woman with curly black hair and huge, round glasses. But her voice could boom like thunder. She used it practically every time I gave her a report. That's just the way she was, even though I worked hard to connect with her. A week after I started she asked me to go in the helicopter with her so I could see what she was seeing and have a different perspective on the job. It was a good idea; who doesn't want to go on a chopper ride?

The helicopter cab was as small as a roller-coaster car. The radio between the two seats had to be removed so I'd have someplace to sit. It was a gorgeous spring day and I brought a camera to take pictures. Roz asked the pilot to fly near the Statue of Liberty, which was covered in scaffolding. We flew so close I thought we were going to hit it. Not once during the flight did Roz yell at me.

And it did help me do my job better. But I thought that after some good one-on-one time we would have bonded. Not happening. Never happened. It was strange, because one of the things a lifetime spent with my mom taught me was how to handle volatile personalities. It made me someone who understands people. It's a valuable skill. At the time, it might have been my only skill.

But Roz wasn't swayed by my charm. And at times she was just plain unreasonable. Once, she was doing the 6:40 update and after she was off the air I jumped on the two-way to give her some accident reports, giving her plenty of time to put it all together. I pushed the radio button and said, "Roz." Then there was silence. So I pushed it again a couple of seconds later and said, "Roz." Nothing. I tried one more time. Finally, she screamed, in her southern accent, "Stop calling my name! I am not deaf! I can hear you perfectly fine. If I don't respond right away just wait before calling me again because I am getting ready for a report!" But the next report was ten freaking minutes away!

After that, whenever I called her I had to time it. "Roz?" Then I'd wait a full minute before saying it again if she didn't respond. "Roz?" I waited. That was fine if we had plenty of time between traffic updates. But sometimes info came in late between our segments and I had to get it to her right away. We'd have a minute before she went back on the air and I'd have vital accident updates that the listeners of WNBC needed to hear so they could get to work on time. This was traffic, goddammit. I'd hit the two-way. "Roz?" Nothing. So now I had to ask myself: *Do I risk getting yelled at by Roz for asking her to respond before enough time has elapsed? Or do I risk not getting her the accurate information so she sounds like she's with it on the air?* It was like *Sophie's Choice.*

Usually I'd let her do the report. And then she'd yell at me because she didn't have what she needed. "Gary! I want to tell you right now that there is an accident on the GCP and I asked for this info and I have none of it."

It was a difficult position but I didn't want to fuck it up. I soon realized why my interview with Meredith was so weird. She was asking me all these questions about how I handled myself when getting screamed at because Roz was always screaming. Eventually I learned that the two people who had the job before me were women who'd left the building in tears. But this was the other benefit of growing up in my house: If I couldn't get Roz to chill, I at least knew enough about ignoring yellers to turn my back and do my job.

Still, I couldn't stand her. She was a big star at the station and had this patter with Imus whenever she went on the air. He'd say something clever about traffic and then she'd say, "Oh, Imus, you are so funny." He'd follow that with, "Roz, you are crazy." It was so phony, because as soon as she snapped the microphone off she got back on the two-way and started yelling at me.

Her tirades, however, started getting out of control. Shadow Traffic had volunteers all over the area who called in with reports. These were just people with two-way radios who figured out our frequency and tapped into it. There was a guy with a thick Jamaican accent who loved to check in every day, whether there was an accident or not. "All right, mon, I'm on the GCP passing Frankie Lewis and all clear, mon. Out." I think he just liked saying the code words. One day I was at my desk and Imus's producer told me I had a call on line three. My first thought was, *How did Mom get this number?* I hadn't given it out to anyone. I was done with work before most of the people I knew woke up. Besides, I didn't even have a phone at my desk. Then I freaked, worried that maybe something had happened to her, that she was having an episode or had been hurt. This all came to me in a flash, just a few seconds. I picked up the receiver. A man said, "Gary?"

"Yeah," I said.

"Why do you let that bitch talk to you like that?"

"Who is this?" I asked.

"You don't know me," he said. "But why do you let that bitch talk to you like that?"

"Who?" I asked. I had no idea who this was.

"Roz," he answered. "I hear her screaming at you every morning and it is fucking ridiculous."

Then he hung up. I realized he was one of those random guys listening on the two-way radio. And he was right. One morning after she had finished yelling at me over the two-way radio I just started muttering under my breath. "Fuck you, bitch, I can't stand you." I gave the two-way radio the finger. Then I turned around and standing behind me was Imus. He just started cracking up. I don't think he ever said a word to her about it.

I got so bad with Roz that it reminded me of when I was in grammar school. I'd come home with knots in my stomach, unsure of the mom I'd get when I walked through the door. Was it the yeller? The woman who was depressed? The one who was buzzing? I didn't know which Roz was getting onto the helicopter each day, either. I ended my shift thinking, *A day not getting yelled at by Roz is a good day.*

The best part about my job was that I worked at WNBC. I had my fucking ID and when I strolled to my desk I passed the bulletin board with all the job listings at the station. I began to live for those listings. Once you were in the door you had the inside track on all the other open gigs. Being the traffic boy wasn't what I was meant to do with my life.

Chapter 18

Piloting the "N" Car

THERE WERE A LOT of fresh-faced college grads working at WNBC in the '80s. We all thought we were too hip for the place, but we loved radio and couldn't believe that we were working at a 50,000-watt station. In a lot of ways, it was just like the record store; we all became friends. I met my future roommate, Greg, there. He was a quiet, red-headed kid who worked in the engineering department. He had a high voice and later became a regular on the Stern show at NBC, filling in when our usual engineer would go on vacation. We lived together for four years and are still great friends.

My buddy Bernard, a promotions intern who eventually became Imus's producer, married the hot chick from accounting. We hung out at night and shared a house in the Hamptons for a couple of summers.

It didn't matter that we weren't getting paid shit. My fifteen hours barely covered the cost of my monthly pass on the Long

Island Rail Road. I still humped it back on the 9:15 A.M. most days to go work at the kennel supply store. I even kept that crappy overnight shift at the automated station WCTO through the summer, four months after I took the WNBC job, although partly that was to prove to the jerks that I could last there longer than three months.

When I wasn't rushing back to Long Island, I hung at WNBC long after my shifts were over. I wanted to meet people and I needed to know everything about what happened there. There wasn't an aspect of working in radio I didn't find interesting. I became friendly with the prop master for NBC-TV, an old guy who had been there since it was the Blue and the Red networks. I spent some afternoons in the basement of the building talking to him, listening to his stories from the early days of radio and TV. Every trunk stacked in his storage room held a million different stories.

I was around so often that even Imus grew comfortable with me. Back then he had agreed to do a PSA for the American Cancer Society about quitting smoking. He tried stopping for a while. But eventually he picked up the habit again and still had to do these PSAs. So he did them while he had a cigarette dangling from his mouth. That's part of the beauty of radio.

I was a smoker, too. Back then you could light up in your cubicle without breaking the law. I had an ashtray on top of my desk, and I kept my cigarettes perched next to it. One day Imus came out of the studio and, as he walked by my desk, I heard him mumble something. Then he turned back and grabbed one of my cigarettes. He did that every day for a week, just mumbling and taking my cigarettes. One morning when he picked up my pack I looked at him and said, "Did you quit smoking or just quit buying?"

"Fuck you," he said in the nicest way anyone could possibly say it. Later that day his producer handed me three packs of cigarettes without a word. I felt like I was in the club after that.

The best part about working the morning shift was being done by 9:15. It meant I could volunteer for just about any other job at the station that needed free labor. When my shifts were over I hung out with my friend Lori in the promotions department. She always had a task no one else wanted to do.

Every summer NBC did a big promotion where you put a bumper sticker on your car and then drove around hoping to be spotted by the station's "N" car. At the time it was for Stroh's beer. Listeners went to convenience stores like 7-Eleven and picked up a Stroh's/WNBC bumper sticker. Then the station sent out the N car, searching for people that had the bumper stickers on their cars. During the day, Imus or the DJs or who-ever was hosting a show would say, "Okay, the N car is going to be driving around Livingston, New Jersey, between three and seven this afternoon, so be listening." Then, if the guy in the N car saw the bumper sticker, he'd call in to the show, give the license plate number of the car he saw with the bumper sticker, and, if the driver was listening and waved when his license plate was read on the air, he got paid some cash. Lori needed drivers for the N car, so I did that a few days a week. I earned minimum wage, and was happy to get it.

It was a great job. I got to drive around, listen to the radio, and occasionally I got on the air. I called in to the station from a car phone that took up the entire middle console between the two front seats. It was fucking enormous. The first thing the manager of the N car told me was that I couldn't call my friends while I was driving around, because it cost about $150 an hour to use that thing.

Usually I was in the N car after my shift, for WNBC's mid-day show, which was hosted by Captain Frank. He was a real religious guy. Every call began and ended with him saying, "God bless you, Gary, God bless you." Then it went something like this:

"How you doing in the N car today?"

"I'm great today, Frank."

"Are you following a car?"

"I am, Frank."

"Okay, driver, wave to Gary to win your sixty-six dollars. Are they waving, Gary?"

"They sure are, Frank."

Then they'd win sixty-six dollars (WNBC was at 660 on the AM dial). Once a month, the station gave away $660 and at the end of the year it offered up $6,600.

Pretty soon people around the building got to know me. They may not have known my name, but they knew I was that kid at Roz's desk or the guy who drove the N car.

Every once in a while, I got to drive the N car during Howard's afternoon show. Howard Stern was the guy everyone at WNBC talked about. Imus was the legend, a big star in New York. My dad listened to him in the mornings on a transistor radio in his bathroom while he was shaving. But Howard was the guy who was off-the-map crazy. To be honest, I didn't listen to him that much because I was still a radio snob. I listened to music or one of the rock stations. I didn't listen to talk radio.

But so many people kept talking about him that I grew a little jealous of this guy Lonnie, who interviewed for a traffic assistant position at the same time I did, and got to work the afternoon shift, while I was stuck on the morning show. Then, one day, Lonnie asked me if we could switch. He had a doctor's appointment. I said of course. And when I went in that afternoon the first thing that struck me was how different the vibe was with Howard than with Imus. It was relaxed and fun. No one told me not to look at Howard.

Working that shift happened to be the first time I heard the show. Howard did a bit about wondering why people always check out the Kleenex after they blow their nose, and then throw it away. The whole thing was just great, observational humor. When he walked out of the studio to go to the bathroom, he had to walk right by my desk. I told him I thought it was really funny. He didn't blow me off or just say thanks and keep walking. He stopped and started talking to me. "It's crazy, right? Everyone looks. What do they expect to find?"

Not too long after that, I happened to be driving the N car during Howard's show. He hated going to the N car. He wanted to do what he wanted to do and he saw the whole give-away as a pain in the ass. I'd drive around for three hours and Fred would keep telling me, "We are coming to you soon, real soon." Then he'd finally call me to say, "Looks like we are not getting to you today."

When he did get to me, it sure didn't end with a "God bless you, you've won sixty-six dollars!" Once I was following a woman who had the bumper sticker on her car and I called in to the show with her license plate number. Howard picked up and said, "If you're driving this car, wave and win." But the woman didn't wave. Howard kept asking her, but she clearly wasn't listening. Now he was pissed—and smelled opportunity. "What kind of moron would get the bumper sticker, put it on her car, and then not listen to the radio station when she's driving around? Who would do such a thing? That is just idiotic. What a moron!"

I just kept following, waiting for my instructions. "Gary," he said. "I want you to keep following her until she pulls over. We'll check back with you. But let us know when she does. Then hand her the phone so I can yell at her."

Every few minutes they would come back to me, hoping she would pull over before they went off the air at seven. They were nearly doing the sign-off when the woman finally pulled over. I swerved across traffic, got to the side of the road, and practically jumped her. I have no idea why she didn't run away from me, but when I asked her to come to my car and take a phone call, she agreed. Then Howard blasted her. "What kind of moron are you? We've been asking you to wave for three hours.

You blew your chance to win a lot of money. We've been asking you to wave for hours."

"I'm so sorry, I can't believe it," she answered. "It's my husband's car. I had no idea he even had a bumper sticker on there."

"Well, that's too bad. You had a chance to win sixty-six hundred dollars if you had just waved to me once." He was lying. "Why would you do this? You should feel terrible."

Then he hung up. The woman was practically in tears. So was I. I had never laughed so hard at anything on the radio.

GARY'S REVERSE BUCKET LIST

The Most Amazing Things I've Done That I Never Thought I'd Do

1. Shooting a machine gun out of a Black Hawk helicopter just north of Kandahar, Afghanistan
2. Being in the No. 1 movie in the country
3. Seeing the Red Hot Chili Peppers play on the North Pole
4. Meeting President Bill Clinton
5. Defeating Weird Al Yankovic on *Rock & Roll Jeopardy*
6. Winning two hundred thousand dollars for LIFEbeat on *Don't Forget the Lyrics*.

Chapter 19

Dial-a-Date Is a Serious Turn-on

AFTER THE N CAR EXPERIENCE, I listened to Howard as often as I could. But what truly converted me from afternoon music snob into a full-fledged fan was the Friday Dial-a-Date segment. One Friday they had on a millionaire, who fielded calls from three women who wanted to go out with him. Each one sounded hotter than the next and was willing to prove it. One girl called herself the snow bunny and she talked about how she didn't want to work. She just wanted to ski and have fun and marry a rich guy.

During the bit, Howard pretended to put each girl in the shower and made her convince the guy how hot she was while the water was running. Fred would play sound effects of a shower stream the entire time, and this ski bunny woman didn't let up. She gave everything she had to this call. I was listening to the radio, and I was getting worked up.

But it wasn't just the soft-core porn aspect to that particular show that made me a believer. It was also funny and witty and full of satire. The comments Howard made to the girls and what he said about the millionaire all spoke to larger issues than just some broads looking to score a date with a rich guy. I felt the way I did when I listened to Bob Grant with my dad while I was growing up. Howard attacked callers. And he didn't just passively let something develop; he aggressively led the segment into something that would be interesting and provocative. He exposed people's prejudices. The more I listened the more I realized what he was doing. Good or bad didn't matter as much as being interesting. If something stunk it was lost from the show; if something was good it stayed. But anything that was interesting, that made people think or say, "I can't believe he did that," at the very least got a chance. Dial-a-Date was provocative in a fascinating way.

This was August 1984. And my life was about to get a whole lot more interesting, too.

I had been working as Roz's traffic whipping boy for five months, enduring her rants nearly every morning. But I was doing enough each week—between N car promotions and just hanging around the station—to know there was more out there for me. Every day I walked by that job posting board and prayed I would find something that spoke to me.

One afternoon I saw an opening for a producer's job. Soupy Sales had been hired to do a midday show. I went to Lyndon, Imus's old producer, who was now running programming for the station. He was the guy who told me never to look at Imus. He was kind of aloof, but I realized he was a good guy. I told him I wanted to apply for the job. But I was already too late. He had given it to another young producer, named Lee Davis.

I really liked Lee. He went on to become the general manager of WFAN. But at the time he was a roving producer, filling in for people wherever they needed him. His most recent job had been as a really low-paying, low-level assistant for Howard. Almost immediately, when Lyndon told me Lee had gotten the Soupy Sales job, I blurted out, "Then I want Lee's job." I still don't know what made me think to say that.

"Really?" Lyndon asked. "You want that job?" He seemed surprised because it was barely a step above what I was doing.

"Yes," I said. "I do."

"Okay, let me talk to some people and see what I can do."

I don't even think you could call what Lee had been doing a producer's job. It was more like a paid internship, because the salary—$150 a week; $114 after taxes—was barely the living wage. To call it a salary was almost illegal. It was closer to allowance. But that didn't matter; every person my age working at WNBC Radio wanted that job.

But I needed this job. And decided it was mine to lose. The months I had spent in the office, hunched over in my cubicle listening to traffic scanners, had been building to this moment.

I knew that Fred and Robin and Howard took a car service in to work together every day and usually arrived at around 12:30. I put on some nice clothes and went to stalk them. I waited, and waited, and waited.

And that was the one day Howard was out sick.

Instead, Fred and Al Rosenberg, an old Imus sidekick who did voices for Howard, took pity on me. Actually, they were just bored. Since Howard was out that day, they didn't have much to do and there I was, with my poufy hair and John Oates mustache, looking as eager as ever. I was fresh meat.

Back then, everything Howard did that made him so popular with listeners—yelling at callers, faux porn from Dial-a-Date—made him an enemy of WNBC management. Fred would tell you that there was outright contempt for everyone who worked on the Stern show, from the receptionist on up. Their offices proved how little they were liked. My interview took place in what Fred liked to call "the converted supply closet." And it lasted more than an hour. The two of them asked me about every single thing I wrote on my résumé. When they saw the line for the Adelphi movie I worked on called *Intimate Companions,* Fred wondered if it was about bestiality. Both of them were just fucking with me. Fred especially. No one likes to break people's balls more than he does. And when he's bored, forget it.

I know that part of it was just Fred being a wise-ass but the other part of it was like a hazing. They wanted to see where I was coming from and what my response would be to outrageous behavior. They weren't the McLaughlin Group—they didn't want someone who would cast judgment over everything they did on the show. They needed an ally in their battle with WNBC.

After I interviewed I heard they had narrowed it down to me and one other candidate, a kid who worked the day shift on the news desk at NBC. A couple of days after my interview I was listening to Howard and, suddenly, this other guy was on the air. Howard was interviewing him, asking him why he wanted the job. I thought to myself, *Fuck, he works during the day and he's got the inside track!* I was totally bummed because he got this face-to-face with Howard and I didn't.

Then Fred asked me to come back. He's always had a thing against kids who are spoiled. That kid was making less than two hundred dollars a week as an assistant but he wore a Rolex. Big strike against him. But there was more to it. Fred felt that anyone who seemed nice and down-to-earth and came from within the building deserved a second look.

Now I had to figure out what to wear. Because this time I was meeting with Howard. I had listened to the show; they didn't seem like suit people. So I went with my standard Record World outfit. Nice pants, nice shirt, Capezio shoes, and a skinny tie.

When the day came, I realized this could be a life-changing moment. I was going to have a sit-down with Howard to discuss how I felt about the show and what I could do to make it better. Instead he just looked at me and asked if I wanted the job. I said, "Absolutely." Then he told me it wouldn't be glamorous or glorified. It would be about me doing the grunt stuff that needed to get done.

I understood and I didn't care. I didn't leave with an offer, but I felt better about my chances.

Word got around that I was interviewing with Howard. And I was pretty shocked by how people reacted. I was a lowly traffic assistant who had become a loyal Stern listener. He was doing cool stuff and I wanted to be a part of it. I had no idea how much people within WNBC hated him.

When I took the job with Roz I had to join a union, NABET, the National Association of Broadcast Engineers and Technicians. In broadcasting, unions have a lot of power and everyone's role is clearly defined. If you handled any kind of equipment—like the traffic scanner—you had to be a member. It was insane how detailed the restrictions were. If I was in the field reporting a story I had to get permission to hold my own mic. But if I didn't have written permission to turn the volume up on the headphones myself, I'd have to ask a sound engineer on site to do it for me.

One afternoon, shortly after I spoke with Howard, the shop steward of the local chapter of NABET came by my cubicle and said, "Hey, Gary, can I speak with you for a minute?" I had never spoken to the guy, but said sure. Then he led me to an old NBC greenroom that hadn't been used in years. We sat on the couch and he said to me, "Word is going around you are up for a job with Howard."

"I am," I said. I knew the union hated Howard because he

turned everything on its head. He didn't care about who was allowed to hold what microphone. He just wanted to make great radio, and worried about consequences later.

"Well, I just want you to know that the union does not look kindly on him. And if you work for him it will seriously damage your future in the NABET."

Really? NABET? I was trying to get out of NABET.

The next day Judy DeAngelis, a high-profile reporter for WNBC, came by my desk. "Do you have a second?" she asked, and led me to the same greenroom I had gone to with the guy from NABET. "I heard you might go work for Howard Stern."

"It's possible," I said.

"Well, I don't think they are nice people," she said. "You seem like a nice kid and you're just getting started and you should give it a second thought. Because they are really not very good people."

What the fuck? Two people in senior positions at WNBC who had barely spoken to me were now telling me not to work for Howard. More than anything, it made the Stern show even more enticing. I thought, *This must be some fucking show if they are telling me I don't want any part of it.* It's like when your parents tell you not to look at porn online. It becomes all you want to do.

A couple of days later I got a call from Fred. He wanted me to come back and see Howard again. This time he told me to try to dress a little bit nicer. "This is a professional organization."

I didn't think twice about it and just did as Fred told me: I put on the gray, pin-striped suit. It was August 31, 1984, and it was brutally hot. I had pit stains when I walked into Howard's office, and Fred, who was there, too, just started laughing hysterically. I think he was a little shocked that I took him seriously. But it made him think, *This sincere little fucker wants the job.*

Howard said to me, "You're hired—temporarily. Let's see how it goes for a month." The whole thing lasted thirty seconds.

I didn't care how long it lasted. And I didn't have any expectations. All I thought was, *I have my NBC ID and a full-time job at the station.* The next time I looked for a job and someone asked me if I had experience, I could say yes.

Little did I know that, twenty-six years later, I'd still be waiting for that opportunity.

Chapter 20

Boy Gary, Tassels, and a Snow Bunny

BEFORE I GOT THE JOB, whenever I hung around the station in the afternoons looking for stuff to do, I'd see Lee prepping the studio for Howard. Every day he walked by with a drum, a cymbal, a sound machine, a megaphone, and some papers piled on top of it all, which were notes Howard wanted in front of him during the show. It was a long walk for Howard from his office to the studio. He had to trek down a narrow hallway, then through the main hallway on the second floor, past reception, and finally through to the studio, accessible only with a key card. It was a haul if he had to carry all that stuff, too.

On my first day, I became the carrier of the drum, the cymbal, the sound machine, and the megaphone. I felt so happy and proud. I felt like I was carrying the Olympic torch in the opening ceremonies. I was the new producer. During his reign, Lee had come to be known as Boy Lee on the show. And, as I carried the props into the studio, Lyndon saw me, stared for a second, and said out loud, "Boy Gary? Naaah, it will never stick."

The show started at 3 P.M. The intro was Ronald Reagan introducing the Boston Celtics during a visit to the White House after they had won the NBA title, and butchering every single player's name.

After the intro, Howard came on the air at 3:04. I really wanted to be there when Howard flipped the microphone on my first day. I thought maybe he'd mention me or have me on to talk for a minute. But at 2:45 he handed me an envelope and asked me to run it up to his agent's office at Forty-fifth and Madison. That was a fifteen-minute walk. There was no subway that went directly there. And if I took a cab I'd get stuck in traffic. I decided the only way to get it done and be in the studio when we hit the air in nineteen minutes was to sprint. So I did. I ran faster than I ever had in my life, a blur of black hair.

My hustle paid off.

I was panting and sweating, but I was there. And instead of getting made fun of for looking like I was about to die, Howard praised me on the air. "I am impressed with this new boy," he said. "I gave him an errand to run and he ran it twice as fast as Lee ever did. This Boy Gary, he may turn out to be pretty good."

Then he asked me about being Italian and if I was circumcised. And finally Robin pointed out that I looked like John Oates down to the last hair follicle.

I had arrived.

I was on the air almost daily from the start. The only person who enjoyed that more than me was my mom.

Her son was on the radio and people were recognizing his name. She felt she was, by proxy, worthy of attention, too. I was still humping it back to Uniondale at the end of every shift—

the job didn't pay enough for me to get my own place in the city—and one afternoon my mom made me go to the beauty parlor during one of her Saturday appointments to "say hello." In twenty-three years she had never asked me to say hello to anyone, but she'd been telling all the ladies about her son who was on the radio and now she wanted me to meet everyone. What was I supposed to do, tell her all I did was carry the cymbals? I walked in, waved to the ladies under the dryers, and walked out. I'm not sure how it went over, but at least my mom felt like a celebrity. My father loved to bust her when she'd mention five or six times in one conversation that I worked for Howard Stern. She'd act surprised at any hint of recognition from strangers and then my father would say, "Ellen, you haven't stopped telling them where Gary works! Of course they're going to ask you about it." The fact that I was sharing some of the most embarrassing moments of my life for the entertainment and mockery of millions of listeners never seemed to bother her much.

My father barely listened to the show at first. But I knew how happy he was that I had waited and worked to land my dream job. He always told me, no matter what I did, I was selling a product. And if you didn't believe in what you did, people would see right through you. He saw how much I liked my job and was happy and proud, which made me feel the same way. Even if I still couldn't afford to move out of his house.

That was a bummer. I was working on the coolest, hippest show in radio, the right-hand man to a guy on the verge of becoming a superstar. And yet I went to bed every night in Uniondale. My new hours meant I couldn't keep my job at the kennel supply store—my perennial backup plan—but I made some cash moonlighting as an assistant to a DJ at a Long Island club on Friday and Saturday nights. I didn't care. I was finally in. I'd have done anything for an opportunity like this.

Booking guests was the hardest part of the job, mainly because of Howard's rep. It was unfair. Howard is rarely ungracious with guests. He just asks them every question he can think of. But, in his first couple of years with WNBC, he publicly clashed with management and had some pretty outrageous bits, so celebrities were wary.

The first call I ever made was to Steve Martin's publicist. He had a big movie coming out that fall, *All of Me,* in which he played a lawyer whose soul is taken over by a very old rich woman who wants to live on. Hilarity ensues. Martin had been a famous comic for almost twenty years at that point, and he'd been one of the biggest movie stars of the early '80s because of *The Jerk.* When I asked his publicist if we could get him on the show I could practically feel her hatred through the phone. "You will never get a guest the caliber of Steve Martin on the show."

That was brutal. From then on, I usually started a call by saying, "Hi, I'm Gary Dell'Abate with WNBC," because those letters carried some weight. And no one hung up on me, at least not right away.

Dial-a-Dates were a lot easier to set up.

We did the segment every Friday. After four or five of them I set up the dates for everyone at the same time and place. If no one got along, at least there were ten Stern fans hanging at a bar or a restaurant who could have a good time. It was my job to pick the location, set the time, and then meet everyone on their big group date. I was the chaperone. And by the time I started working on the show there was a pretty big backlog of contestants waiting to go on their dates. At the top of the list: the ski bunny and the millionaire.

The restaurant the station had a deal with was a French place on the Upper East Side. But it wasn't your typical escargot, white-tablecloth joint. It was a French revue, like a burlesque show, where women walked around topless. Basically it was a classy strip club, but instead of giving lap dances and wearing pasties, the girls wore tassels.

I was looking forward to meeting the ski bunny; she was the reason I fell in love with the show and, for that matter, probably had my job. And she didn't disappoint. Everything she did was intended to leave an impression, including showing up half an hour late so she could make an entrance. She wore a Jackie Kennedy pillbox hat with a veil and white gloves that were pulled up to her elbows. She was small and thin and blond. A perfect-looking WASP, really cute and well put together.

There was only one problem: Her date was a no-show. I had to give her the news. I walked up to her and said, "Hi, I'm Gary."

"Where's my date?" she asked.

"I don't think he's coming."

The look on her face was devastating. I thought she was going to cry. It was as if she had never been stood up before. She wheeled around and walked toward the front door, but I felt bad so I chased after her.

"Listen," I said. "This guy is an asshole and you look beautiful and dinner is free. Why don't you at least sit and hang out for a while."

I honestly had never seen anyone that upset about a busted blind date. But she agreed to come back to sit with me. And since we were the only two people who weren't matched up, we spent a lot of time talking to each other. I told her about my job and how excited I was. She mentioned to me that she spent a lot of time in Long Island but was staying in Manhattan at her grandfather's that night. When she told me his name and his job on Wall Street, I think she expected me to recognize him. But I was clueless.

At the end of the night Ski Bunny asked me to walk her to her grandfather's place, a gorgeous building on Park Avenue.

The guy was clearly loaded. But I didn't get a stick-around vibe, so I shook her gloved hand, said thanks for staying, and caught the train back to Long Island. I didn't think I'd ever talk to her again.

Which is why I was so surprised when, at noon the next day, I got a call from the WNBC receptionist. There were a dozen purple roses waiting for me at the front desk. When I picked them up, there was a card attached that read, "It's okay for a lady to give flowers to a gentleman." I called Ski Bunny to say thanks. This was a Friday afternoon; we decided to go out on Saturday night.

Later that Friday I went to the club where I DJ'd on Long Island and had a drink. I was telling a buddy at the bar about Ski Bunny and mentioned her grandfather's name. My friend said, "Do you know who that is?"

"No, I have no idea."

"He's one of the richest guys in New York."

Her grandfather, it turned out, was a Wall Street tycoon. And when I picked her up on Saturday night, I realized how rich she really was. She lived on the North Shore of Long Island, about an hour from Uniondale, in a really rural area. The house was a bona fide mansion, with a circular driveway and a front hallway as big as the entry at Rockefeller Center. She was the only one home.

We got into my pimped-out Firebird and I took Ski Bunny to the club I worked at, where the admission and the drinks were free. As we were driving I asked her if she had a boyfriend and she said, "Nope. I was dating someone but we broke up."

We stayed late at the club. And then we headed to a bar not too far from her house, a real dive. Soon she asked me to drive her back home and when we got there she mentioned that she was alone for the weekend. I was in!

I spent the night and was feeling pretty good. Until eight o'clock the next morning, when I heard someone pounding on the door and ringing the doorbell. "Open the fucking door! Open the fucking door!" the guy was yelling.

I got up to go to the window but Ski Bunny grabbed my arm and said, "Don't, I'll handle it." Then I realized: It was the ex-boyfriend. When she went downstairs I looked out the window and saw that he was holding a tire iron and looked like he wanted to take out the headlights of my Firebird. I heard Ski Bunny say, "It's over, leave me alone, it's over." For some reason, as she repeated that, it clicked with him, because he dropped the tire iron, got into his car, and peeled out of the driveway. I didn't see much reason to stick around after that.

The roads leading away from her house were winding ones cut out of a dense forest. When I turned on to the main road I heard a noise coming from the woods. I looked in my rearview mirror and saw a car parked behind the bushes. It was the boyfriend, and he was peeling out behind me. Within seconds he was practically on my bumper. He was trying to run me off the road!

Holy shit! There were no driveways for me to pull into and I couldn't exactly pull over. I drove as fast as I could, the whole time thinking I was going to get into an accident. I was sweating my balls off. To any farmer plowing his fields that morning it must have looked like we were drag racing.

Then I remembered: One of the landmarks I passed on the way to Ski Bunny's house was a police station. As I rounded a bend in the road, I saw it, and made a sharp turn into the parking lot. The boyfriend whizzed by, glaring at me. I never got out of my car. I just sat in that lot, panting, my heart pounding. I waited a half hour before getting back on the road, and I checked my mirrors every couple of seconds until I pulled into my parents' driveway in Uniondale.

But the drama wasn't over.

Later that night I was watching a game on TV with my dad when the phone rang. I heard him say, "What? Huh? No, you've got the wrong number." A few minutes later the phone rang again. My dad got up to answer it again and told the caller, "Nope, you've still got the wrong number." Then it happened again and this time my dad said, "Look, there is no [Ski Bunny's name] here."

It was the boyfriend, calling my parents' house, looking for Ski Bunny. After my dad hung up on him, the boyfriend called again. This time, though, my mom answered. And I was psyched. A prank caller who wouldn't stop? This was her specialty. This was the conspiracy she had been waiting her whole life to unravel.

"Ski Bunny who?" she asked.

"And what do you want with her?" she continued.

"And how do you know this girl?"

I had no idea what the guy was saying back, but my mom was unfazed. She never raised her voice; she was too curious to get hysterical. Her only goal was to get to the bottom of this mystery and find out who this girl was, why this man kept calling for her, and how it was going to spell the end for all of us. The rapid-fire questions kept coming until, finally, I heard my mother say, "Hello, hello?" The boyfriend had hung up. He crumpled under my mom's interrogation.

The Pitch

2009

I love the Mets. That comes from my father. He grew up a Dodgers fan and when the Bums left Brooklyn for Los Angeles he just waited, like so many New Yorkers, for the town to get a new National League team. Rooting for the American League Yankees wasn't an option. Even when the Mets debuted in 1962 and lost 120 games, fans loved them because they had waited for them for so long.

Every year, my dad would take me and my brothers to Shea for the old-timers game. Just the boys. Since the Mets didn't have any old-timers they invited old Dodgers and New York Giants. We saw guys like Duke Snider. My first game is still so vivid to me. We walked through the gate, out of the darkness of the concourse and into the light of the field. The grass was greener and the dirt browner than it ever looked on television. Then a great thing happened to me: It was 1969. I was eight years old, just learning about the intricacies of baseball and really appreciating it, and the Mets won the World Series. That will make you a fan for life.

When the Mets played the Red Sox in the 1986 World Series I got a single ticket to the first game. I went by myself with a flask of vodka because it was freezing. I got hooked up with two more tickets for Game Six, so I took my dad. He parked at my apartment on 105th Street and then we walked to the subway from there. "How much is a subway these days?" he asked.

"When's the last time you took a subway, Dad?"

"Nineteen fifty-six."

"How much was it then?"

"A nickel."

At K-Rock our promotions people were always pestering the Mets folks to let one of us from the show throw out a first pitch. For years this went on. And when I got to know some people there I started nagging, too. Finally, late in 2004, they decided to give me a shot. The situation was perfect: The Mets were out of it, it was late in the season, and so Shea wasn't too crowded. My parents, who had moved to Florida, flew up for the game. I even got this great picture of my mom hugging Mr. Met on the field. I wasn't nervous at all. But when I stood on the mound the distance to the plate seemed pretty far. So I moved off the pitching rubber at the top of the mound to the front edge of the dirt, where it meets the grass. I threw a strike to the catcher that was just a little high. It was a great day, everything I wanted it to be.

On the show that Monday we barely even talked about it. Howard wasn't interested and the only person who made a comment was Artie. He had seen a picture of it, and noticed that I wasn't standing on the mound, so he gave me a hard time about moving closer to the plate. But it was a blip on the radar. No one cared, except for me.

Cut to the winter of 2009. I was contacted by the folks who run Autism Awareness Day. They were hoping to bring attention to the cause by sponsoring the first pitch at a Mets game on May 9. They asked me to do it, since I would talk about it on the show. I said absolutely. I love the Mets. I love throwing out the first pitch. I love a good cause. This was going to be great.

As soon as I mentioned it on the air, Artie said to me, "Throw it from the rubber this time. Don't be a pussy." I laughed. And I didn't think about it again.

Cut to the first week of April. I would be throwing out the pitch in five weeks and I wanted to practice. I took Jackson out to the front yard, marked off sixty feet, six inches, the official distance from the mound to home plate, and started to throw. I was doing great. Some were a little high, some were a little low, but mostly they were on target. Jackson barely had to move. But after about ten minutes of warming up, I remembered Artie's words. *Throw it from the rubber this time. Don't be a pussy.* The very next pitch was way high. Hmm, strange. I thought about what he said again and the pitch was way too low, bouncing off the dirt to Jackson.

As I wound up again, I could hear people saying that George W. Bush might have lost the 2004 election if he had thrown a bad first pitch while campaigning. Then I started thinking about the roar of the crowd. The Mets had just opened Citi Field. And it was early in the season. Unlike last time at Shea, where I had practically grown up, I'd be pitching in an unfamiliar environment, in front of a packed stadium. My next throw was twenty feet to the right.

The beauty of being on the show is that it's a great forum for working out your issues. So I figured if I talked about how nervous I was becoming it would help me calm down. Well, that was silly. As soon as Howard mentioned it, a couple of weeks before the pitch, Artie just piled on. He said, "Mets fans are the worst. You'll get booed no matter what.... Be a man.... It doesn't matter, you'll choke anyway." I didn't feel any better. I felt much, much worse. Every time I went out to practice, my throws became progressively less accurate. I was like Nuke LaLoosh in *Bull Durham* who beans the mascot in the head. I might throw four of five decent pitches. But as soon as I thought about Artie or the crowd or that moment, it was like I was driving blind. I was just all over the place.

The more nervous I got, the more it became a bit on the show and the more Artie came after me. The people from the Autism Society were psyched because we were talking about it on the air so much. But it got so bad, the woman who ran the program called me and said, "I don't want this to be a source of stress for you. If you want you can bring your kid out, I'll bring my kid out, and we can have them throw the pitches."

When I mentioned this to Artie he said, "You can't give it to your kid. Don't be a pussy."

Why did I keep talking about it on the show? And why did I keep listening to Artie? I don't know, but at this point I knew I couldn't get out of it. And I needed professional help.

Jackson was playing baseball at Bobby Valentine's Sports Academy in Stamford, Connecticut. Bobby Valentine had once been the Mets' manager. Mitch, the guy who ran the place, listened to the show, heard how nervous I was, and offered to work with me. I went over there one afternoon and, at first, I was wild. None of my pitches went anywhere near the target. But after a few minutes I settled down and threw five strikes in a row. Mitch told me my form was fine, I was in good shape, and that I shouldn't psych myself out, because I'd have no problem doing this.

Then I went home to practice some more and I couldn't have hit my house with a ball standing two feet in front of it. I was freaking out.

A week before the pitch, the Mets invited me to come to a game. We were going to have a press conference about Autism Awareness Day and then I was going to go onto the field so the local news could shoot me practicing. I wasn't worried about the cameras. I was just anxious to get on the mound. Just having that moment and getting comfortable in those surroundings would put my mind at ease. I brought Jon Hein with me. On *The Wrap-Up Show* he too had been telling me I had to calm down, that I was just psyching myself out, that I could do this. That actually became the mantra everyone I knew repeated to me. Hein, Mary, Jackson—they all thought I was allowing it to get to me. "It was just the stupidest thing ever," Mary still says.

It would all be better once I had those practice pitches, I told myself. And then they canceled the practice pitches. It had rained the night before. The field was still a little wet and the grounds crew was working on it. Hein could see my body slump when they gave us the news.

We took our seats for the game and I was anxious to see the first pitch. If someone else went out there and flubbed it or bounced, I'd relax a little. The guy who got the call that day had caught Gary Sheffield's five hundredth home run. He sauntered out to the field in his jersey and his hat and I thought to myself, *Okay, this is just some Joe Blow, he won't be any good.* Then he went into a full windup, as if he were facing a real batter. In that moment I was thinking, *What a freaking tool, this is going to be great.*

He threw a perfect strike. *Fuck me!*

I went home that afternoon and threw ten pitches with Jackson and Lucas. Five were right on target. And five looked like a guy throwing back a grenade that just landed at his feet.

With less than a week to go it was time for the heavy guns. First I spoke with a sports psychologist. Seriously. He asked me what my fears were. When I told him I didn't want to embarrass myself he said, "Okay. You are a husband and you are a father and a good brother to your brother who passed away. Look at why you are at this event. You're doing it for charity. Who cares what happens. It will be just one small part of your life." I thought that was a good philosophy. I felt a little better.

Next, I planned one more warm-up with Mitch at the Bobby V. academy the Friday before the game. I happened to have been in Toronto that Thursday night to see Springsteen and, after an early morning flight, I'm pretty sure I was still hungover when I went to practice with Mitch. But I threw okay. And he repeated the mantra to me: "Calm yourself down, you can do this, don't be crazy, don't psych yourself out."

I was starting to believe. But, just to be safe, I wanted to throw from an actual mound at least once before the game. That afternoon Jackson and I went to the local high school. We couldn't get on the field because there was a game. But Bobby Bonilla, who had played for the Mets, was there because his kid was on the high school team. We talked about the pitch for a few minutes and seeing a former Met felt like good luck.

But I knew it would take more than luck to get the ball across the plate. We were scheduled to leave for the game at eleven. I made Jackson go out to the front lawn one more time. He squatted down, I wound up . . . and threw a perfect strike. My son gave me a huge thumbs-up.

"We are done," I said.

"Just one?" Jackson asked. "No more?"

"Why mess with it?"

We went home and piled the whole tribe into the car: Mary, Jackson, Jackson's friends, Lucas, and Lucas's friends. Jon Hein bought tickets to the game; he was going to meet us there. I was ready.

We walked into the press room and who was there, waiting to support me? Artie. He was not being a dick, but his mere presence was unnerving. The guy who had been my biggest detractor, the ultimate Yankee fan, was going to be sitting in a front-row seat. I seriously started to freak out. And no one was all that interested in calming my nerves.

Next to Artie was John Franco, the former Mets reliever, the quintessential Italian ballbuster. He could tell I was losing it and left the press room with me for the walk through the tunnel toward the field. He draped his arm around my shoulders and whispered in my ear, "Don't fuck this up. You can't fuck this up." Then he stood behind me and pretended to massage the knots out of my shoulders, "Release the tension. And don't fuck this up," he said. He was killing me.

When we got on the field it was just a pig fuck. José Reyes, the Mets shortstop, was in center field, and David Wright, the third baseman, was near second as they played a long-distance game of catch. Sebastian Bach of the '80s hair band Skid Row was walking around getting ready to sing the national anthem. Rob Smigel, the guy who voices Triumph the Insult Comic Dog, was there because he has a kid with autism. And fucking Artie was just walking around home plate. Triumph, Sebastian Bach, Artie, John Franco, all my kids' friends. It was like a goddamn Fellini movie. The whole thing was swirling around me and I could feel myself starting to hyperventilate. I was desperate for a paper bag to breathe into.

One of the Mets reps handed me a ball and told me to go stand by the Mets dugout. But all the action was by the visitors' dugout. That's where everyone was hanging out. It was much worse being alone, with nothing to concentrate on but me and the pitch. This was where it got really bad. When I get nervous, I dry heave. Standing there by myself, I started to retch. If you didn't know any better, it looked like I was coughing. But Hein, who was in the stands nearby, knew what was happening. By the time they called my name to go to the mound my body was like rubber and I was so nervous my legs were shaking. I asked myself, *For what?*

I stood there as they announced the cause I was pitching for and then I lifted my arm into the air, showing everyone the ball. I always thought the first pitch happened fifteen or twenty minutes before the game. But the game was about to start. Players were running out to their positions. John Maine, who was pitching for the Mets that day, was behind me, getting ready. I had become friendly with him because he is a fan of the show, but his head was so into the game he didn't even acknowledge me.

I wound up and I swear to God when I threw the ball I couldn't feel my body. Using a contorted half pitch, half push, I just closed my eyes and hoped it would go somewhere near the plate. When I opened them I realized it didn't get anywhere close. In fact, it was so far to the left of the catcher that the umpire, who was standing four feet away and putting his mask on, had to put his hands in front of his belly to protect himself. It was a knuckler. The ball bounced off his fingers to the ground. The crowd went, "Ohhhhhhhhhh."

I turned my back to home plate, bent over with my hands on my knees like I was sick to my stomach, and then walked off the mound and gave a thumbs-up. The first thing I saw when I was able to focus again was Artie, doubled over in laughter. *Ahhh, fuck,* I thought. Mary greeted me right away and said, "Don't worry. Are you bummed?"

"I am so bummed you can't even believe how bummed I am." Then I had to look at Jackson. "Are you just embarrassed?"

"You really psyched yourself out, Dad," he said. I later worked up the courage to watch the video Jackson shot of the pitch. I could hear Jackson saying, "Come on, Dad, you can do it, you can do this." Right after the pitch, all you hear is: "Ugggghhhhhh."

Many people have tried to evaluate what went wrong. But Howard's father pinpointed the problem: I started to pitch it and then, mid-motion, I decided to lob it.

I had thrown a bad pitch. I assumed the worst would be that I would get grief for it on Monday and that would be that. That changed before I even walked off the field. While heading up to the suite we had for the game I saw a kid I used to coach in youth football. "Mr. D., did you throw out the first pitch?" he said.

"Yeah, I did."

"Wow," he said. "You can't throw."

Kevin Burkhardt, roving reporter for the SNY sports television channel, interviewed me later that day during the game broadcast. I thought he'd want to talk about the Autism Society, but after one question he said to me, "You threw out some first pitch." Then he showed it on the screen for all to see again. "What are you thinking right now?"

All I could say was "I was really hoping that would not end up on television."

After the game Hein came up to me and was being so kind. Too kind. I needed a drink. We went to a barbecue in Connecticut after the game. Everyone asked me how it went and when I said bad and they asked how bad and I said *so* bad, someone poured me a scotch. I was feeling a little bit better. The moment had been left behind at Citi Field in Queens. Until 6:25. My cellphone pinged and it was a text from my buddy Booker at K-Rock. "Dude," he said. "They just showed your first pitch on TV."

"What channel?" I asked.

"The local news on CBS."

Oh motherfucker! Are you kidding me? Okay, I said to myself, at least it is contained to the tri-state area.

That night Howard and his wife saw the pitch on the highlights. Beth said, "He throws like a girl. I guarantee I could throw better than that. I've never seen a pitch like that."

Howard called me when I was already two scotches in. I sounded so bad he couldn't even give me shit. He decided to save it for Monday morning.

The next day was Mother's Day. I was just moping around. "What is your problem?" Mary asked me.

"Did you see what happened yesterday?" I asked.

"So what," she said. "It was an honor. No one else was asked to throw it."

It didn't matter. All day I was trying to assess the damage. In the afternoon I turned on the Mets game. I wanted to watch the pregame show to see if they mentioned it. If they didn't, it was probably over. And, much to my relief, no one said a word. Then the game started. And before the opening pitch the announcers said, "We have to show you what happened yesterday."

They saved my pitch for the actual broadcast! It was too good for the pregame show. I lost my shit. And so did Mary.

"Are you going to ruin my whole Mother's Day?" she said.

"Yes, well, my whole life is ruined," I said as reasonably as I could.

"We are talking about a pitch!" she said, and then she walked out of the room.

I had to face everyone at work the next day. As soon as I walked in I saw Will sitting at his computer. He is a big sports fan. I knew, in the split second that I saw him, that his reaction would be a good gauge of how bad things were going to go. And it was bad. He looked at me as if my parents had been killed in a car accident. His eyes showed nothing but sadness for me. I would have rather been teased.

When the show started, Howard, who doesn't care about sports, recounted a conversation he had had with his father the day before. It began harmlessly, with his dad saying he was just watching the Mets game. Then it quickly led into the pitch. Howard said how his dad told him that I had thrown "the worst pitch ever. I never saw a pitch like this in my life."

"Wow," Howard told his dad. "This is Gary's worst nightmare. I'm thrilled because we just found the first two hours of Monday's show. It's the single most embarrassing moment in the history of first pitches."

Then he just handed the show over to Artie. He was brutal. "I just saw Lance Bass throw out the first pitch," he said. "Gary was so nice. He was doing this for Autism Day and threw it like he was autistic."

Artie's a great storyteller and he told a doozy about an older guy who was an usher at Citi Field. I knew this usher from Shea. He's a great guy and he happened to be on the field for the pitch. I noticed him talking to Artie and, afterward, the expression on his face was as if he had just watched the Zapruder film. During the show Artie added the dialogue that I missed while I was walking off the mound:

Artie: "Man that pitch was so gay."

Usher: "That pitch was gayer than a guy sucking another guy's dick. And I should know—I was a cop for years and saw a lot of guys sucking dick."

That hurt. A lot. I always liked that guy and I couldn't believe he would take a shot at me like that.

I was down, and Artie was pummeling me. I worried about my kids going to school and being made fun of. Even though they told me everything was fine and no one made a big deal about it, Artie said, "They're lying. They are miserable."

It's still a sore spot for me. But, on the air at least, I really had no choice but to take it. We've mocked so many people. When Chris Rock threw out the first pitch at a game once and it was less than stellar I destroyed him.

Over the next three weeks, the video went viral. It wasn't just that I looked so bad and it was embarrassing. It hurt my credibility. I'm the guy on the show who knows sports. I love sports. People assumed because I couldn't throw a pitch, I couldn't have a discussion about sports anymore.

The world was divided into two types of people: the ones who were nice and tried to make me feel better (but only made it worse), and the guys who laughed at me and thought I was a fucking tool. Mary was in her own get-the-fuck-over-it category. The Thursday after the pitch I had to coach one of Jackson's baseball games and I was afraid to warm up with the kids. I wondered if everyone was going to be looking at me funny. My saving grace was that a prominent married guy in town had just been busted for trolling for hookers online and was on the front page of the *New York Post*.

For a month I was in a funk. The turning point came on Memorial Day. I was at a neighbor's barbecue. Another neighbor whom I respect a lot and coached with was there, too. He is levelheaded and empathetic. He told me that he felt for me. He said he watched me out there every day working with Jackson in the front yard. Then he told me that he'd played soccer in college. He was a goalie at a small school that had made it to the title game. Late in the game he lost his concentration for less than a minute, a few seconds tops, but it happened to be the exact moment when someone took a shot. It went right by him. "I was the villain on campus for a few weeks," he said.

He was the first person after the pitch who didn't mock me

or try to tell me it wasn't a big deal or pretend to be nice. He just had a conversation with me about it. And he told me that one day I would feel better. He was right. Pretty soon I stopped thinking about it every minute of every day.

And then, a few months after the pitch, I found out that the famous usher whom Artie quoted had actually never said anything. I was doing a Gadget Gary segment for the CW11 TV station in New York, and the usher's son worked there. He came up to me and said, "My father never said that stuff. He wanted to call the show but decided not to because he didn't want to draw attention to it." Later that summer, when I was back at Citi Field for a game, the usher apologized and told me how bad he felt because he had never said anything.

Not that I'm over it, nor ever will be. Whenever anyone makes a bad first pitch—Shawn Johnson, the mayor of Cincinnati, please watch, theirs are worse than mine—I know that a reference to me and the video of my pitch is coming next. I actually haven't thrown a ball since then. I can't do pitching practice anymore for Little League. And if I am coaching third base and the ball rolls my way, I just lob it back to the pitcher underhanded. The pitch has seriously traumatized me.

In the winter of 2010 I actually got a call from someone at the Autism Society asking me if I would throw out the first pitch again in the upcoming season. He was really pressuring me because it would attract so much attention and raise so much money, but I couldn't do it. I get the dry heaves now just watching other people throw out a first pitch.

But some good did come of it. I put the ball and the jersey that I wore that day up for auction at a LIFEbeat charity event. Hein tried to keep me from doing it because he thought I'd want to hold on to them for sentimental value. "I never want to see these things again," I told him. One of the show's sponsors paid eighteen thousand dollars for it. He takes the ball around the country with him when he travels and, if he sees a celebrity, asks them to take a picture with it. I've got one of Tony Hawk smiling with the ball.

I'm glad it brought someone some joy.

I'D BE A LIAR if I told you that a week into my job with Howard I could look ahead and see where I am today. When I started, I loved working for everyone in Howard's orbit. He and Robin and Fred were maestros in the studio, riffing perfectly and setting one another up for comedy gold. They'd only been together for a couple of years at that point, but they had the rhythm of well-trained sketch artists. I was just the interloper who had thirty days to prove himself. But I was determined to make myself valuable during that month. If it worked out, great. If not, maybe they'd still like me enough to recommend me for another radio job.

The way the offices were set up, I sat on one side of the building near Fred and Howard. Robin was on the other side, in the newsroom. Because of that, I didn't have as much interaction with her as I did with Howard and Fred. You could always hear her coming because she has that incredible laugh that filled the halls. But those first couple of years, she was the one who reminded me most of my mother. I didn't know how Robin was going to react to me day-to-day. I remember one afternoon I got to work and Fred met me at the front door. "I hear Robin and Howard talking in Howard's office," he said. "There's a lot of yelling and your name keeps coming up."

When Howard called me in it turned into a screaming match between Robin and me. I can't remember what we were fighting about. Finally Howard said, "I don't know what the fuck is going on but figure it out." I was a kid in my early twenties and what I cared about most was drinking and hooking up. After I read Robin's book, I realized she was actually doing a very good job of putting on a good face while dealing with a lot of personal shit. We get along great now, but sometimes I got on her nerves.

Howard had created the kind of environment where everyone could be themselves and contribute to the show. He was so normal and funny and had such a good vibe, but he also had a very clear picture of what he wanted. He'd listen to all of our ideas, pick the best parts of each one, and incorporate them. I was used to working for Roz—someone who didn't accept anyone's opinions except her own.

In order to secure my place at the show, I had decided I should follow Fred around like a puppy. I spent more time watching him than anyone else because he clearly knew a lot about producing radio. Getting to see him work every day made me realize that he was a much more important element of the show than a listener might think. Plus, I could see that he needed a hand.

For his part, Fred wanted to show me the ropes so I could free him up to do more writing and segment producing. He knew that was why Howard hired me: to take care of stuff around the office so the creative people could be as creative as possible. If Fred said, "Hey, we need two baked potatoes and four ounces of turkey with no salt," my attitude wasn't *Are you kidding me?* It was *I'll get it for you as fast as I can.* I could see Fred was getting bogged down in nuts-and-bolts stuff and it was keeping him from being creative.

I watched Fred write some bits and Howard would voice them. Then Fred would do the background tracks for song parodies and harmonize with himself, layering one vocal on top of the other. Sometimes, if he required crowd noise we needed to make our own. Fred would grab people as they were walking by or call people from their desks into the studio to get a good buzz going. And if no one was around, he built the crowd himself, standing in different parts of the studio and at different distances from the microphone. He'd do a high voice and a low voice, then have the engineer layer one on top of the other until, like magic, you had a crowd of people where once there had just been a single guy behind a microphone.

He was so technically sound, an unbelievable writer and producer. Not the kind of producing I do, but producing pieces, telling engineers how to make them. No matter how pressed he was for time—the show would be starting in half an hour and an engineer would decide that that was when it was time to take a break—Fred would still calmly explain to me what was happening.

After working on the show for just three weeks I already felt an intense loyalty to it. The guys had really taken me in. All around me was this corporate environment—I was dealing with a station lawyer about a half-dozen daily issues regarding the show and I worked with music directors and the station general manager. But within the confines of the show it was very loose and comfortable. The only goal was doing something interesting and unique and entertaining. How we got there or who came up with the idea was secondary. Everyone found a way to contribute, on the air and off.

One afternoon Howard decided we were going to do something that had never been done on radio before: convince a woman to get naked on the air. Just because none of our listeners could see what we were doing didn't mean we couldn't be titillating and push the envelope. He announced the contest, and we had three women call in who wanted to do it. It really didn't take much convincing. I took their numbers, called them back, and set up the times for them to come in the next day.

Before the show that afternoon, Howard pulled me aside and said, "Listen, this isn't a circus, okay? I want you to put newspaper over the windows. Do not let anyone who doesn't need to be in the studio get inside the studio."

"Absolutely," I said.

We went on the air. The girls were inside. And it was crazy. The way Howard described them was brilliant. You didn't need to see them to get a clear picture of how good they looked. A steady stream of people—mostly the other young producers and assistants I had been working with for the past year—were coming up to the door trying to get into the studio. And I told all of them to turn around. That wasn't too hard.

But then the lawyer I worked with every day came by. "I need to get in," he said.

"I can't," I said. "Howard told me not to let anyone in."

"I am the lawyer," he said again, calmly but more forcefully. "You need to let me in."

"Why?" I asked.

"Because," he said, "I am the lawyer and I need to see if there is anything indecent happening in there."

I don't know where I got the balls to say what I said next.

"Well," I said, "you don't really need to *see* if something indecent is going on. You need to *hear* if something indecent is going on. If you want, you can sit across the hall and listen on some headphones."

He was pissed. He stared at me. And then he audibly grunted and turned on his heels to go to listen to the show.

Afterward I told Howard what happened. He told me I did the right thing, but two other things happened because of it: One, he saw that I had his back. Two, I saw that he had my back for having his back. There were no repercussions for what I did. And I realized, from then on, in any dispute between Howard and management, I was always going to side with Howard. If I had to put my eggs in one basket, without a doubt they were going in his.

Even after that incident, though, I still wasn't sure if I had a full-time job. I had been working on the show for nearly a month. And I was literally counting the days until those four weeks were up. I figured Howard and Fred were, too, and then we would have a conversation about how I was doing, what I needed to do to get better, and whether I had a long-term future at the show.

The show ended at 6:54:30 on the dot and at the end of every day I would grab the drum and the cymbal and walk back to Howard's office with him. We'd do some small talk about the show. But at the one-month mark I was too anxious. I just blurted out, "So, what's the story?"

"About what?" he said, kind of confused.

"About me," I said. "You guys told me I was being hired on a temporary basis for a month. Well, it's been a month. Am I hired?"

He looked at me like I was an idiot. "What are you talking about? You got the job."

Chapter 22

Things Were Better When They Were Bad

IN 1996, AFTER THREE KIDS and forty-five years of marriage, my parents should have been getting a place in Florida and settling into their twilight years.

Instead, they got divorced.

All those years while I was growing up, when my dad came home from work and my mom laced into him, he had threatened to walk out. But he never did it. Even after we were all out of the house, I kept waiting for him to call me and say, "I'm done." Once Steven died, though, I assumed the trauma from that would keep them together forever.

So when my dad told me over the phone that he was leaving my mom, I thought he was bluffing.

But he wasn't. She had had a complete mental breakdown—I can't even tell you what it was about—and he had had enough. The fact that it took forty-five years was actually impressive.

When I called my mom she was in a rage. She wanted re-venge, the way she did when she felt wronged by a neighbor or one of her sisters. "I want to call Dominic Barbara," she said. Dominic is one of the most powerful divorce attorneys in New York, famous for representing Mary Jo Buttafuoco, and a regu-lar on the show.

"Don't call Dominic," I said. "He handles really high-profile divorces for people who have a lot of money. You guys don't have any money at all."

She ignored me, looked up his number herself, and called him. Dominic called me and said, "Don't worry, I'm going to take really good care of your mother."

"I wish you had told her you were too busy," I said.

For some reason I thought this would be easy. My father had decided to give my mom the house and whatever money he had in his savings account. He told me, "No matter what hap-pens, she is still your mother. I spent most of my life with her and I'll always care about her."

How he found the strength, I have no idea. Because my mom was out for blood. She wanted to go to court and get even more. As much as I tried to tell her there was nothing left to get, she didn't want to listen. When I was a kid her rages would subside, eventually. But this was different; for the first month after my dad moved out of the house, she was in a constant pique. It was as though she were banging pots 24/7. Only now I was an adult, not a six-year-old kid at the kitchen table afraid to speak up. I could see that she was being irrational and I could tell her what I thought, because I could escape. "Mom," I said, "you're going to go to court and have to give a lawyer a third of whatever you get, which is nothing, because there is nothing left."

My father really had given her whatever he had. He was liv-ing in an apartment on Long Island with four other guys. He wouldn't even let me come see it. He had just wanted out.

When my mom realized she wasn't going to go to court she began accusing Dominic of screwing her over. At one of their meetings he pulled out a tape recorder and turned it on, just to capture her tirades. But he did eventually get her to sign the papers. With the stroke of a pen, I was a child of divorce.

That was a serious pain in the ass. Even if you're thirty-five years old and have your own family, dealing with parents who are no longer together is complicated. Especially when they aren't talking to each other. For Jackson's second birthday we had two parties—one with my dad on Saturday and one with my mom on Sunday. We celebrated Easter on Saturday and Sunday, too. And Christmas became a two-day event. It was insanity. Finally, after almost a year of this, I told them I couldn't take it anymore. They needed a thaw, if for no other reason than that it was making my life very difficult. They agreed to try.

It helped that, in 1997, my mom moved to Lantana, Florida, right near West Palm Beach. Except it wasn't anything like West Palm Beach. She had bought a prefabricated house that arrived on a truck and was planted on top of a concrete slab. Mary made fun of me. "Your mom is moving into a mobile home," she said. I'd get defensive. And then one day, shortly after settling in, my mom and I were on the phone and she rushed me off. She had to get to the local motor vehicles department before it closed—her house needed a registration sticker.

You'd think having her in Florida would have made my life easier. No such luck. We were on the phone four nights a week—she didn't know who to pay for the gas or the mortgage or the phone. And I couldn't leave her hanging out to dry. Look, our relationship wasn't black-and-white; no one's is with their mother. She was still my mom. Someone had to help her. Besides, if I didn't, they would have kicked her out of her mobile home. Then she'd have to move in with me.

The move did improve her relationship with my father. When she came to visit for the holidays or one of the kids' birthdays, the two of them got along much better. The distance seemed to mellow them both. More and more, when she was back in Florida, he was the one she called to explain how to pay a bill or navigate tricky issues with the car or the house. One day in 1999, a week before Mary, the kids, and I were scheduled to go to Lantana for Easter, my father was visiting us in Connecticut. We were driving around town, running errands.

"I was talking to your mother," he said. "She wants me to come down."

"To do what?" I asked.

"To live."

There was a very long pause between us.

"As a couple?" I finally asked. "Or just to live in the same house?"

My father broke out laughing. "I don't know."

By the time I got down there the next week, he had moved into the mobile home. It was as if the divorce had never happened. They were back together, unmarried and living happily ever after.

"I think there is something wrong with your father." It was my mother, calling me from Florida. "He fell."

This was in November 2005. My dad was eighty-one.

"Well," I said, "he's getting old."

"No," she said. "There is something going on."

My mom is an alarmist, but she also has a sixth sense for knowing when something is seriously wrong with her loved ones. Like the day Steven passed away.

Thanksgiving was just a few weeks away and my parents were scheduled to visit us in Connecticut. I decided not to push for answers. If my mom was right, I'd see for myself. After they arrived, I kept my antennae up for anything strange. My dad looked alert and strong. I chalked it up to my mom overreacting.

At Christmas they went to visit Anthony in Texas. "There is something wrong with Dad," Anthony said when he called me. "He fell."

It wasn't just that he fell, he was thin. It had only been a month since I'd seen him and now Anthony thought he looked sickly. We were worried. But getting my dad to the doctor was nearly impossible. He thought doctors were unnecessary. I couldn't recall him seeing a doctor once while I was growing up. I hadn't even seen him take a day off. When he was out of work he still woke up early every day, put on a coat and tie, and went to hustle at flea markets. Once he moved down to Florida, rather than live off social security, he took a job as a concierge at a luxury building in West Palm Beach. He sat at a desk every day letting very rich people know when their packages arrived. The man did not stop. That's how you survive World War II.

For several weeks Anthony and I tag-teamed him, really beating him up about seeing someone. "If it were the other way around," I told him, "you'd be all over me to go." I think he knew he was sick. He didn't want to have it confirmed.

But he couldn't ignore his own kids, especially when I flew down there and escorted him to an appointment. He was asked about his symptoms and if he had been a smoker. When you're that age and have been smoking as long as my dad had, doctors are inevitably looking for answers that lead to one diagnosis: cancer. They found what they were looking for after a chest X-ray, which revealed a small white spot on his lungs.

It's hard to think of your parents as frail and dying. And possibly scared. My dad had been a rock my entire life, someone we clung to when my mom was swirling out of control. He had almost always kept his sense of humor no matter what kind of abuse was being heaped on him. When she was especially unhinged he could give me a look or make a sly comment that made me realize we were in this together. I wanted him to know that if he was sick, that was still the case.

In March, a few weeks later, we met with an oncologist, a very sweet Indian man. First he drew two circles on a piece of paper, which he told us represented my dad's lungs. Then he started drawing smaller circles inside the two lungs, until they were completely filled. Our mind-set since the initial diagnosis had been, Expect the worst, hope for the best. Now we were getting the truth. "Those are cancer," he said, pointing to the small circles. "And it is bad."

The doctor was very matter-of-fact, which I could tell my father appreciated. My father never sugarcoated the truth and he didn't want it done for him. The doctor continued: "You could do chemotherapy. And you could do radiation. But, honestly, they won't help much." In other words, my dad had been given a death sentence. The challenge wouldn't be healing and living; it would be comforting while dying.

I listened but it felt surreal, like I was watching it from above. My dad sat stoically, as he did when he was at his happiest or saddest. My mom fainted. That became the scene.

After she came to we went home and my father walked outside. He lit up a cigarette. At this point what did it matter? I followed him out and tried to have a conversation with him. "I am really sorry this is happening," I said.

He took a deep drag, looked at me, shrugged, and said, "What are you gonna do?"

It wasn't flip. It didn't sound like someone saying, "I don't give a shit." It was more like, this is happening, and running around the house screaming won't help because at the end of the day, we are going to be in the same position. But I did want to scream. Before I could he said to me, "Listen, I want your mother taken care of. I have put some money aside for her."

"How much is it?" I asked.

"Fifteen thousand dollars." It was all the money he had saved working as a concierge.

"Where is it?" I asked.

"It's in a shoe box in the house."

I couldn't believe it. That mobile home was made of paper. The first thing I did was go into the house, grab the money, and put it in the bank.

Mary, the kids, and I visited in late April while school was out. My dad was showing signs of the disease, breathing through a mask connected to an oxygen tank, needing a walker. I had to leave before the others to get back to work and when Mary drove me to the airport I just broke down, sobbing hysterically. I believed I was never going to see my father again. I couldn't stop crying. When I got back to New York I called his primary care doctor. I said, "I know you guys aren't God and you can't predict the future. But how long do you think he has left? How long are we talking?"

"Two to twelve weeks," he answered.

This was insane. Two weeks! I started making more visits, hoping he'd last until the next one. I went down the last week in May and we had perfect Florida weather. He convinced me to take him to the place he loved more than anywhere else: the track. It wasn't the horses, we bet the dogs that day, but the rush was the same.

This was where all the old-school degenerates were, retirees from New York who grew up playing the ponies at Aqueduct. My dad, shuffling behind his walker, breathing through a mask, fit right in. He even had a track-issued, preloaded cash card, his own betting debit card, so he didn't have to walk to a window. He could just slip it into a machine, like an ATM, and punch in his bets.

The track had grandstands set up all around the edge where bettors could sit in the sun. But he and I sat inside, where it was air-conditioned, right next to one of the betting ATMs. He'd pull himself up by his walker, shaking from the effort, put his card into the slot, and make his bet. Then he'd walk to the bathroom, come back, and watch the race. That was his pattern, just like any bettor.

When we talked, it wasn't about his condition or anything heavy, but about the races. It was a relief to forget for an afternoon. I had no interest in being at the track—this was one habit we never shared—and yet I wasn't in a hurry for the day to end. When it did he said, "Thank you for coming. I know this must have been boring for you."

He held on through the summer. My mom cared for him just as she had my brother. After the initial diagnosis, her strength was remarkable, like a worker bee. She dragged him to appointments, made him comfortable, and took care of paying the bills. I always marveled at how a phantom slight from a neighbor could set her off but in moments of true crisis, when someone in our family was physically suffering, she found composure.

In August my father entered the hospital. We all knew he wouldn't be coming home. One afternoon I answered the phone and it was my mom. "Hold on, I'm with your father," she said. "He wants to tell you something." I could hear her put the phone down to his ear. His breathing was shallow and weak. Then he whispered to me, "I love you."

This was completely unlike my father. I don't know that he had ever said that to me before. I knew it was true; he had shown it a hundred different ways during my life. He didn't need to say it. But he must have felt compelled to do it. Which made it even scarier. I thought, *Those are the last words I'll ever hear my father say.*

After my mom hung up the phone she said to him, "It's okay, Sal, you can let go. You can let go." With all the strength he could muster he lifted his frail arm and waved her in. He wanted her close, right next to his mouth, so she could hear what he had to say. When her ear was inches from his face he whispered, "Shut up."

Fucking brilliant. That was their relationship.

The next morning, during a break for the now-defunct *Friday Show*, my mom called. I picked it up in my office and closed my door. "Your father passed," she told me. I went into producer mode and spent several minutes making funeral arrangements. Then I took a deep breath and went back out. I didn't tell anyone, not even Howard. I just finished the show. What was I going to do? It wasn't a shock. He was still going to be dead in an hour when we were off the air. Besides, my father wouldn't have walked out in the middle of work.

We had the funeral on a bright and sunny August day in Uniondale. Members of the U.S. Army played taps and handed my mom the flag that draped his coffin. I eulogized him, talking about how he had been our rock at home, how I always appreciated that he spoke to me like an adult, even when I was a kid. I told the story about him throwing the radio off the roof of his building after losing a bet in the Bobby Thomson game. He had been so admired and respected, especially by my mom's side of the family.

A relative told me a story I had heard about my dad years earlier. A cousin of mine had married a bad guy and it went south quickly. They got divorced, but the ex-husband wouldn't leave her alone. The guy worked in a flower shop in the city, and one day my dad walked in and quietly asked if he could talk to him outside. My father was known for being mild-mannered, so the guy agreed. As soon as they hit the sidewalk my dad threw him against the wall and said, "If you ever bother my niece again, I will fucking kill you." Then he walked away. Problem solved.

Two of my cousins, who had served in Vietnam, talked with reverence about what a hero he had been. They meant in World

War II. They didn't know how much more true that was at home.

My father was the second person I was close to who passed away, the first being Steven. Steven was so young when he died, and the wake was full of sadness and talk of what could have been. But my dad's wake was truly a celebration of his life. I missed him, but I wasn't consumed by grief. There were so many people around in the days after he passed recalling his greatness, I was filled with pride, not sadness.

It wasn't until weeks later, as the baseball season waned and the football season began, that I realized how much I would miss him. As I got older I didn't call my dad for advice: I called him to talk and shoot the shit, the way you would call a friend. He was unconditionally on my side. No matter how much crap I took at work or what was happening at home, he was always proud of me. I never had to be on the defensive with him, which made the conversations so comfortable and light. Mostly we loved catching up about the Mets and Jets and how they were both perpetual disappointments.

The first time I wanted to call him—following another Mets collapse—I remembered something I had heard on the radio after Tiger Woods's dad had died. A show host said, "You are not a man until your dad dies." At the time I thought it was such bullshit. Just something stupid someone says to lend gravity to a moment.

But after my father died I believed it. If your dad is around you can always call him if you need to, no matter how grown-up or successful you are. But now I had no safety net. I was my own man.

I just hoped I was the man he wanted me to be.

Almost a year later, in June 2007, I was sitting at home on a Wednesday night when my cellphone rang.

"Hi," said a voice at the other end. "I am calling from the hospital. We just wanted to let you know that your mother is improving and—"

So many times during my life I had expected a call telling me that something had happened to my mother. Maybe it came with her volatility. I worried she'd hurt herself—or make someone so mad they'd hurt her. But as she got older the fear subsided. She was around fewer and fewer people to piss off. I had relaxed. I shouldn't have. Or so it seemed.

"I'm sorry," I interrupted. "I don't have any idea what you are talking about."

"No one told you?"

"Told me what?!"

Earlier that day my mom had been in a serious car accident in Boynton Beach. She pulled out of a strip mall parking lot into a busy road, tried to make a left, and never looked to see if another car was coming. She got hit. Hard. The injuries she sustained were so serious she needed to be helicoptered to a major trauma center. She had a broken leg, a broken wrist, and severe head injuries. The administrators handling her case mistakenly thought I had been called right away. "She is out of danger," I was told. "But she will need to be here for several more weeks."

On the phone, her situation sounded bad. When I arrived at the hospital the next afternoon, it looked so much worse.

She was in the ICU, connected to miles of tubes, a bandage around her head, her limbs immobilized. As soon as I walked in, I choked up. I said, "Hey, Mom." It seemed like she recognized me, but she couldn't speak. There was pressure on her brain. The doctors kept repeating the same phrases to describe her condition: "There was bleeding around her brain . . . she suffered a hematoma . . . she had a severe head injury."

"What does all this mean for her life?" I asked.

"We don't know," they answered. "The brain is a tricky thing."

"When will she recover?"

"We don't know. The brain is a tricky thing."

"Will she ever walk again?"

"We don't know. The brain is a tricky thing."

They also didn't know how tricky my mom's brain was before the accident. I worried about how she would be rewired.

After a couple of days she became more aware, but she was still struggling. When I asked her a question her answers were barely audible grunts. She had no memory of the accident.

Anthony had flown in from Texas and he and I beat ourselves up after getting her full diagnosis. Just a few weeks earlier we had talked about making her quit driving but didn't act on it, so we were feeling guilty. She had always told us, begged us actually, to keep her out of a nursing home. Now we were told she'd be in the hospital for three weeks and after that, she wouldn't be able to take care of herself for some time. Or possibly ever again.

Now we were facing the fact she wouldn't be able to drive and would be living alone in Florida, potentially addled. She might not even be able to make a cup of coffee for herself. Anthony and I looked into the options for post-hospital care. The only acceptable one—other than one of us moving to Florida—was hiring around-the-clock nurses, for six thousand dollars a month.

When my mom was released she still was far from herself. Anthony had a great word to describe her: *pliant.* My mother had never been pliant in her life. She had made reinforced steel look soft and flexible. But he was right. In the hospital we noticed that she had developed a very strange smile, fake and clownlike, plastered on her face. It would spread across her cheeks when we'd walk into the room.

At one point, while helping her settle in at home, Anthony asked her if she was comfortable and she emptily replied, "Oh yes." Her demeanor was sweet and light and accommodating.

We assumed it was the painkillers and the lingering effects of the head injury. We tried to appreciate it—she was acting like the mom we had always wanted—because we knew it wouldn't last. Eventually her senses would return.

That first week, I knew the home health aide wasn't going to work. My mom's nurse was a three-hundred-pound Haitian woman who had been on the job for years. It seemed like she'd lost interest in taking care of people. She was supposed to be walking my mom around every day, but whenever I called all I heard in the background was Rachael Ray. I'd ask my mom if she had been out and she'd cheerily tell me no, as if she couldn't be happier about it. It was all very strange and frustrating, especially trying to gauge what was happening from Connecticut.

A couple of weeks later I got a call from someone at the company that managed the nurses. The representative began apologizing profusely. I didn't understand why, and then she told me they were replacing my mom's aide. Apparently there had been an argument. My mom had called the aide a bitch. The aide then threw something at my mom.

I called my mom. "Did you call this woman a bitch?"

"Yeah," she said, as bright as sunshine.

"Why?"

"I don't know," she answered. Then she started laughing.

Part of me couldn't have been happier. The outburst made me feel that she was on the road to recovery. But I also realized that twenty-four-hour care wasn't going to work out. It was costing a fortune and, if my mom was getting her pepper back, I wouldn't be able to manage it over the phone.

I knew she needed to go into a home. If you've got more money than Warren Buffett there are plenty of options, but none of us did. We couldn't find any places we liked near Austin, Texas, by Anthony, and only saw one place that was in the right price range near me, in Connecticut.

It was a gut-wrenching decision. I knew in my heart that she needed to be closer to one of us. Neither Anthony nor I could monitor whether she was getting proper care if she was down there alone. But when I told her she'd be moving to a facility near me in Connecticut, part of me felt like I was breaking bad news to a child. "We are going to keep your house. It may be temporary," I said. "Or it may be permanent. We are going to have to wait and see." Two months earlier she had been completely independent, living alone, driving to do her errands, living a full and healthy life in a house of her choosing. Now she was being taken to a strange place where she'd live in one room, with a roommate—the exact scenario she had begged Anthony and me to avoid. We felt like we had no other choice.

Yet when I told her, she didn't resist, for which I was relieved. But I also thought she was acting strange. She had been out of the hospital a month and, except for the flare-up with the aide, her personality had vanished. There was no pepper, no anger, just placid acceptance. I called Anthony and said, "Man, what's up with Mom? She's still not herself. She's being way too nice."

He had noticed it, too. While we liked it at first, the dramatic makeover was starting to freak us out. We weren't used to her being pliant. I had spent my life managing difficulty and rage, waiting for the mercury to get to the tip of the thermometer and explode.

I braced myself for the explosion the day she moved into the home. But when I picked her up at the airport—I had paid an aide to help her fly up from Florida—she was thrilled to see me. At the home a team of people met us at the door and greeted her as if she were an arriving dignitary. Complaints were kept to a minimum.

I installed Sirius in her room and showed her how to find the Sinatra station. The old cabinet from our house with the built-in record player fit snugly against the wall. She lined the shelves with pictures of me, Anthony, my dad, and Steven. Pictures of her grandkids and drawings they had made for her were scattered on top of her dresser. During our visits she smiled, the same empty smile I first noticed right after the accident. All she did during the day was watch TV, despite the efforts of the staff to get her out. The home organized field trips to the beach nearby and to baseball games. For entertainment, an organist visited the home and played songs from around the world—a Mexican hat dance one minute, "Volaré" the next. Some days the staff invited a guy named Nick the Balloonatic to come in and make crazy hats out of balloons. I'd walk into the lobby and see all these people in wheelchairs with wacky balloon hats on their head. It reminded me of a five-year-old's birthday party.

I had actually been worried that my mom would think the social life at the home was beneath her. But she just didn't participate in any of it. It's not that she had lost her will—she was happy, laughing and reminiscing during our visits—she just seemed to have lost interest.

Anthony and I started calling her robomom. She was no longer recovering; she had changed. A couple of months after she moved into the home, we sold her house in Florida. We knew she wasn't moving back.

The difference in her personality was never more obvious to me than the Memorial Day after she had moved into the home. Mary, the kids, and I had gone to a parade in town in the morning. Afterward I went to visit my mom. She asked me what I had done that morning and I told her, "We went to the parade."

A look crossed her face; a darkness filled her eyes that I recognized from when I was younger. "I like going to parades."

"I know, Mom," I said. "But we were running late and I just decided it would be easier if I came to see you this afternoon."

"Oh," she said. "Okay."

That was it. Before, in another, more chaotic life, the answer would have been a full-throated "I like parades, too! And I am stuck in here all day by myself and you take your family to the goddamn parade and leave me here!" It would have been an afternoon of guilt and bitterness. Now, it was all just okay.

I'll ask her now if she remembers beating our neighbor with shrubs or throwing Chuck Taylors at a sales clerk and she'll wave me off with a smile and say, "Oh yeah, that," as though it was a one-time incident, not the moments that shaped me.

It's times like these when I think, *I miss my mom.* And there's the rub. I spent my entire life praying for the mom I have today. The one who doesn't cause any drama, the one who smiles and says okay to everything I do.

But I don't want her.

The accident knocked the crazy out of her, but it also knocked out the good. She's missing the fire and spunk and wit and sarcasm that made her so great, if also volatile. I actually miss the theatrics. I miss hearing her use swear words so creatively that Richard Pryor would blush. I miss the challenge of negotiating her moods. That's why, whenever I kiss her good-bye and walk out the door of her building, I thank God I grew up the way I did.

Otherwise you'd be calling someone else Baba Booey.

Special Chapter for the Paperback Edition

Baba Booey's Afghanistan Journal

July 2, 2008

It was mid-morning and we were moving at what felt like warp speed in a Black Hawk helicopter, about seventy-five miles north of Kandahar. The sun was beating down and it was fucking hot. It was always hot in Afghanistan. It seemed like there were only three settings for summer in this part of the world: Hot; Oh my God it's hot; and Oh my God it's fucking hot. Apparently there's no such thing as a breeze in the desert.

I had on a long-sleeved Jets shirt and a pair of jeans—U.S. Army policy required that we wear long sleeves and pants in the helicopter—and I was sitting in the third row of the Black Hawk, next to Artie. It was the third day of a USO tour of Afghanistan that Artie had organized. There were five of us there—Artie had gotten his comedian friends Dave Atell, Nick DiPaolo, and Jim Florentine to perform, and I was there as emcee. We had just done a show at a forward operating base in Qalat, a hundred miles north of Kandahar. Our ears were covered by headphones and we were slicing through the air, just seventy or eighty feet off the ground. At one point the pilot spotted a nomad in the sand carrying a backpack, and then the exchange between him and his co-pilot went something like this: *The bottles—were they water? Or were they gas?* The difference was life and death. Luckily they determined with binoculars that the bottles were filled with water.

As we neared the base in Kandahar the pilot screamed over our headsets, "Do you guys want to fire the machine guns?" I admit my first reaction was a little panicked: *Why would they let us do that?* I guess we weren't deep in enemy territory . . . and we weren't on full alert. I reasoned that if they were expecting trouble, we probably wouldn't have been there in the first place.

"Fuck yeah!" Artie shouted, jumping into the gunner's seat at the side of the helicopter. The moment was classic Artie. I figured we'd each shoot for about five seconds. But Artie sat down and squeezed that trigger, firing nonstop for thirty or forty seconds. He just whaled on it and never let go. *BADADADADADADADADADADADADADADADA.*

When I got my chance I went for more of a *BADDA BADDA BADDA* thing. I aimed at the sand. I aimed at the sky. It felt like I was maneuvering a videogame device. I am a liberal pacifist. But I got that gun in my hand and understood everything any proud member of the NRA feels. The gun was vibrating, the helicopter was whirring, the sand was flying. I am an adult who's gotten to do a lot of cool shit in my life, but this was the only thing I could think of that made me feel like a kid. It was like getting a toy on Christmas and playing with it for the first time. I'm the kind of person who often loves things more in retrospect, after I've had a chance to consider the experience. But this time I told myself to live in the moment: *Love it right now; don't wait.*

And I did. It was awesome.

Three months earlier I had heard that Artie had been working with the USO for a while to organize a trip to entertain the troops in Afghanistan. As it started to come together, I realized that I really wanted to go, too. I thought of my dad, who was just a teenager when he shipped off for World War II. And I thought of my kids. I wanted to teach them about giving back and how important it is to support the troops. And to be honest, I thought if I went it would yield some good stories for the show.

When I first mentioned the idea to Artie, he wasn't into it. He said he felt funny about bringing a guy with kids on the trip. "None of the other guys on the trip have anything to lose, you know?" When I went home that night and talked it over with Mary—probably something I should have done before asking Artie to take me—she was as excited as I was. Neither of us was really nervous; we both just thought it would be an incredible experience for me that I could then share with our kids. But soon we learned that there had been an attack near one of the places where Keith Urban had performed while he was on his USO tour—and it was also a location scheduled for Artie Lange's Operation Mirth tour.

So I started to get a little bit nervous.

For a couple of months Artie and I went through the paces of planning the trip. I got about $500 worth of inoculations and worked on my act. I was getting up there with professional comedians, so I felt like I had to have a role. We decided I'd warm up the troops. Since it was just a couple of minutes and people would know me from the Stern show, I didn't expect it to be that hard. Besides, I had some experience doing this for guys from the show when they went on the road. I'd even done it for Artie in Tampa once. Another time I volunteered to open at a fund-raiser for a school on the Upper East Side. Turns out they had some pretty good headliners, including Susie Essman from *Curb Your Enthusiasm*, Joy Behar, and Mario Cantone. Before the show, Susie asked me, "How much time do you do?"

"I don't do any time. I'm just doing this as a favor to get the ball rolling," I said.

I went onstage, did a few jokes, and then thanked everyone for coming. Susie walked out doing a real slow clap and gave me a totally emasculating look. "Thanks, Gary, for that amazing warm-up."

But I could do five or six minutes for the troops if I had to. Of course, before I ever got onstage, or even left for Afghanistan, things got uncomfortable. About a month before our trip, Howard took a call on the air from a listener who said, "Gary always has to do everything Artie is doing. Artie has a cupcake, so now Gary has a cupcake. Artie is going on this trip, so now Gary has to go on this trip."

Then Artie acted like he was put out that I had asked to go. "What was I going to do?" he said. "Say no?"

"Well," I responded, "if you don't want me to go, I don't have to go."

"No, no, I want you to come. It'll be cool. We'll have fun."

But right up until the moment we left, he made me feel like I had weaseled my way onto the trip.

I got over it, though. As the trip drew nearer, I spent a lot more time thinking about Jackson and Lucas and how it would affect them. Half an hour before I left, Lucas asked me if we could play one last game of pool. I hadn't realized how hard he was taking it. Sometimes I forget how sensitive he is. Apparently some kid at his school had told him I might die in

Afghanistan. I had to reassure him that I would be in safe areas, protected the entire time, but it still scared him. He was tearing up a little as we played, and that made me sad. Maybe I was being selfish. I kept telling myself that I was doing this for my sons, but the truth is, I was doing it for me, too.

June 29

We left the night before from Newark Airport. The first leg of the trip was to Frankfurt, where we were supposed to connect to a flight to Istanbul. And from there it was on to Afghanistan. Piece of cake, right? As though flying into a war zone is an everyday thing. I got lucky at the airport because a woman at the counter recognized me and bumped me up to first class. I even got some PJs and slippers and a good night's sleep.

I was traveling with Nick and Dave, who sat behind me in business class (Artie and Jim were on different flights). I've got mad respect for those guys. Nick is irritated by everyone and everything. His kinetic energy and biting humor kill me. He's completely politically incorrect and at the opposite end of the political spectrum from me—which I love, because that's just another way of saying he's honest. Dave I didn't know as well when the trip started, but he was a veteran of these tours, so I was in awe of him.

Honestly, as we flew around the world, it wasn't even the destination that made me nervous. It was what I had left behind. Jackson had put a note in the book I brought with me, telling me how proud he was of what I was doing. I had no cell service and my BlackBerry didn't work, so I felt completely cut off from my family and my life. In Frankfurt I decided to check out the business-class lounge so I could log on to a computer and check in with Mary. As soon as I walked in, I saw Jim Florentine. We said hello and then I asked him, "Where's Artie?"

Without saying anything, he just nodded in a way that made

me look to my left, and then he smirked, like he knew I would enjoy what I was about to see. There was Artie, lying on a bench on his back. He was snoring and his shirt was up over his belly and his hands were resting on his stomach. He looked like Fred Flintstone. I couldn't stop laughing.

When I checked my email I found a message from Mary informing me that everyone missed me, the Mets had lost, and the electrician had sent a bill for $2,300. Maybe I was better off not checking in.

Once we arrived, my biggest fear wasn't the potential for bombs, bullets, and mayhem. It was performing. I only had to fill a few minutes, but I am not a stand-up and have never really enjoyed doing it. I desperately wanted to earn my keep on the trip and set a good tone for the troops. If I were emceeing for Carrot Top it would be one thing. But I had a lot of admiration for my fellow travelers on Operation Mirth. And I had even more respect for the guys who were serving.

I wasn't for the war when it started and wasn't for the war when I decided to go to Afghanistan. But I was curious to see if this trip would make me rethink it all. Everyone I knew who had gone on trips like this kept telling me it would be a life-changing experience. I am a cynic at heart and not at all religious. A life-changing experience? I wasn't sure I was capable of one . . . much less in three days.

From Istanbul, we landed in Kyrgyzstan, a former Soviet republic that was now independent, in the middle of the night. We'd be staying at a U.S. Army base there for one night. We had no idea what to expect as far as accommodations went; we'd been warned there would be times that we'd be bunked down in tiny tents in the middle of sandstorms. But our rooms were shockingly good, like dorm rooms, with clean beds and showers. I was exhausted and we had plenty of time to rest, but I don't think I slept more than two and a half hours that first night. I was too anxious, especially about our first show.

June 30

By 10:30 that morning, Dave, Nick, Jim, and I were all up and ready to go. Artie was still sleeping. So our USO guide, Jeff Anthony, gave us a tour of the base, introducing us to the bigwig colonels and the troops. Jeff is a fifty-year-old, no-nonsense ex-Marine who has seen his share of USO tours. He couldn't have been nicer or better equipped to handle our nerves. But I got the feeling he was a little weary, especially since our tour itinerary called for four shows in four different locations in just three days. Most tours plan on four shows over six days.

Our recognition factor was high, which put me at ease. People knew Dave from *Insomniac* and Nick from *Tough Crowd*. They recognized Jim if you said he was the voice of Special Ed on *Crank Yankers*. When it was time to eat breakfast, Jeff told us to sit with the soldiers and not keep to ourselves. It never dawned on me to do that, actually. I thought we'd be annoying, but that was the lightbulb moment of the trip for me. Life on the bases can be pretty boring and tedious. I realized that the fifteen minutes the troops spent talking with us broke up the monotony.

No one wanted to talk about politics or the war or why they were there. The truth was, they were just happy to see someone from back home. Sitting with us—with anyone who visited—gave the soldiers an opportunity to tell their stories. I'd ask where they were from or how long they'd been in. I'd ask about their family back home. From there conversation flowed: There was the woman from Maryland who was a second gunner, a guy from Georgia with two years of college under his belt who was a medical technician. I hung with a Mets fan from Pennsylvania. I argued with a Reds fan from Cincy who couldn't stop smiling.

Dave was really amazing at making people feel comfortable. The base had these gazebos for smoking and he was always out there. That seemed to be the place to be, even if you didn't smoke. We'd sit out there and within minutes there'd be five or six soldiers hanging out. Moments like that were unforgettable.

Artie got up at 4:30 that afternoon. Our show time was 6 P.M. Suddenly I felt anxious again about going onstage. Artie made me nervous. It wasn't anything he said, just a general vibe. I felt like I didn't belong because I wasn't a comedian. But the other guys reassured me and helped me organize my set. I had come with some jokes I had written and some that Sal had written. They were funny enough, but the guys helped sharpen them.

Then, just a few minutes before we took the stage, one of our hosts gave us some unexpected ground rules. We were told that dick jokes were off-limits. So were masturbation jokes, sex jokes, and basically anything else that might offend someone, because there were women in the audience. These guys do a lot of dick jokes, masturbation jokes, sex jokes, and, well, jokes that might offend women. So this instruction threw everyone off.

I went out and did my intro, which was quick because of my nerves. Jim came out next, and after about thirty seconds of trying to keep it clean you could see a light go on in his head where he just decided, *Fuck it,* and he did a bunch of the masturbation jokes. It was like a cloud had been lifted. Nick went on next and pushed it a little more, followed by Dave, who completely blew the doors off whatever rules we were supposed to follow. The last guy in the show was Artie, who came on and did all the gay jokes he wanted. Everyone in the audience laughed—and none of us were sent home.

That first night I remember walking offstage feeling like I did okay, like I deserved a beer.

So I had one. The beers were huge on the base. A full twenty-four ounces, and higher in alcohol content than the average beer—7 percent instead of 4–5 percent. The soldiers are only allowed two beers in any twenty-four-hour period and need to have their ID cards scanned in order to get one. I was about to pop open my second beer when Jeff gave us word that our flight to Kandahar, the next leg of our trip, was leaving at 2 A.M., rather than 7:30 A.M. as had been scheduled.

We had to be in the takeoff area at 11:30 P.M. for security reasons. When we arrived they kept us in a large waiting room with rows of seats and a TV. They started playing *Mr. Brooks* with Kevin Costner, which I love, but I was so tired I stretched out on a row of seats and passed out. We hadn't even been overseas for twenty-four hours and already it felt like I'd been gone for weeks. I had packed a lifetime of experiences into our first day on the ground.

My nap lasted no more than thirty minutes before I was shaken awake. It was time for us to board. We were loaded onto some old-school army buses for the short drive to the plane. When we arrived we saw that the rest of the soldiers heading to Kandahar had saved the front row of seats for us. The plane was packed, all these kids going off to fight. And it was exactly what you'd expect from a military aircraft, nothing modern or luxurious about it. Imagine if you took the paneling off the inside of an airplane and you could see all the wires—that's what we were flying on.

But it was so cool. We took turns going into the cockpit and checking out the view. It doesn't matter how old you are, that kind of thing fills you with wonder and makes you feel like a little kid.

By the time we landed it was 5 A.M. We were loaded into a couple of hardcore SUVs to be transported to the base. Security was definitely tighter here.

As soon as we got out of the car, we could feel the grit. It wasn't sand like at the beach. It felt like ground-up rocks, very fine and very sooty. It stuck to your body. If you cleaned your hands off inside, as soon as you stepped back outside they were covered in this stuff.

We were exhausted when we arrived at the base, but we waited twenty minutes for the food tent to open before settling into our rooms. When it did, I had a shockingly good omelet. At one point, Artie took his sweatshirt off and his T-shirt accidentally came off, too. He was standing there for a good minute with nothing on above his waist, and everyone around him started to applaud. We were bringing good cheer and we hadn't even been there a half an hour.

After breakfast we settled in to sleep. I roomed with Jeff and Jim, since I was pretty sure Artie snored. As soon as my head hit the pillow I was out. I slept seven solid hours, the best sleep I'd had since leaving home just a couple of days earlier (though it seemed like weeks). When we woke up, it was time to tour the base and meet some more soldiers.

July 1

It's funny: You embark on a trip like this with such reverence for what these people are doing, and you're prepared for everything to be so solemn and serious. But the troops saw us as happy diversions. The weight of what was happening didn't carry over into their daily lives, probably because the danger had become so routine. The colonel who gave us our tour turned out to be a huge Stern fan. He asked me about the Sirius-XM merger and about Jimmy dating Robin. He wanted to know if Sal was still married. He took us to see the Predator planes. Those things are an amazing feat of technology: unmanned, flying up to 25,000 feet, with a camera that can see people and what they are up to on the ground.

We posed for pictures with the planes. We met a woman who flew the planes remotely. We climbed in the cockpit and took pictures. It looked like a gaming console. After that, it was on to armored vehicles that looked like regular tanks but could sustain a blast from the most powerful land mines. We definitely don't have those in Connecticut.

Unfortunately, Artie didn't join us. He slept through both days of meet-and-greets. In my opinion, he missed the best part of the trip.

Later that day, we learned there'd been a suicide bomber jailbreak about twelve miles from the base we were on. Four hundred of the "worst of the worst" Taliban had escaped. Being there brought the threat home in the most powerful, immediate terms. Even though I wasn't a supporter of the war, I could see what it asked of our soldiers day after day, all in the name of fighting for their country. It made me think of what my father and his generation went through, and it was eye-opening: so many young people, then and now, who had a clear sense of purpose, who signed on for a mission greater than any individual, and who shared a willingness to sacrifice all in the name of country.

After our tour with the colonel, we cleaned up for our second show. It was July 1, Canadian Independence Day, and there were a lot of Canadians on the base. We were all feeling pretty good, especially after the success of our first show. And for that second show, we didn't get any censorship warnings. We were told to expect about 750 people. Less than ten people had showed up when we started the show (though before it was over another 250 soldiers came). And it smelled like shit, literally. Turns out we were downwind from the shit pond, where all the waste from the base goes, and every night at six o'clock the wind blew the stench overhead. It was really bad. My best joke was a lame reference to the shit pond.

July 2

In the morning, we rode to our next gig in three Black Hawk copters—the coolest vehicle I've ever been in and the most amazing ride I've ever had. We flew over the countryside, which reminded me of the mountains outside Las Vegas. Then, in the vast desert, you start to notice tiny makeshift tents and a few people milling around; you spot clay huts that you can't imagine could house people; you see a goat herder with his goats. The pilot told me he sometimes flies really low to buzz the goats and watch them scramble and bump into each other. These are very young guys. One of the gunners was just two weeks from turning twenty. He couldn't drink legally, but he could shoot people with his machine gun.

We landed at the forward operating base in Camp Lagman in the town of Qalat, where we played to about 150 American soldiers. The stage had been put together that morning, and the steps were tractor-size tires with plywood thrown on top. I felt like I had my best set of the trip, and afterward Artie told me that I was a really good emcee. That made me feel better.

On the way back we took turns shooting up the desert with the Black Hawk's machine guns. And when we arrived at the barracks, the colonel who was in charge of the Predators

stopped by to meet Artie. It turned out that the night before, when we did the gig, the Predator had gone up. The colonel had the plane take a picture of us performing, and he presented it to us. The Black Hawk pilots also gave us a gift: the American flag that had been flying on the helicopter. We took pictures with the flag on the Black Hawk and they folded it up and presented it to me to bring back to the Stern show studio. It still sits on a bar in our studio, folded in a commemorative case.

July 3

Precise travel schedules don't exist when you are traveling in and out of Kandahar. It's deliberate. Jeff explained to us that having planes arrive and leave at the same time every day would give the enemy too much information. So flights come and go as they come and go.

That day we were supposed to begin our journey home. We were told to arrive at the base's airport at around 10 A.M. Our goal was to get back to Kyrgyzstan, where we'd catch a commercial flight at 3:30 A.M. to Istanbul and from there head to JFK. Kyrgyzstan was just two hours from Kandahar; we had plenty of time.

We spent some quality time at the base airport, which the American soldiers called "the Taliban's Last Stand." The building looked like it was a thousand years old, and it was pockmarked by bullet holes. Before it became the waiting room for flights, it was the last Taliban stronghold before the Americans seized Kandahar. A serious battle had been waged here. We ordered Domino's pizza from the base, played poker, and spent a lot of time wiping sweat from our faces. It was one of those Oh-my-God-it's-fucking-hot days.

All of the guys on the trip had spent a lot of time on the road—appearances, comedy shows, whatever. We were used to the pace of traveling and flying overnight, we knew how to deal with flights getting screwed up. The military had told us we might have to wait a long time, but after a few hours, I began to wonder, *Is my long time the same as their long time?* To me, four hours is a long time to wait. We got a little antsy. The soldiers waiting with us seemed used to this; they said that at times they'd had to wait for days. No one with any power was telling us where the plane was and everyone else had come to terms with that—except for us. We just kept playing cards. Artie asked if he could hold people's guns.

The plane finally arrived at 4:00 in the afternoon, six hours after we reported to the airport. Still plenty of time to get to Kyrgyzstan. But when we boarded, the pilots told us we weren't going directly to Kyrgyzstan, we were first going to Bagram Air Base in Kabul, about three hundred miles from Kandahar. We'd get on another plane from there to Kyrgyzstan. Frustrating, but clearly the military had bigger priorities than getting us home in a timely fashion. Besides, it was just a one-hour flight from Kyrgyzstan to Kabul. Not a big deal.

Our flight to Kabul was hot. Brutally hot. Hotter than I have ever felt. So hot I couldn't stop sweating, even though I did my best not to move. At one point the pilots said they had room for two people up front, where it was air-conditioned. Since it was Artie's trip, he grabbed a seat and took Nick with him. They were having a great time looking out the window and playing with the dials. Meanwhile, I couldn't read because sweat was pouring down my face and into my eyes, making them burn. But the flight was just an hour. Another quick hop and we'd be in Kyrgyzstan, headed home. Of course, it was the army's schedule, which meant there was no schedule. We just hoped that a plane would arrive at some point within the next five or six hours.

While in Kabul we toured the beautiful USO center there, named for Pat Tillman. The NFL donated a ton of money to build it, and it's filled with some of his football memorabilia. But mostly we waited. And waited. And waited. And began to freak out a little bit. Everyone kept making the same nervous joke about being stuck there forever. It was getting dark and late. Suddenly making our 3:30 A.M. flight in Kyrgyzstan didn't seem like such a sure thing. Four hours, five hours, six hours passed. Seven hours passed.

July 4

At 1:30 in the morning our plane finally arrived. Weirdly, all the soldiers on board had beards. Turned out they were special ops; without the beards, locals wouldn't speak to them. Their commander stood up and addressed his troops: "If you look around today we have some special visitors on this flight. So watch what you say."

It didn't matter. By the time we took off it was 2 A.M. We had just ninety minutes to make our flight in Kyrgyzstan. We'd been waiting for sixteen hours. We were all too anxious and self-absorbed and desperate to get out of there to listen to any secret plans from special ops.

We landed at a little after 3 A.M. We had to cross from the military side of the airport to the commercial side. We got to customs at 3:15. There was no one in the airport, just us and the customs guys. Through the window we could see our flight on the runway, idling. As we ran to the door the customs agent screamed in Russian. We had no idea what he said, but we understood it to mean, "Stop or I will kill you!" They wouldn't let us on the plane. Motherfucker!

Jeff, our USO guy, spoke through an interpreter and tried to find out what our options were. The next flight to Istanbul was at 6. Not so bad, just a few hours away. Oh wait—hang on. More confusion: the flight was at 6 *P.M.*—fifteen hours away. That hurt to hear. But wait—what? Not 6 P.M.? When was it? The next flight to Istanbul was the next morning, at 6 A.M., *twenty-seven hours away*. We were stuck in Kyrgyzstan for another whole day.

We were shocked, trying to comprehend all this, and pissed,

but to varying degrees and in different ways. Jim and I were the least bothered, taking an it-is-what-it-is approach. None of the people working at the airport were going to bend their will or find us a new airplane just because we were mad. Dave was pretty mellow, too. Nick was more visibly frustrated. But Artie just lost his shit. He was in his own stratosphere. He stormed around the airport, throwing his luggage, cursing at everyone. Jeff told us we had to get him under control, so, one by one, we all tried talking to him and calming him down. He was stomping around like a bull, actually snorting. When it was my turn to walk into the ring I said, "Artie, get it together. If you get arrested here there is really nothing anyone can do for you." He told me the same thing he told everyone else: "I don't give a shit."

After we got Artie to calm down we went to this dank old airport bar for a drink before heading to the base. It had bad yellow lighting and everything seemed to have a film of dirt on it. There was one other guy in the bar, a seedy-looking dude. When we sat down at a table, we barely noticed him—except for Artie. None of us knew this at the time, but somehow Artie was able to communicate to the bartender that he was looking to score some Valium. The bartender didn't speak English. Artie didn't speak Russian. But when Artie said "Valium," it was like he spoke a universal language. The one guy in this airport bar in Kyrgyzstan happened to be a dealer who had fifteen Valium on him. Artie bought all fifteen off the guy and downed twelve of them right there with a swig of Scotch. I didn't even see it happen. The only one who did was Nick, who really wasn't sure of what he'd seen until we got back to the base.

That's when Artie began slurring his words badly. At that point Nick said, "I think I saw him take something at the bar." You know how it is when you have that one friend who's really drunk and has to crash, but you're not ready to go home? So you have to take him back and make sure he's safely asleep, and then go back out? That's what we tried to do with Artie. We just wanted to get him back to the base and in bed.

On this trip I was videotaping everything I could for the show. I was interviewing Artie the whole time during his drug haze. Then, just as we walked him to a room on the base, he started to yell at me, accusing me of taking advantage of him in his condition. He called me a cocksucker and a piece of shit. Then he finally passed out in his room. Relieved, we stepped outside and started walking toward the mess hall. But before we even reached the entrance, we heard a noise, turned around, and saw Artie headed our way. Uh-oh.

He came straight up to me again and got right in my face. "You piece-of-shit cocksucker!" he screamed. "You know what you are doing. I know what you are about. I don't trust you. I should kick the shit out of you right now."

I felt horrible. In his mind, I think he believed he'd done me a favor by letting me come on the trip, which he had. And he knew I was sensitive about it. When you are mad at someone, you go right for the jugular. But I don't want to say I was hurt. Once I said I was hurt by something he said on the air and his response was "What are you, like a bitch? Girls get hurt, men don't get hurt. Grow up." So let's just say I looked at him in a different way after that. It was a turning point for me in how I thought he really felt about me. He offered a weak apology the next morning. I was surprised he even remembered it. But I know I'll never forget what happened. It's like when a friend is drunk and they say what they are really thinking. It made me see him in a different light and question what our relationship really was. I still don't know the answer to that question.

At that point Jeff, who was as nice as they come but is also a former Marine, grabbed Artie by his shoulders and bull-rushed him back to the room. Jeff stood him up against the wall and said, "Listen, motherfucker, you have to man the fuck up and sleep this off!"

Finally Artie relented. The rest of us went back to breakfast, ate quickly, and then went back to our bunks. We slept the entire day. Later that night, we got up and wandered around the base. When Artie apologized for screaming at me, none of us could believe he remembered a thing. You gotta hand it to him: he had total recall.

July 5

Unfortunately, our adventures weren't quite over.

The next morning, as we approached customs for the second time, we were told our visas had expired. The only way to get new ones, the agents said, was by going to a government office in downtown Bishkek. It was 5:10 A.M. Our flight left in fifty minutes. We were staring down a group of big, beefy, ruddy-faced men who barely spoke English. I started to panic. We all did, except for Jeff, who calmly asked, "Can I speak to your boss?"

A few seconds later, the boss walked out. His English was better. So was his disposition. He calmly explained that, yes, our visas had expired. But he could help us renew them right there, on the spot, for a mere $45 each! No paperwork. Just cash. It was a textbook old-school shakedown. Jeff paid the money and we sailed through, on our way home at last.

As I sat on the plane and drifted in and out of sleep, I thought about the trip. I had seen three sunrises in five days, more than I've seen with my wife. But it was a scene that happened while we were at the base in Kyrgyzstan the night before that stood out.

Around midnight, Artie and I passed a group of soldiers, maybe thirty or so. One guy called out, "Hey, come and hang out with us." So we walked over. They were from Fort Hood in Dallas. Man, they looked young.

We started shooting the shit and Artie had them laughing. He told jokes and sort of did his act, but it didn't seem like his act. It was very natural and funny. He had them laughing hard.

It was a beautiful moment—completely organic and unscripted. It was the reason we came. Artie was on a roll. I took a step back and watched him doing his thing. I saw the joy and relief he brought them, and I knew this would be a bright spot in their endless tours of duty. *They will really remember this,* I thought.

So will I.

REJECTED BOOK TITLES

Monkey Boy:
The Tale of a Horse-Toothed Creature from the Jungle

Ass Camping:
How to Make It Last for Eighty Years

How to Do Everything Wrong and Still Succeed in Business

Hello, Hello

Too Fat to Pitch

The Tooth, the Whole Tooth, and Nothing but the Tooth

Lord of the Chimps

Mein Caps

Dark Side of the Tooth

Green Teeth and Ham

War and Teeth

Memoirs of a Dumb Fuck

The Connecticut Ape:
How an Italian from Long Island Erased His Past to Become a WASP

A Farewell to Teeth

How Green Were My Choppers

The Apes of Wrath

BABA BOOEY'S DESERT ISLAND DISCS

Born to Run, Bruce Springsteen

Aja, Steely Dan

London Calling, Clash

Hotel California, Eagles

Thriller, Michael Jackson

Marshall Mathers Show, Eminem

Revolver, Beatles

Rubber Soul, Beatles

Live at the Fillmore, Allman Brothers Band

Sinatra's Greatest Hits, Frank Sinatra

Led Zeppelin IV, Led Zeppelin

BABA BOOEY'S
MUST-HAVE JUKEBOX SONGS

1. **"Suspicious Minds,"** Elvis Presley

2. **"My Way,"** Frank Sinatra

3. **"Mack the Knife,"** Bobby Darin

4. **"Be My Baby,"** Ronettes

5. **"Only the Lonely,"** Roy Orbison

6. **"Don't Stop Believing,"** Journey

7. **"I Shot the Sheriff,"** Eric Clapton

8. **"Alone Again (Naturally),"** Gilbert O'Sullivan

9. **"Rock and Roll Heaven,"** Righteous Brothers

10. **"Radar Love,"** Golden Earring

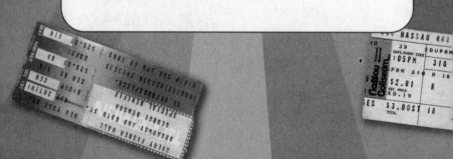

STUMP THE BOOEY: THE HOME VERSION

1. He helped write "Wild Thing" and "Funky Cold Medina" before scoring his own Top 10 hit. Name the artist and the song.

2. Ray Parker, Jr., had a huge hit with the song "Ghostbusters" from the blockbuster movie of the same name. He was sued by one of the bigger artists of the '80s, who claimed the song was a case of copyright infringement. Name the rocker and the song.

3. Everyone knows the name of the first video ever broadcast on MTV. It was "Video Killed the Radio Star" by the Buggles. What was the second video played?

4. One of the biggest hits of the '80s features backing vocals from the New Jersey Mass Choir, *Dreamgirls* star Jennifer Holliday, and the Thompson Twins. Name the song and the band.

5. Roy Orbison had a resurgence in popularity in the '80s as a member of the Traveling Wilburys, along with Tom Petty, George Harrison, Bob Dylan, and Jeff Lynne. Sadly, Orbison died soon after the release of the first Wilburys album. How is the late Orbison represented in the video for "End of the Line"?

6. Tom Tom Club featured half of one of the defining art rock bands of the '80s. Name the two members and the band they came from.

7. This song was originally written by David Foster for the Canadian athlete Rick Hansen, who at the time

was going around the world in his wheelchair to raise awareness for spinal cord injuries. His journey was called the "Man in Motion Tour." It was also the title track to one of the defining movies of the '80s. What was the hit single and who performed it?

8. He had four hits with three different bands. The first was with a one-hit-wonder band in the '70s. The next was with an English New Wave band in the early '80s. The last two were as the lead singer of a band founded by the guitarist for one of the '80s' biggest bands. Name the singer, the bands, and the four songs.

9. Guitarist David Howell Evans is better known by what name?

10. This '80s New Wave band's debut album is based almost exclusively on the writings of *Primal Scream* author and psychologist Arthur Janov. Name the band, the debut album, and the two members of the group.

11. This performer was sitting around his house late one night watching a slasher movie when he decided to write a goof song about a homicidal killer. A few weeks later he heard about a movie that needed some songs for the soundtrack. He asked his wife to send three songs. She sent the three songs, but accidentally sent the song about the homicidal killer as well. It became one of the biggest hits of the '80s and a defining moment in the film. Name the song, the artist, and the movie.

12. The director of the Talking Heads videos "Once in a Lifetime" and "Crosseyed and Painless" had a one-hit

wonder all to herself in the '80s. Name the artist and her hit. Hint: She also choreographed the videos.

13. This '80s heavy metal hair band featured a Hollywood legend in their videos. He was the uncle of the band's manager. He was also rumored to have the biggest schlong in Hollywood. Name the band, the legend, and the video.

14. Of all the popular TV theme songs in the '80s, only one was able to reach the top spot on the *Billboard* chart. What was it?

ANSWERS

1. Young MC and "Bust a Move."
2. Huey Lewis and "I Want a New Drug." Lewis and Parker settled out of court and the terms of the deal were confidential until 2001, when Lewis commented on the payment in an episode of VH1's *Behind the Music*. Parker subsequently sued Lewis for breaching confidentiality.
3. "You Better Run" by Pat Benatar.
4. "I Want to Know What Love Is" by Foreigner.
5. All the Wilburys are playing on a train and when it's Orbison's turn to sing, the train goes through a tunnel. All you see is a rocking chair with his guitar in it and a picture of him on the wall of the train.
6. Husband and wife Chris Frantz and Tina Weymouth of the Talking Heads.

7. The song is "St. Elmo's Fire," performed by John Parr.

8. Paul Carrack hit as the lead singer of Ace with "How Long" in 1975. He hit again with Squeeze on "Tempted" in 1981. Then he did it two more times with Mike + the Mechanics: once in 1985 on "Silent Running" and again in 1989 on "The Living Years." Mike is Mike Rutherford, the lead guitarist of Genesis.

9. The Edge, of U2.

10. Roland Orzabal and Curt Smith are the two members of Tears for Fears. The album is called *The Hurting*.

11. Michael Sembello had to change the lyrics to the song "Maniac" for the 1983 movie *Flashdance* from "He's a maniac, maniac that's for sure / He will kill your cat and nail him to the door" to "She's a maniac, maniac on the floor / And she's dancing like she's never danced before." I'm sure he's glad he did since the song was No. 1 for two weeks in September 1983 and is one of the highest-grossing songs ever written for a film.

12. "Mickey" by Toni Basil.

13. Ratt's video for "Round and Round" features Mr. Television himself, comedian Milton Berle.

14. Theme from *Miami Vice*, by Jan Hammer.

Acknowledgments, Part 1

Howard Stern has been my boss for twenty-seven years, but he's much more than that to me. Part dad, part big brother, and part good friend, he's taught me so many valuable things over the years. He's truly the King of All Media, and his accomplishments as an entertainer have been well chronicled, but it's his achievements as a person that have had the greatest effect on me.

I was a dumb twenty-three-year-old kid living in my parents' house when I met Howard. He was the example I learned from. Howard taught me how to treat people with respect, and as his fame grew he never lost sight of how to treat his staff. I've never seen him act "too big" for anyone.

Howard jokes that he tips well because he's "Howard Stern," but the truth is that he appreciates how hard people work and he'll never treat anyone like they are beneath him. He taught me how to be a good dad, a good worker, and a good person. And I wouldn't be Baba Booey, much less telling my story, if it weren't for him.

Thanks, Voff!

Acknowledgments, Part 2

To my brother Steven, who I miss every day.

To my brother Anthony, who laid the foundation for my insane music knowledge and was invaluable to helping me fill in the blanks. Thanks for listening and helping.

To super-agent Don Buchwald, who believed in me and changed my life. And to Tony Burton, who takes my call ten times a day and pushed to help me get this done.

To Richard Abate, who told me what this book should really be and then talked me into it! And to Julie Grau, for walking me through this process with a smile and keeping us all on track.

To Chad Millman. We clicked right away. This could never have been done in such a short time without your amazing work ethic.

To Fred Norris, who has treated me with respect since the day I met him.

To Robin Quivers, who is like a sister to me. *The Howard Stern Show* is a family, and it wouldn't be the same without you in it.

To Jon Hein, who counseled me through this endeavor from start to finish. A great friend with great advice, and a pretty good on-air partner, too!

To Ross Zapin, my friend of twenty-plus years and a great sounding board. HOW R YA????

To Jason Kaplan, Will Murray, JD Harmeyer, Steve "No Longer an Intern" Brandano, and Tracey Millman: the best crew I've ever worked with.

To Richard Christy, Sal Governale, and Benji Bronk, who make me laugh every day.

To Scott Depace (yes, even Scott), Doug Goodstein, Mike Gange, Brian Phelan, and all the guys at Howard TV I've worked with over the years.

To Tim Sabean (the best programmer ever and all around good guy), Artie Lange, Mel Karmazin, Scott Greenstein, Tom Chiusano, Ronnie Mund, Scott Salem, Jim McClure, Jared Fox, Teddy "On the Board" Kneutter, Toni Coburn, Jeff Schick, Rob Fichtel, the Howard 100 News team, the Tapes team, Bubba, Ferrall and their respective crews, and my entire Sirius family.

To Karen Rait, Rob Cappilli, and the gang at Record World; Conan Curley, Andre Gardner, Nancy Z., Laura Lackner, Ralph Cirella, and Megan Pinto; Laura Van der Veer, Maria Braeckel, Meghan Walker, and Dan Zitt at Random House; and Ethan Wilson at the New York Mets.

And to anyone I forgot (and I'm sure that I did), I apologize. I know you'll give me shit on the air. Instead of being pissed off, buy the book and write your name on the line below:

_____

(YOUR NAME HERE)

Photograph Credits

*All photographs are courtesy of the author,
with the following exceptions:*

GARY DELL'ABATE is the producer of *The Howard Stern Show* and co-hosts *The Wrap-Up Show* on Sirius XM Radio. He and his wife, Mary, have two sons, Jackson and Lucas, and live in Connecticut.

CHAD MILLMAN is a senior deputy editor at *ESPN The Magazine* and writes a column for ESPN.com that explores the culture of sports gambling. He is also the author of *The Odds* and *The Detonators* and co-author (with Chuck Liddell) of the *New York Times* bestseller *Iceman*. He lives in New Jersey with his wife and their two sons.